EDITORIAL

This issue of *Endnotes* has been a long time coming. Its publication was delayed due to experiences and conversations that compelled us to clarify our analyses, and at times to wholly rework them. Many of the articles in this issue are the products of years of discussion. Some articles spilled over into such lengthy pieces that we had to split the issue in two. *Endnotes* 4 will therefore be forthcoming, not in another three years, but rather, in the next six months. Here, by way of explanation for the delay, we describe some of the questions and quandaries that gave birth to this issue and the next.

1 NEW STRUGGLES

The first two issues of *Endnotes* called for a renewed focus on the struggles of our times, unencumbered by the dead weight of outmoded theories. However, we ourselves provided little analysis of struggles. Partly, that was because class conflict was at a low ebb at the time we were writing, and that made flights of abstraction more attractive. But it was also because we didn't know what we wanted to say about the struggles that were ongoing, and we thought it best not to pretend otherwise. We began this journal as a place for the careful working out of ideas. We didn't want to rush to conclusions for the sake of being topical.

That said, the milieu of which we form a part — the so-called communising current — did offer an analysis of struggles, which we found attractive.

[1] R.S., 'The Present Moment', *SIC* 1 (November 2011), 96.

Participants in the milieu observed that, even in factory struggles, the re-emergence of an affirmable working class identity seemed to be off the table: workers were self-organising, but without illusions about the revolutionary potential of such self-organisation. For example, in certain factories — in South Korea, in France, in the US, and elsewhere — workers took over their workplaces, not in order to run them on their own, but rather, to demand better severance pay. Meanwhile, many struggles were erupting outside of the workplace — concerning students, the unemployed, racialised minorities — with no interest in finding their way in. Workers in what were once bastions of working class strength (industry, construction, mining and utilities) could no longer offer up their struggles as a container for the needs of the class as a whole. Struggles over "reproduction" were supplanting those over "production", even if the former seemed to lack the power vis-à-vis capital historically wielded by the latter.

The communising current also provided the following analysis of these struggles. They seem to hobble forward on two legs. Their first leg is the *limit* of struggle: acting as a class means having no horizon outside of the capital–labour relation. Their second leg is the *dynamic*: class belonging is then experienced as an "external constraint", as something to be overcome. In the anti-globalisation movement, the dynamic of class struggle became autonomous from the struggle itself: the abandonment of a class position served as the basis from which to attack capital. The present crisis was supposed to force the legs of class struggle to walk together. Struggles were expected to re-emerge within the workplace, around a structurally "illegitimate" wage-demand.[1] The forms that had characterised class struggle since the restructuring (radical democratism, activism) were to be overcome in a return to basics: abandoning a class position, from within the workplace, was going to be possible only as the generalised overcoming of class society.

That wasn't what happened. Instead we got the Arab Spring, Indignados, Occupy, Taksim, as well as plenty of riots. As we discuss in "The Holding Pattern", in this issue, these struggles seemed more like a transformation of the anti-globalisation movements, as well as their extension to a wider portion of the population. That is not to say that recent struggles undermined the theory of communisation (or that dynamic struggles won't re-emerge within the workplace). Much about these movements confirmed the communising perspective: an intensification of struggle was not associated with the return of a workers' identity. As we argue, it was precisely the unavailability of a constituting identity — around the working class or otherwise — that was at play in the dynamics of the movement of squares.

In light of these struggles, it seems clear that now is not the time for pronouncements, but rather careful analysis. In *Endnotes* 1 and 2 we tried to dismantle the twin traps set for us at the end of the last century: tendencies to either (1) stray from an analysis of capital's self-undermining dynamic, in order to better focus on class struggles occurring outside of the workplace, or else (2) preserve an analysis of crisis tendencies, but solely in order to cling to the notion that the workers' movement is the only truly revolutionary form of class struggle. We managed to evade these traps, towing along some meagre analytical tools. Now is the time to put those tools to work, to try to understand the new sequence of struggles in its unfolding. We must be open to the present — its tendency to surprise us, to force us to reconsider every supposedly fixed truth — while remaining intransigent about the revolution as communisation: there will be no theoretical compromises.

Editorial

2 SURPLUS POPULATIONS

Endnotes 2 emphasized the role of surplus populations: populations with tenuous connections to waged labour. Surplus populations have been expanding due to a secular decline in the demand for labour, attendant on a reactivation of the contradiction of capitalist society. This social form, based on the centrality of labour, undermines that centrality over time. Capitalist growth thus undoes the terms of the relation on which it is grounded: the production of surplus populations alongside surplus capital is the final result of the immediate process of production.

That doesn't mean, however, that the surplus population is going to become a new revolutionary subject. On the contrary, the growth of surplus populations undermines the consistency of the revolutionary subject, as such. It is no longer possible to see capital as a mode of production with a future, integrating more and more people into it through "development", i.e. industrialisation. Instead, the industrial working class is shrinking, almost everywhere. The workers' movement, which previously organised itself around the hegemonic figure of the semi-skilled worker, can no longer provide consistency to the class. Nor can any other subject present itself as the bearer of an affirmable future.

The growth of surplus populations is precisely the disintegration, the decomposition of the class. Thus, the surplus population is not affirmable – not only because it is a position of subjective destitution, or abjection – but also because it is massively internally differentiated within itself. More than that: its growth *is* the increasing differentiation of the class as a whole. What role do surplus populations play in struggles, today? "A Rising Tide Lifts All Boats", in this issue, provides a case study of the 2010–11 British anti-austerity movement and riots and enquires into the empirical applicability of the "surplus population" category.

3 THE GENDER DISTINCTION

Since the publication of our last issue, "Communisation and the Abolition of Gender" appeared in the anthology *Communization and its Discontents*.[2] This text was the product of a ripening debate with *Théorie Communiste*, which has since turned a little rotten.

In their attempt to reconcile a feminist dual-systems approach with their previously elaborated theory, TC got lost in a debate with themselves about how many contradictions there are in modern society. For us, it makes no more sense to speak of a contradiction between workers and capital than it does to speak of one between men and women. In fact, the only "contradiction between" is the one with which Marx begins volume one of *Capital*, namely, the contradiction between use value and exchange value.[3] Ultimately, capitalist social relations are contradictory because they are based around the exchange of equivalent values — measured by the socially necessary labour time of their production — and, at the same time, they undermine that basis, since they tend to displace human labour from the production process (that expresses itself, paradoxically, as overwork for many and un- or underemployment for others).

The economy is thus a social activity that is based on a *logical* contradiction, which unfolds, in time, as unfreedom, as a practical impossibility for human beings to be what they must be: "The working population therefore produces both the accumulation of capital and the means by which it is itself made relatively superfluous; and it does this to an extent which is always increasing."[4] This contradiction gives rise to multiple antagonisms, within capitalist societies, of which the class antagonism is one. Others exist around: race, gender, sexuality, nation, trade or skill, religious faith, immigration status, and so on. It would be impossible to think all the antagonisms of capitalist society if antagonism

[2] Benjamin Noys, ed., *Communization and its Discontents* (Minor Compositions 2011), 219-236.

[3] The notion of a 'contradiction between classes' appears to be of strictly Maoist lineage. Some have defended its Marxian imprimatur by pointing to a passage in the Penguin translation of the *Grundrisse*, where Marx refers to a 'contradiction of capital and wage labour' ([MECW 29], 90, Nicholaus trans.). But the term here is *Gegensatz* (opposition), rather than *Widerspruch* (contradiction). We can find no reference in Marx's work to a contradiction between 'capital and labour', or 'capitalists and workers'.

[4] Marx, *Capital*, vol.1 (MECW 35), 625. On the logical character of contradiction in Marx and Hegel see

Editorial

and contradiction were not clearly demarcated (otherwise it would be necessary to come up with a different contradiction for every antagonism).

Richard Gunn, 'Marxism and Contradiction' *Common Sense* 15 (1994).

The point is that social antagonisms, in capitalist society, are articulated and rearticulated in relation to capital's contradictory logic. As "The Logic of Gender" demonstrates, in this issue, gender in capitalist societies is constructed around the distinction of spheres, one of which we call "directly market-mediated" and the other "indirectly market-mediated". This distinction is not separate from class society. Instead, it is fundamental to the production of value. The capitalist mode of production could not exist without a distinction of spheres, which until now has never been rigorously defined. In this issue, we devote ourselves to a clarification of concepts, to understanding the basis and transformation of the gender relation in capitalist society. This clarification allows us to better grasp the processes of de-naturalisation of gender — what Butler calls its troubling — as well as the complex dynamics, first, of gender's ongoing deconstruction (the loosening of compulsory heterosexuality, the possibility of affirming gender-queer and trans-identities) and, second, gender's constant re-imposition, especially in light of the recent crisis and austerity measures.

4 NON-CLASS IDENTITIES

This interest in gender is part of a more general theoretical turn. The workers' movement privileged the class antagonism above all others because it saw the working class as the future of humanity — if only it could be freed from its connection to capital. The affirmation of class identity was supposed to be the only possible basis on which to overcome capitalism. Insofar as workers self-identified along other lines, that was considered a false-consciousness, which was opposed to a true, class-consciousness. The effect of this orientation was often to emphasize the struggles of certain workers (white, male, citizen) over others within the class. Equally, that pushed the struggles of those "others" into channels where they ended up replicating the productivist perspective of the workers' movement: women demanded that their labours in the home be recognised as productive, via the wage; formerly colonised populations undertook their own programs of heavy industrialisation, with all that that entailed, namely, a vast toll of human suffering.

In spite of all that, participants in the workers' movement expected that other forms of identity – non-class based identity – would disappear with the further development of the productive forces. The movement described non-class identities as atavistic holdovers from earlier modes of production. There was no need to consider them as anything other than moribund. But capitalist social relations do not necessarily undermine non-class forms of identity. On the contrary, capitalist social relations transform, or even modernise, at least some of those identities. To be done with the workers' movement – to recognise that there is no longer a class fraction that can hegemonise the class – means that it is necessary to rearticulate the relation between class and non-class identities. "The Gender Logic" is part of this theoretical effort. Chris Chen's "The Limit Point of Capitalist Equality", an intake in this issue, is another.

It is imperative to abandon three theses of Marxism, drawn up in the course of the workers' movement: (1) that wage-labour is the primary mode of survival within capitalist societies, into which all proletarians are integrated over time, (2) that all wage-labourers are themselves tendentially integrated into industrial (or really subsumed) work processes, that homogenise them, and bring them together as the collective worker, and (3) that class consciousness is thus the only true or real consciousness of proletarians' situations, in capitalist societies. None of these theses have held true, historically.

Editorial

On the one hand, many proletarians lived out large parts of their lives outside of the capital–labour relation, languishing in the home as housewives. On the other hand, in workplaces, capital profited from the employment of workers who were not formally free (or not entirely so): slaves, "natives", the undocumented, women. In the course of the twentieth century, "race" continued to play a major role in determining who would be formally free, who would get work, and especially, who would get "good" work when it was available. Processes of racialisation and abjection have been intensified – though also transformed – during this period of the disintegration of the capital–labour relation, when many proletarians find themselves excluded, partially or fully, from that relation.

5 STRATEGIC VISIONS

In "Logistics, Counterlogistics and the Communist Prospect"– another intake in this issue – Jasper Bernes argues that the global restructuring of capitalist production, in our times, is capital's response to a situation in which labour has become super-abundant: capital leverages huge wage differentials across the globe, in order to reduce costs and control outbreaks of labour unrest. Supply chains exist largely because capital makes use of them to arbitrage labour markets. For that reason, the logistical infrastructure provides no prospects of a new collective worker appearing on a global scale. It has, rather, undermined such a possibility, by further fragmenting the working class. Bernes thus concludes that supply chains are strategic objects of contemporary struggles only insofar as they may be interrupted.

Bernes's article is in part a response to Alberto Toscano, who has criticised the "partisans of communisation" in several recent pieces. He accuses them of lacking a properly strategic orientation, that is, an orientation towards doing whatever "needs to be done to *prepare* the kinds of subjects that might take communising action".[5] For Toscano, there is a lot of preparatory work to do: for example, we need to figure out how to read the logistical infrastructure, not as something that needs to be torn down, but rather, as a site of "anti-capitalist solutions".[6] Since the communising current lacks a positive conception of how to get out of capitalist society (that is, other than abstractly negating that society) Toscano has called it an "intransitive politics", and he links this perspective, symptomatically, to a lack of a strategic thinking.[7] With this label, Toscano elides two ideas, one concerning the transition from revolution to communism (the "transitional state"), and the other concerning the transition from present-day struggles to revolution ("transitional demands"). With respect to the latter, it is of course true that the revolution will not fall from the sky. It will not come from nowhere and suddenly be everywhere. If revolution is to emerge at all, it will do so only in response to the limits that actual struggles confront, in the course of their unfolding. The rupture must be a produced rupture. That is the "transitive" position that *Endnotes* has put forward since its inception.

But that position is precisely the one Toscano rejects. For Toscano does not see how it is possible for revolution to emerge out of the limits of present-day struggles. He cannot lay "all trust in a kind of learning-by-doing that seems wantonly indifferent to the gargantuan obstacles in the way of negating capital"; with respect to that negation, "you can't make it up as you go along"; and again, "the path is not made by walking it".[8] Apparently, the path will have to be made by individuals who are able — somehow — to chart out the way for proletarians to take, in advance. Here, we enter the cunning world of the strategists. In "Spontaneity, Mediation, Rupture", in this issue, we attempt to reconceive the relation between struggle and revolution through a re-articulation of central concepts from the history of revolutionary theory. An open-ended approach to struggle is necessary, one that is neither carelessly dismissive nor naïvely affirmative. Class struggle

[5] Alberto Toscano, 'Now and Never', in Noys, ed., *Communization and its Discontents*, 98.

[6] Alberto Toscano, 'Logistics and Opposition', *Mute* 3:2 (January 2012).

[7] Toscano, 'Now and Never', 87.

[8] Ibid., 99.

is not simply the site of a spasmodic reaction to capital's impositions, but the place where the contradictions of capitalism play out, in ways that are immanent to proletarian experience. It is only in the course of intensifying struggles that the strategic questions of an era can be asked and answered, in a concrete way; only here that tactics, strategies and forms of organisation — and even the meaning of communism itself — can take concrete shape. Strategies emerge as responses to the specific limits of a sequence of struggles. They cannot be imposed from the outside.[9]

6 COMMUNIST PROSPECTS

Endnotes 3 thus tries to fashion tools with which to talk about present-day struggles — in their own terms, with all their contradictions and paradoxes brought to light, rather than buried. The question remains, how do those struggles relate to revolution? Here, we insist: revolution is a possible outcome of struggles today, but only as communisation. That's because the revolution will have to be the abolition of the value form, for that form is no longer a viable way to organise our existence. Direct human labour accounts for a diminishing portion of social production, while an imposing mass of technologies and infrastructures, destroying the ecological conditions of human life on earth, confronts us as the primary force in social life. Yet the buying and selling of labour still structures every aspect of lives, and capital remains our main mode of interaction with one another. How might we actually get on without it? There are no easy answers — especially considering that the reproduction of each of us, today, depends on a productive apparatus flung far across the continents. The question of revolution is nonetheless still posed — abstractly, speculatively, but necessarily so — by the contradictory character of the central relation on which society pivots. And this question can only begin to approach concretion in struggles themselves.

[9] Toscano sees our perspective as abstract (in its 'intransigence' and concern with 'theoretical purity'), but it is Toscano who poses the problem of revolution in an abstract manner, by suggesting that a solution could be found to strategic problems in abstraction from the concrete ways in which those problems emerge in the course of actual struggles.

THE HOLDING PATTERN

The ongoing crisis and the class struggles of 2011–2013

In 2007, following the deflation of the housing bubble that had held it aloft, the world economy plunged into a deep depression. Homeowners found themselves underwater. Firms were inundated. Unemployment shot upwards. Most dramatically, the financial architecture of the world economy nearly collapsed. Pirouetting their way onto the scene, government ministers undertook coordinated action to prevent a repeat of the 1930s. Shortly thereafter, those same ministers were forced to implement austerity in order to assure bondholders that they remained in control of the slow-motion catastrophe. Public employees were sacked; those that persisted saw their wages slashed. Schools, universities and hospitals faced massive cuts. Meanwhile, in spite of the crisis, food and oil prices remained elevated. Unemployment, too, remained stubbornly high, and youth unemployment above all. Finally, despite the best efforts of politicians — or perhaps, precisely because of those efforts — some national economies found themselves mired in not one or two but three separate recessions, in the space of a few years.

Under these conditions, increasing numbers of proletarians have been forced to rely on government assistance in order to survive, even as that assistance is under threat. Outside of the formal wage relation, informality is proliferating, from under-the-table work to petty crime.

Yet, in spite of all that, both wage-earners and the unwaged mostly responded to the onset of this crisis — which is itself merely the latest consequence of a decades-long economic decline — by adapting to it.[1] Of course, that was not universally true: many proletarians set about defending their conditions of life. In 2008–10, there were demonstrations, some of which included blockades of roads and refineries. There were riots, as well as incidents of looting. General strikes stopped work for a day. Students occupied universities, and public sector employees occupied government buildings. In

[1] On the long-term decline, see below, p. 24, as well as 'Misery and Debt' in *Endnotes* 2.

response to plant closures, workers not only took over their workplaces; in a few locales, they also kidnapped bosses or burned factories down.

Some such actions occurred in response to police killings or workplace accidents. Many more had as their goals to stop the implementation of job losses and austerity, and to reverse rising inequality and corruption. However, as *Kosmoprolet* noted, "conventional means of class struggle were unable to put enough pressure behind their demands anywhere and the protests failed in every respect despite the enormous mobilisation efforts".[2] Then, in 2011 – a year portentously accompanied by earthquakes, nuclear meltdowns and floods – a wholly unanticipated form of struggle washed onto the shores of the Mediterranean.

[2] Kosmoprolet, 'The Crisis, Occupy, and Other Oddities in the Autumn of Capital', *Kosmoprolet* 3 (2011).

1 THE MOVEMENT OF SQUARES

Starting in Tunisia, the movement of squares spread throughout the Middle East and across the Mediterranean before arriving in the anglophone world as Occupy. In reality there were more differences than similarities among the many square movements, such that it might seem foolhardy to try to generalise across them. Yet it is not we, the commentators, who draw the connections, but the movements themselves, both in the form of their emergence and in their day-to-day practice. An internationalist phenomenon from the beginning, the movement of squares linked struggles across a mosaic of high- and low-income countries. Oakland and Cairo were suddenly "one fist".

Unlike the anti-globalisation protests – but like the anti-war movement of 2003 – a growing conflictuality was not contained within one city, nor did it hop sequentially from one city to the next. Instead, occupations proliferated across city centres, attracting precarious wage-earners and frightened middle strata, as well as organised labour, the slum-dwellers and the new homeless. Nevertheless, besides chasing a few ageing dictators down from their perches, the movement of squares achieved no lasting victories. Like the 2008–10 wave of protests, this new form of struggle proved unable to change the form of crisis management — let alone to challenge the dominant social order.

However, the movement of squares did change something: it allowed the citizenry — a cross-class formation — to come together, to talk about the crisis and its effects on everyday life (in North Africa, it really freed them to do so). Previously, such discussions had occurred only in private: individuals were made to feel personally responsible for unemployment, homelessness, arbitrary police violence, and debt; they were never given a chance to discuss collective solutions to their problems. For that reason alone, all the talk of occupy was no trifling matter.

As the occupations unfolded, occupiers' own activity became the main topic of debate. What should they do to defend the squares against the police? How could they extend the movement into new areas? The popularity of such discussions, even outside of the occupations themselves, suggested that a growing portion of the population now recognised that the state was powerless to resolve the crisis. At the same time, no one had any clue what to do with this knowledge. The occupations became spectacles. The occupiers were spectators of their own activity, waiting to find out what their purpose had been all along.

The main problem the occupiers faced was that the very manner in which they came together made them too weak to pose a real threat to the reigning order. The occupations concerned everyone, but — with the exception of the homeless — they concerned no one directly. The occupiers found one another, but only by abandoning the concrete situations (neighbourhoods,

The Holding Pattern

schools, job centres, workplaces) that might have provided them with leverage. As a result, occupiers controlled no material resources and no choke points or territories, aside from the squares themselves.[3] It was rare for people to arrive at the occupations as a delegate of a neighbourhood or workplace, let alone some other fraction of the social body. The occupiers had little to offer one another but their own bodies, their "indignant" cries echoing across hitherto barren central plazas. Outside of certain cities in North Africa, occupiers largely proved incapable of transmitting their indignation from the squares into everyday life, where self-activity would necessarily involve larger numbers and more substantial risks.

In this context, the occupiers opted for a set of negative demands: *ash-sha'b yurid isqat an-nizam* (the people want the regime to fall) and *que se vayan todos* (they all should go). However, to get rid of governments, to reverse austerity, to lower the price of food and housing — even under the most favourable conditions, what might these demands achieve? If they could prevent the implementation of austerity, occupiers might be able to spook holders of government debt, thereby forcing the state into bankruptcy. To drop into the abyss: not even the most opportunist political parties — with the possible exception of the Tea Party in the US — have been willing to take up that call.

And yet, without the ability to demand a reflation, let alone re-industrialisation of the economy, what is left but the sectional interests of various fractions of the proletariat (and other classes)? If they have no choice but to accept the economic status quo, how can these fractions divide up a limited set of resources — of both public handouts and private employment — without antagonising one another? It is easy enough to say that there is nothing left to do but make the revolution, but which revolution will it be?

[3] Holding the squares meant more in some places than in others. In Tunis and Cairo, the police were not only pushed out of the squares. They were prevented from entering the surrounding area for weeks or months. By contrast, in lower Manhattan an area of only 100 by 330 feet was (more or less) 'liberated'.

In the twentieth century, proletarians were able to unite under the flags of the workers' movement, with the goal of rebuilding society as a cooperative commonwealth. The coordinates of this older form of liberation have been thoroughly scrambled. The industrial workforce was formerly engaged in building a modern world; it could understand its work as having a purpose, beyond the reproduction of the class relation. Now, all that seems ridiculous. The industrial workforce has been shrinking for decades. The oil-automobile-industrial complex is not building the world but destroying it. And since countless proletarians are employed in dead-end service jobs, they tend to see no purpose in their work, besides the fact that it allows them to "get by". Many proletarians today produce little more than the conditions of their own domination. What programme can be put forward on that basis? There is no section of the class that can present its interests as bearing a universal significance. And so, instead, a positive project would have to find its way through a cacophony of sectional interests.

In lieu of that, the movement of squares took shape as a new sort of frontism. It collected together every class and class fraction that had been negatively impacted by the crisis, as well as by the austerity measures that followed corporate bailouts. Thus, the sinking middle classes, the frightened but still-securely employed, the precarious and the newly unemployed, and the urban poor – individuals from these groups came together as an impassioned cross-section of society because none of them could accept the options that the crisis had put in front of them. However, their reasons for not accepting those options were not always the same. In North Africa these fronts could be mobilised to topple governments, but in this case their success was precisely their factionalisation.

Our contention is that the movement of squares took this form for a reason. In essence – although certainly not in every manifestation – its struggle was

The Holding Pattern

an anti-austerity struggle. That it was such a struggle should strike us as odd. Every talking head seemed to know, in 2008, that a deep recession, comparable to that of the 1930s, should elicit not austerity but its opposite, namely massive fiscal spending. Certain low-income countries (China, Brazil, Turkey and India, among others) took this route — often in a limited way, and sometimes only after experiencing deep recessions. But crucially, the high-income countries did not go down that road. Where is the much vaunted green capitalism, which was supposed to set the global economy on a new path? The last few years seem to have provided the chance for capital to wholly reinvent itself as humanity's saviour. That hasn't come to pass. Our sense is that it is precisely the depth of the crisis that has forced states in high-income countries into slashing budgets. They are locked into a dance of the dead.

As we will show below, those states have been made to dance in the face of two contradictory pressures. On the one hand, they have had to borrow and spend, in order to stave off deflation. On the other hand, they have been forced to implement austerity, in order to slow the growth of what were already massive public debts (attendant on decades of feeble economic growth). This spinning-in-circles has not resolved the crisis. However, it has blunted its fallout, so that it has become the crisis of certain individuals or sections of society — and not of society as a whole.

That is what has given struggles an odd character: by implementing austerity, in the face of the crisis, the state made it seem as if it also had the power to reverse the crisis. In short, it seemed as if the state was acting irrationally. According to occupiers everywhere, if the state was acting irrationally, then that had to be the result of corruption: the state had been captured by moneyed interests. Whereas, in fact, what appeared to be the state's strength was actually its weakness. Austerity is a symptom of the inability of the state — in the face of decades of slow growth and periodic crisis — to do anything except to continue to temporise. That, it has done, for now. Order reigns.

2 A HOLDING PATTERN WITH A GRADUAL LOSS OF ALTITUDE

The present economic malaise certainly began as a financial crisis.[4] Mortgage-backed securities and credit default swaps suddenly became the topics of an endless televisual discourse. Lehman Brothers collapsed. AIG was loaned $85 billion. Reserve Primary Fund "broke the buck", causing commercial paper markets to seize up. Acting as lenders of last resort, central banks were able to keep financial flows from freezing entirely — thereby averting a repeat of the Great Depression. Where do we stand now, four years after the end of the "Great Recession"? How are we to understand the crisis? Was it merely a momentary setback along the highway to the Chinese Century? Recent developments suggest otherwise.

After recovering in 2010 from two years of deep recession, GDP-per-capita growth-rates in the high-income countries began to decelerate in 2011 and 2012.[5] In the latter year, they grew at a meagre rate of 0.7 percent. The recovery has been historically weak — the only rival, in terms of the length and severity of this downturn, is the Great Depression — and is weakening further. In fact, in the high-income countries as a whole, GDP per capita in 2012 was still below its 2007 peak. That has made it extremely difficult to reduce unemployment (especially given that, in the interim, labour productivity has continued to rise). Unemployment levels peaked at 10 percent in the US and over 12 percent in the Eurozone — they have hardly fallen to the present.[6] In some hard-hit countries, unemployment is much higher. In mid 2013, it continues to grow: in Cyprus, unemployment levels have reached 17.3 percent; in Portugal, 17.4

[4] An earlier version of this section appeared as a dispatch on the *Endnotes* website (endnotes.org.uk).

[5] All statistics taken from the World Bank, *World Development Indicators*, 2013 edition, and the IMF, *World Economic Outlook*, 2013, unless otherwise noted.

[6] In the US, unemployment levels have fallen to 7.3 percent (in Autumn 2013); however, this fall was only achieved through a massive reduction in the labour force participation rate (LFPR). The latter fell from 66 percent in 2007 to 63 percent in 2013. That's the lowest LFPR, in the US, since 1978. In fact, 2000-2013 saw the first sustained

percent; in Spain, 26.3 percent, and in Greece, 27.6 percent. Youth unemployment, in those same countries, has reached astronomical proportions: 37.8 percent, 41 percent, 56.1 percent, and 62.9 percent, respectively.[7]

More potentially explosive are recent developments in the so-called emerging markets which seemed — for a moment at least — to be capable of pulling the entire world economy forward. Now, all are slowing down. In Turkey and Brazil, per-capita GDP growth-rates fell precipitously, in 2012, to 0.9 and 0 percent, respectively. The Chinese and Indian juggernauts are also decelerating. In China — despite one of the largest stimulus programs in world history — economic growth rates fell, in per capita terms, from 9.9 in 2010 to 7.3 in 2012. In India, growth rates fell further, from 9.1 in 2010 to 1.9 in 2012 (the latter is India's lowest per capita growth rate in over two decades).

Nevertheless, in spite of the extremely weak recovery and stubbornly high unemployment levels, a new consensus reigns in the high-income countries: the Keynesian moment is over; governments need to cut back on spending.

As the crisis evolves past its opening act, it is becoming clear that the real problem is not a failure to regulate finance. If anything, the banks are now too cautious, too reluctant to take on risk. The real problem is the growth of surplus populations alongside surplus capital.[8] *Misery* is the long-term tendency of the capitalist mode of production, but misery is mediated by *debt*. Massive pools of surplus capital formed in the 1960s, and have only expanded since then. Internationally, these pools appear mainly as an excess of dollars: eurodollars in the mid-1960s, petrodollars in the 1970s, Japanese dollars in 1980s and 90s, and Chinese dollars in the 2000s. As these dollars scour the earth in search of returns (because they were not used to purchase goods), they have caused a rapid decline in the price of money, and thus, in turn, they have blown up a series of bubbles, the largest of

fall in the LFPR since women joined the labour force *en masse* in the mid 1960s.

[7] Statistics taken from 'Unemployment in the Eurozone', *The Washington Post*, August 11, 2013.

[8] On surplus capital and surplus population, see 'Misery and Debt' in *Endnotes* 2, and figure 1, opposite.

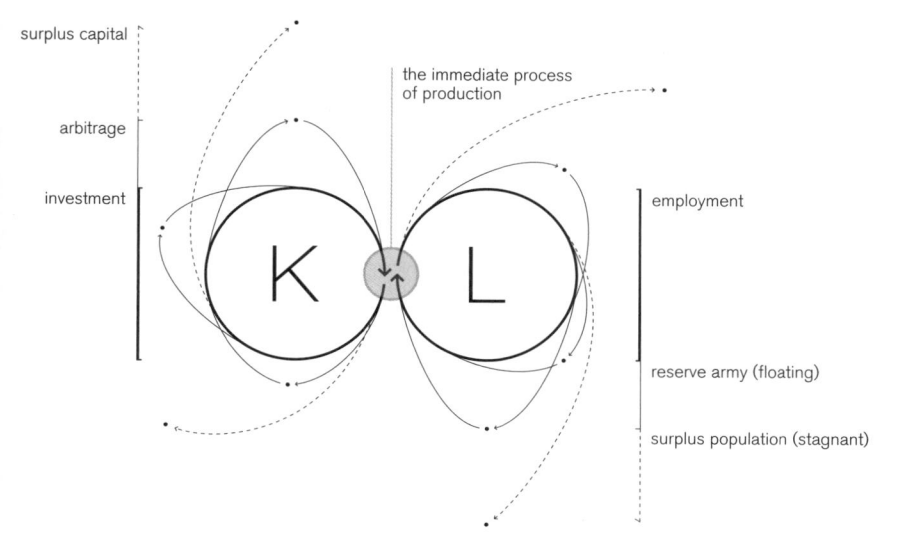

Figure 1: Surplus capital and surplus population as disintegrating circuits of capital and labour

which, in the last century, were in Latin America in the mid-1970s, Japan in the mid-1980s, and East Asia in the mid-1990s. In the lead up to this crisis there were the US stock market and housing bubbles of 1998–2007.[9]

As US stock market indexes and house prices climbed ever higher, individuals with assets felt richer. The value of their assets rose towards the sky. Rising asset values then led to a long-term decline in the savings rate. And so – in spite of declining rates of investment, a long-term slowdown in economic growth-rates, and an intense immiseration of the workforce – bubble-driven consumption kept the economy ticking over, and not only in the US. The US economy sucked in 17.8 percent of the rest of the world's exports in 2007. US imports were equivalent to 7 percent of the rest of the world's total GDP in 2007. Suffice to say: it was a huge stimulus to the world economy. But debt-based consumption in the US was not allocated equally across the US population. Proletarians increasingly find that they are superfluous to the capitalist production process; the demand for

[9] See Richard Duncan, *The Dollar Crisis* (Wiley 2005) Chapter 7, 'Asset Bubbles and Banking Crises'.

The Holding Pattern

their labour has been low. Consequently, workers' real wages have been stagnant for going on 40 years. That has caused a massive shift in the composition of demand, in the United States. Consumption increasingly depends only on the changing tastes of the super-rich: the top 5 percent of income-earners account for 37 percent of US spending; the top 20 percent of income earners account for more than the majority of spending – 60.5 percent.[10]

Now, with falling housing and stock market prices, the wealth effect is moving in reverse.[11] Households are paying down already accumulated debts. They are trying to reduce their debt-to-asset ratios. As a result, businesses are not investing, no matter how low the interest rates fall. And we still have a long way to go. Total debt – state, businesses and households – is roughly 350 percent of GDP in the US. In the UK, Japan, Spain, South Korea and France, total debt levels are even higher, up to 500 percent of GDP.[12] De-leveraging has only just begun. Meanwhile the slowdown in high-income countries has been transmitted to low-income countries by stagnant or declining US and EU imports. The result is pressure on government spending, from two directions:

1) Governments are forced to spend in order to prevent the return of recession. If they are unable to pass large stimulus programs, then they rely on automatic spending increases (or the maintenance of spending in the face of falling revenues). Gross debt to GDP in the G7 countries rose from 83 percent in 2007 to 124 percent in 2013. Over the past six years, the US government took on a debt larger than the entire yearly output of the country in 1990, just in order to prevent the economy from going into a tailspin! Why are economies running so hard to stay in place?

In essence, there has been little private borrowing – in spite of zero percent short-term interest-rates and historically low long-term rates. That people continue to save rather than borrow, across the private economy,

[10] Robert Frank, 'U.S. Economy Is Increasingly Tied to the Rich', *Wall Street Journal*, August 5, 2010.

[11] Robert Brenner, 'What's Good for Goldman Sachs is Good for America', 2009 (sscnet.ucla.edu), 34-40.

[12] Charles Roxburgh et al., 'Debt and Deleveraging: Uneven Progress on the Path to Growth', *McKinsey Global Institute*, 2012 (mckinsey.com).

has opened up a so-called "spending gap". The private economy would shrink if the government did not step in to fill that gap. The purpose of fiscal stimulus today is not to restart growth. That would only happen if people spent the money that the stimulus put in their pockets. Instead, households are using that money to pay down debts. In the present crisis, the point of state spending is to *buy time* – to give everyone a chance to reduce debt-to-asset ratios without causing deflation.[13] By lowering asset values, deflation would make those ratios even worse, causing a debt-deflation spiral.

Meanwhile, at the heights of the international economy, certain states are experimenting with other ways to restore health to private balance sheets: they are trying to raise asset values rather than lower debts. The US Federal Reserve and Bank of England, with other central banks have engaged in "quantitative easing". They purchased their own governments' long-term bonds, lowering interest rates on those bonds. Investors were thus pushed out of bond markets, where yields were falling, into riskier assets. Temporary success was reflected in a return of rising stock prices. The hope was that rising prices would reduce debt-to-asset ratios of businesses and wealthy households – not by paying down or writing off their debts, but rather by re-inflating the value of their assets. The problem is that the effects of quantitative easing seem to last only as long as the easing itself. Stock markets aren't rising because the economy is recovering. A spate of bad news – and worst of all the news that central banks will end quantitative easing – causes these miniature stock-market bubbles to collapse.

More than that: it is only now becoming clear how much of an effect quantitative easing has had, outside of the US and UK, that is, on the world economy. Most importantly, it caused the prices of commodities (e.g. food and fuel) to rise immensely – immiserating the world's poor, and inducing the food riots that directly preceded

[13] See Richard Koo, 'QE2 has transformed commodity markets into liquidity-driven markets', *Equity Research*, May 17, 2011

	2008	2009	2010	2011	2012
Canada	-0.5	-3.9	2.0	1.5	0.6
France	-0.6	-3.6	1.2	1.5	-0.5
Germany	1.3	-4.9	4.3	3.0	0.6
Greece	-0.6	-3.5	-5.2	-7.0	-6.2
Japan	-1.0	-5.4	4.7	-0.9	2.1
United Kingdom	-1.6	-4.6	1.0	0.2	-0.5
United States	-1.3	-4.0	1.5	1.1	1.5
Spain	-0.6	-4.5	-0.7	0.2	-1.5
Brazil	4.2	-1.2	6.6	1.8	0.0
Egypt	5.4	2.9	3.4	0.1	0.5
China	9.0	8.7	9.9	8.8	7.3
India	2.5	7.1	9.1	5.0	1.9
Mexico	-0.1	-7.1	4.0	2.6	2.6
Turkey	-0.6	-6.0	7.8	7.4	0.9
Russian Federation	5.4	-7.8	4.2	3.9	3.0
World	0.2	-3.3	2.8	1.6	1.0
High income	-0.4	-4.2	2.3	1.2	0.7
Low & middle income	4.2	1.8	6.3	4.9	3.6

Table 1: GDP per capita percentage growth rates for selected countries, 2008–2013

the Arab Spring.[14] At the same time, QE also gave rise to massive foreign-exchange carry trades: investors the world over have been borrowing at extremely low interest rates in the US, in order to invest in "emerging markets". That strengthened some low-income countries' currencies, severely weakening what had previously been vigorous export machines. States in low-income countries counteracted that weakening with huge programs of fiscal stimulus (partly relying on the inflows of foreign capital to do so). That stimulus explains why low-income countries were able to recover so quickly from the Great Recession, compared to the high-income countries. But they recovered — not on the basis of a real increase in economic activity — but rather, through the sort of bubble-fueled construction booms that pulled

[14] M. Lagi, K.Z. Bertrand, Y. Bar-Yam, 'The Food Crises and Political Instability in North Africa and the Middle East', 2011 (arXiv.org).

	2007	2013	change
Ireland	25	122	+97
Greece	107	179	+72
Iceland	29	92	+63
Japan	183	245	+62
Spain	36	92	+56
Portugal	68	122	+54
United Kingdom	44	94	+50
United States	66	108	+42
Netherlands	45	74	+29
France	64	93	+29
Italy	103	131	+27
Denmark	28	52	+24
Finland	35	57	+22
New Zealand	17	38	+21
Canada	67	87	+21
Australia	10	28	+18
Czech Republic	28	45	+17
Belgium	84	100	+16
Germany	65	80	+15
Austria	60	74	+14

Table 2: Government debt as a percent of GDP for selected OECD countries, 2007–13

the rich countries along in the 2000s. Now, with the possibility that QE will come to an end, it is not only the weak recovery in the US, but apparently also the bubble-fueled recovery in the emerging markets, that has been put in danger. States will have to keep spending to keep the temporary fixes they've put in place from falling apart.

2) But there is a second pressure on governments: in the US and EU, stimulus has given way to austerity, in order to reassure bondholders. In Greece, Ireland, Italy, Portugal and Spain, long-term interest rates rose rapidly, relative to the German ten-year bund. Greece had to default, partially. Elsewhere, austerity measures have been necessary to keep interest rates from rising further. The problem is that government debts were already large

in 2007, at the start of crisis. This fact has been entirely ignored by Keynesians. Over the past 40 years, debt-to-GDP ratios tended to rise during busts, but refused to fall, or rose even further, during booms. *States have been unable to use growth during boom years to pay off their debts, because booms have been increasingly weak, on a cycle-by-cycle basis.* Any attempt to pay down debts risked undermining increasingly fragile periods of growth. As a result, state debts expanded, slowly but surely, in many high-income countries, over a period of decades. But the growth of that debt only mitigated an implacable slowdown in growth rates. Per capita GDP growth-rates fell, decade by decade, in high-income countries, from 4.3 percent in the 1960s, to 2.0 percent in the 1970s, to 2.2 percent in the 1980s, to 1.8 percent in the 1990s, to 1.1 percent in the 2000s.

And so, at the start of this crisis, debt levels were already much higher than they were in 1929. For example, on the eve of the Great Depression, US public debt was valued at 16 percent of GDP; ten years later, by 1939, it rose to 44 percent. By contrast, on the eve of the present crisis, in 2007, the US public debt was already valued at 62 percent of GDP. It reached 100 percent just four years later.[15] That's why rising debt levels have raised the spectre of default, throughout the high-income countries.

High levels of state debt, carried over from previous decades, limit the capacity of states to take out debt today. They need to *keep their powder dry* – to maintain, for as long as possible, their ability to draw on inexpensive lines of credit. States will need credit as they attempt to ride out the coming waves of financial turbulence. Austerity in the midst of the crisis has been the paradoxical result. States need to convince bondholders of their ability to rein in debt now, in order to preserve capacity to take out debt later. Some states (Ireland, Greece, Italy, Spain, Portugal) seem to have already maxed out their credit limits.

[15] We use the US statistics, here, because these are the only ones that allow for a comparison between 1929 and in 2007. But the US is a unique case; because the dollar is an international reserve currency, it is more or less impossible for the US state to be pushed into bankruptcy through over-borrowing.

These two pressures – to spend in order to stave off deflation and to cut spending in order to stave off default – are equally implacable. Thus, austerity is not *only* the capitalist class attacking the poor. Austerity has its basis in the overgrowth of state debt, which is now reaching an impasse (as it had in the low-income countries in the early 1980s).

Greece is at the centre of the resulting austerity storm, having been bailed out twice by the EU and IMF. The first bailout package came in May 2010 and the second in July 2011. That there will need to be a third package, in 2014, seems almost inevitable. In order to win these bailouts, Greece was forced to implement at least five separate austerity packages, the worst of which was voted through in June 2011. Public sector workers' salaries were cut by 15 percent. 150,000 public sector workers are to be laid off by 2015. The retirement age was raised. There was a 36 percent reduction in spending on pensions and social benefits. Many utilities (telephones, water and electricity), as well as state-owned ports, mines, airports, were partially privatised. Income taxes and sales taxes were raised. Deep cuts came, again, in July 2013, when 25,000 public employees were sacked, in spite of high levels of unemployment in the private sector. As a result of austerity, Greek incomes shrank by a fifth between 2007 and 2012. Since that shrinkage also meant a reduction in government revenues, austerity measures have only pushed Greece further from fiscal health. Like so many low-income countries in the 1980s, structural adjustment has made Greece ever more dependent on outside financing.

In Portugal, Spain and Italy, similar austerity measures have been implemented, at a lower level of intensity. But even the US has seen schools closing, rising tuition and health care costs, and disappearing retirement benefits. Public sector workers have been laid off *en masse*; those that remain have seen wages cut.

Coordinated action of central banks, massive assistance to financial firms, increasing levels of state debt, and now — in order to prevent scares on bond markets — turns to austerity: all have prevented the Great Recession from turning into another Great Depression. The way these operations were undertaken has further centralised control in the hands of government ministers in the US and Germany, which function as spenders and lenders of last resort for the world economy. But as is clear — given very high levels of public and private debt, slow or even persistently negative economic growth, and extremely elevated levels of unemployment (especially youth unemployment), in many countries — the turbulence is far from over.

We like to think of the present period as *a holding pattern*. But we note that the economy is losing altitude all the time. For that reason, the holding pattern can only be temporary. Perhaps it is possible, through some miracle, that the world economy will achieve enough speed, pull up on the throttle and soar through the sky. But there are "significant downside risks". The turn to austerity is endangering the stability that it is meant to prop up, since austerity means that governments are doing less to make up for the lack of spending in the private sector. That raises, once again, the spectre of deflation; an indefinite program of quantitative easing remains the only force pushing back against deflationary pressures. Yet, even without deflation, there is still a high likelihood that the present economic turbulence may end with a crash. After all, sovereign defaults — when examined on a world-scale — aren't actually that rare: they come in waves and play a major part in the global unfolding of crises.

Can states somehow defy the working of the law of value, massively increasing their debts without decreasing the expected future growth-rates of their economies? Those who believe they will be able to do so will have their thesis tested in the coming period.

We can't rule out the possibility that they will be right: after all, a massive accumulation of debts – held by corporations, households and states, and always in novel ways – has deferred the onset of a new depression over and over again, for decades. Who is to say whether the present pattern will be maintained only for a few more weeks, or for a few years?

However, if it is to be maintained, this will require that there not be a blowout, somewhere in the world economy, that would test the strength of the world's financial architecture once again. AIG may have been too big to fail, but Italy is too big to save. The Eurozone has been pulled back from the brink a number of times, but the Eurozone crisis has not been resolved definitively. Potentially more turbulent is the possibility that the ongoing slowdown in the BRICs will give way to what is euphemistically called a "hard landing". That already seems to be happening in India and Brazil, but the real worry remains a blowout in China. Massive government stimulus, since 2007, has only exacerbated over-capacity in construction and manufacturing. Banks are hiding huge numbers of bad loans in a massive "shadow banking" sector. Most tellingly, there has been an extremely rapid increase in housing prices – orders of magnitude larger than the housing-price bubble that just popped in the US. The Chinese government reassures us that "this time it's different", but the US government said exactly the same thing in the mid 2000s...

3 THE RETURN OF THE SOCIAL QUESTION

The capitalist mode of production is caught, at present, in a deep crisis; however, we must guard against the tendency to mistake the crisis of this mode of production for a weakness of capital in its struggle with labour. In fact, crises tend to *strengthen* capital's hand. For, in a crisis, the demand for labour falls at the same time as, due to massive layoffs, its supply rises. That alone

The Holding Pattern

weakens the bargaining position of workers. But more so: while it is true that capital suffers losses in the course of a downturn, it is nevertheless the case that individual capitalists rarely face an existential threat as a result of those losses. On the contrary, it is workers who, in a downturn, are threatened with the loss of their jobs – and thus the loss of everything they have. Crises weaken the position of workers, as workers.

That is why, in the midst of a crisis, capitalists can argue – correctly, from the point of view of many workers – that the restoration of the rate of profit must be put before all else. As long as workers accept the terms of the class relation, they find that their lives (even more than those of capitalists) depend on the health of the system. Restoring the profit rate is the only way to create jobs, and in the absence of a massive assault on the very existence of class society, individual proletarians have to try to find jobs or to keep them. It is thus no surprise that many workers have responded to the onset of the crisis by accepting austerity measures. It is because workers are vulnerable, now more than ever, that capitalists and their representatives are pressing their interests; they are defining what it will take to restore the system to health in ways that directly benefit them.

That's why austerity never means just temporary reductions in social spending in the midst of an economic downturn. On the contrary, social-spending programs have not only been cut back; they are being gutted or done away with entirely. In many countries, the crisis is being used as a lever with which to destroy long-held rights and entitlements, including the right to organise. And everywhere, the crisis has served as an excuse to further centralise power in the hands of technocrats, acting in the service of the most powerful states (the US, Germany). These manoeuvres are not merely cyclical adjustments in response to an economic downturn.

They are about restoring profits in the most direct way possible: suppressing wages. The Keynesian notion that, if states were acting rationally, they could somehow convince capital not to press its advantage, in the course of the downturn, is the purest ideology.

[16] Bruno Astarian, 'Crisis Activity and Communisation', *Hic Salta* (hicsalta-communisation.com).

Paradoxically, it is for these very reasons that crises are associated — not with a continuation of class struggle along normal lines — but rather, with "crisis activity".[16] Self-organising struggles break out more frequently: big demonstrations and general strikes, riots and looting, and occupations of workplaces and government buildings. In the midst of a crisis, workers find that they can only lose if they continue to play by the rules of capital's game. That is why more and more workers have stopped playing by those rules. Instead, they are engaged in struggles that challenge the terms of the capital–labour relation (without necessarily challenging its existence).

The question then arises: what specific sorts of spontaneous struggles are proletarians engaged in today? In *Endnotes* 2, we focused on the appearance and expansion of surplus populations, as the human embodiment of capital's contradictions. For that, we were criticised in some quarters. After all, surplus populations make little direct contribution to accumulation; they lack the leverage of traditional productive workers, who can bring the system to halt by withdrawing their labour. Moreover, surplus populations can be marginalised, imprisoned, and ghettoised. They can be bought off with patronage; their riots can be allowed to burn themselves out. How could surplus populations ever play a key role in the class struggle?

In late 2010, surplus populations answered this question, themselves. On December 17, Mohamed Bouazizi set himself on fire outside a police station in Sidi Bouzid. Two days later Hussein Nagi Felhi climbed an electricity pole in the same town, shouted "no to misery, no to unemployment", and electrocuted himself.

The Holding Pattern

Within days riots had spread to almost every city, and within weeks the president had fled. In the month that followed, acts of self-immolation, like signal flares, lit up the slums of North Africa: in Algeria, in Morocco, in Mauritania, and in Egypt.

Abdou Abdel-Moneim, an Egyptian baker, self-immolated on Jan 17, 2011, after being refused an allocation of subsidised flour. Traditional patronage relations were breaking down.[17] That was one side of a vice pressing down on Egypt's poor. The other, signalled by the brutal murder of Khaled Said in police custody the year before, was a ramping up of police repression. Here was the context in which Egypt's young activists — taking their cue from the overthrow of Ben Ali in Tunisia — decided to take their stand against Mubarak. Crucially, they began their marches, on January 25 (a day traditionally reserved for celebrating the police), from Cairo's poorest neighbourhoods, and they added "bread" to their already promulgated demands for "freedom" and "social justice". In response, people from these neighbourhoods spilled out into the streets. Emboldened by the example of Tunisia, this new, amalgamated struggle — bringing together class fractions whose struggles had previously unfolded in isolation — quickly spread to every major city (unlike the failed-strike-cum-bread-riot in Malhalla, in 2008).

And so, if the self-immolations were the initial moment of this struggle, then the anti-government protests that followed were its culmination. The tactics of the current wave of struggle were solidified: (1) mass riots, capable of widespread diffusion, but often focusing on a territory; (2) the transformation of that territory into an occupation, a centre of debate and display (and confrontation with the police); and (3) attempts to extend from that centre out to the surrounding areas, by means of wild demonstrations, neighbourhood assemblies, solidarity strikes, and blockades.

17 Since Egypt imports most of its wheat, rising global food prices in late 2010 helped to undermine the subsidised provision of bread to the Egyptian poor. Flour sold by the government at discounted prices was hemorrhaging into a black market characterised by high prices and rampant adulteration.

Of course, slum-dwellers were neither the only nor even the principal constituents of this new wave. Who else located themselves in the squares? Paul Mason, a BBC journalist who was on the ground for most of the movements, identified three class fractions, which all played key roles in the 2011 movement of squares: graduates with no future, the youth underclass, and organised workers.[18] It is the first in this list — that is, indebted graphic designers, impoverished administrative assistants, unpaid interns and, in North Africa, graduates on long waiting lists for bureaucratic jobs — who take the centre stage in Mason's account. However, looking back on 2011, it is apparent that the struggles of these disaffected graduates only became explosive when they were invaded and overwhelmed by the poor. In Egypt, as we saw, the January protests took off because the young activists started their marches in the slums. The same was true in England: a key turning point in the 2010 student protests was the entry of the young and restless, who came out in force to protest the discontinuation of the Education Maintenance Allowance.[19]

The point here is a more general one: insofar as the 2011 protests generalised, they tended to do so in ways that destabilised their central demands. There was a pressure towards generalisation, which nonetheless failed to unify the class. After all, what does it mean to demand freedom in a sea of Cairo's slum-dwellers? There is no chance that they will be integrated — as normal workers/consumers — into any economy, whether that of an autocratic or a liberal Egypt. By the same token, what does it mean to fight tuition hikes alongside youth from the council estates? They are likely to be excluded from the very economy into which university students are seeking entry. For that reason, alliances between college students and poor youth have been uneasy. Nevertheless, we should be clear: this tension is not the same as the one that rent the 1960s, dividing middle-class from working-class youth.

[18] Paul Mason, *Why It's Still Kicking Off Everywhere* (Verso 2012), 61.

[19] See 'A Rising Tide Lifts All Boats', in this issue.

That's because higher education has been thoroughly transformed in the half-century since 1968. In the rich countries, universities are populated, not only by the children of the elite, but also – and largely – by children of the working class. These students typically work their way through college. Even so, they rack up massive debts in order to get a degree. In that sense, the so-called neoliberal era was not only about the globalisation of misery. It was also about the globalisation of hope. Education plays a central role, here: the American Dream – freedom through private enterprise – universalised itself by means of an expanding access to university education. Get yourself a degree has replaced Guizot's *enrichissez-vous*.

Heeding the call, families everywhere are trying to send at least one of their children to school (even Mohamed Bouazizi was putting money towards his sister's degree). In this context, "the sheer size of the student population means that it is a transmitter of unrest to a much wider section of the population than before. This applies both in the developed world and in the global south. Since 2000, the global participation rate in higher education has grown from 19 to 26 percent; in Europe and North America, a staggering 70 percent now complete post-secondary education."[20] For that reason, the 1990s and 2000s were an era, not only of class defeat, but also of class compromise. Now, that compromise has been shaken, or undermined, by the crisis. The kids are screwed, and that makes a lot of sense: someone had to pay, and it was easier to delete their futures, with a keystroke, than to take away the actual jobs of older workers. In Egypt, today, unemployment is almost 10 times as high for college grads as it is for people who have only gone through elementary school. The crisis played itself out as a generational conflict.[21]

For Mason, it was the "lack of synthesis" between, on the one hand, the struggles of the two youth fractions, and on the other hand, those of the organised workers,

[20] Mason, *Why It's Still Kicking Off,* 70.

[21] To point that out is not to downplay the intergenerational solidarity displayed in these movements. All the square occupations were at least implicitly testament to this; the 'Casseroles' in support of the Quebec student strike were explicitly so. Solidarity, however, presupposes a material separation.

that broke the protest movements' strength: hence, the disjunction between the "black bloc" tearing up Oxford Street and the TUC demonstrators massing in Hyde Park, for the biggest (and most ineffectual) trade-union demo in British history.[22] Hence also, we might add, the strained relation between the ILWU longshoremen's union on the West Coast of the United States and Occupy. From the first port blockade on November 2 against the repression of Occupy Oakland, to the second blockade on December 12 in defence of the union in Longview, tensions rose as both sides feared co-optation. Things played out similarly in Greece. Partly in response to the Syntagma Square occupiers and other social movements, the Greek unions announced one-day general strikes. But in spite of their high turnout those strikes had only a minimal impact, and this impact diminished over time. In response, the unions increased the frequency of the general strikes, at times extending them to 48 hours instead of the usual 24; yet the strikes remained auxiliaries to the mass demonstrations and riots taking place on the same days, in which union stewards were reduced to bystanders.[23]

The strained relation of workers to the broader protest movements was overcome only in Egypt – and even there, only momentarily. In the final days of the Mubarak regime, workers began to form autonomous organisations, separate from the corrupt, state-run unions. More and more workers went out on strike against the regime. Mason describes this process of contagion with a phrase lifted from a psychiatrist interviewed in Cairo: what he saw was "the collapse of invisible walls".[24] This psychiatrist was referring to the walls between fractions of workers. In the hospitals, doctors, nurses and porters all began talking to each other as equals, making demands together. The walls came down.

Mason's central argument is that, if these walls did not come down, elsewhere, this was due to a clash between organisational forms: while the graduates without a

[22] Ibid., 57 and 'A Rising Tide Lifts All Boats', 139-141.

[23] In Spain and Portugal, where the general strikes generated more momentum, it seems to have been precisely because the organising was not dominated by the unions, instead taking the form of blockades involving numerous class fractions.

[24] Ibid, 21.

The Holding Pattern

future and the urban youth-underclass both formed networks, workers continued organising themselves into hierarchies. A deeper limit was confronted here, however, one bearing not only on the form of the struggle, but its content as well. There was a real conflict of interests at stake in the movement of the squares.

Among the protesters, there were those who experienced the crisis as an exclusion from secure employment: students, young precarious workers, racialised minorities, etc. But among those who were already included in secure employment, the crisis was experienced as one more threat to their sector. In short, "youth" were locked out of a system that had failed them; whereas the organised workers were concerned with trying to preserve what they knew to be a very fragile *status quo ante*. That *status quo ante* had to be preserved — not merely against the onslaughts of the austerity state, but also against the hordes of students and the poor who were trying to force their way in. That became clear in the aftermath of the protests, when, continuing an earlier trend, "youth" were easily rebranded as "immigrants", stealing jobs from deserving citizens. Here, we are concerned with the question of the content of the struggle. But what were protesters fighting for, in 2011?

4 TO BE DELIVERED FROM THE BONDAGE OF CORRUPTION

Cairo and Tunis, Istanbul and Rio, Madrid and Athens, New York and Tel Aviv — a great cacophony of demands was on display in the occupied spaces of these cities. But if one demand stood out, from among the many, it was to put an end to "crony-capitalism". The shibboleth of the occupiers was "corruption", to get money out of politics was their goal. In every square, one found signs painted with disgust: corrupt businessmen and politicians had destroyed the economy. Under the cloak of freeing up markets, they helped one another to the spoils. Perhaps that clarifies some of the other generic demands of the movements: demands for "democracy" and "equality" were precisely demands that everybody count as one, in a world where some individuals clearly counted for much more than others.

In opposing corruption, the occupiers found themselves taking up two mutually contradictory positions. (1) They criticised neoliberalism in terms of its own ideals: they wanted to eradicate corruption – handouts for the cronies – to establish a level playing field for the play of market forces. At the same time, (2) they called for the replacement of neoliberalism with a more egalitarian form of patronage: they wanted to redirect government patronage from the elites to the masses (a popular bailout to replace the bailout of the banks). It is worth pausing to consider these demands – to try to figure out what was behind them, and why their appeal was so universal, across the global movement of squares.

Leftists typically think of neoliberalism as a conspiracy to consolidate class power.[25] However, in its self-presentation – as a technocratic agenda – neoliberalism is first and foremost concerned with opposing corruption, in the form of "rent-seeking" by "special interests". What is supposed to replace rent-seeking is market competition, with its promise of fair outcomes. In that sense, neoliberalism is not so much about shifting the balance of power from the state to the market; rather, it is about fashioning a state that is compatible with market society: a capitalist state. The paradox, for neoliberal ideologues, is that their reforms have everywhere led to rising inequality, and concomitantly, to the capture of state power by a class of the extremely wealthy (centred on finance, insurance and real estate, as well as the military and oil extraction). That class has itself come – through dodgy deals and bailouts – to represent the epitome of corruption. Neoliberalism then provides a framework with which to oppose its own results.

The Holding Pattern

25 Neoliberalism has also become a catch-all term for an entire era, one that all-too-easily conflates state policy with economic turbulence, distracting from the capitalist tendencies that really unite them.

But what is corruption, exactly? To define it in a precise way is rather difficult. In many ways, corruption simply names the imbrication of capitalism with non-capitalist old regimes. Corruption is then synonymous with patronage. Non-capitalist elites as well as upstart notables compete to capture fractions of the state. They fight over ownership of income streams — so, for example, elites may control the import of flour or command state-run enterprises that weave textiles. Elites then use state-generated incomes to fund retinues, which trade their allegiance for a slice of the pie. Where property rights are still politically constituted, everyone — from the lowliest ticket-collector to the highest politician — must play the game of bribes and kickbacks.

Modernisation is, in part, a project of eradicating patronage arrangements. By centralising the state, increasing tax efficiency, and replacing direct transfers to constituents with infrastructural investment and targeted subsidies, modernisation supposedly forces everyone to secure incomes, not by state capture, but rather by competing in markets. Of course, modernisation remains woefully incomplete, in this sense. The incompleteness of the modernising project was one of the main targets of neoliberal programs of structural adjustment. But far from implying an end to corruption, the modernisation of the state — now in a neoliberal guise — actually exacerbated it. In the context of a sagging world economy, neoliberal reforms had little chance of expanding participation in markets, in virtuous cycles of growth (that was especially true, since neoliberalism was associated with a decline in public investments in infrastructure, without which modern economic growth is all but impossible).

What neoliberalism achieved, then, was to make corruption more discreet, while funnelling it towards the upper echelons of society. Corruption is now less ubiquitous but involves much larger sums of money. The small-scale bribery of officials has been supplanted by the large-scale bribery of corrupt privatisation deals and public investment projects — which flow to the wealthiest clients. The family members of dictators, Gamal Mubarak above all, have become prime targets of popular hatred, for that reason. The massive payouts they receive look all the more egregious now that (1) the state is supposed to be eradicating corruption, and (2) those lower down are no longer in on the game. This is why neoliberalism is about inequity: when old forms of patronage are undone with the promise that new sources of wealth will come to replace them, the failure of that promise reveals the new as a version of the old patronage, only now more egregious, more *unfair*.

In the high-income countries, a similar process of neoliberalisation took place. The target of reforms in the rich countries was not, however, old-regime patronage arrangements but, rather, social democratic corporatism. The latter had replaced the former in the course of the twentieth century; now, it was itself to be dismantled. Once again, the much-vaunted freeing of the market was supposed to benefit everyone. When economic growth failed to appear, neoliberalism meant only that handouts had been funnelled up towards the top.

That process was perhaps most clear on the Northern and Eastern shores of the Mediterranean, where state funds (and flows of hot money) were channeled into infrastructural investment. From the late 80s to the 2008 crash, the economies of Spain, Greece and Turkey were largely kept afloat by a massive construction boom. Construction is, by its very nature, a temporary form of stimulus: many people can be employed, to build a road network, but only a few are needed for upkeep or maintenance, once that network has been built. For that reason, urban development projects can offset a decline in profitability only temporarily. An infrastructure boom merely defers the crisis by locking up surplus capital in the expansion of the built environment.

The Holding Pattern

When this growth machine runs out of fuel, it sometimes leaves behind impressive but useless ruins. Corruption today appears as empty airports in isolated corners of Spain; half-built tower-blocks overlooking an Athenian port; and plans for a shopping mall in a poor neighbourhood of Istanbul. What makes these projects corrupt is not so much the insider deals that directed government agencies to throw away their money on follies. In truth, those deals appeared as corrupt only retrospectively: when the tourists stopped coming, the housing market collapsed and consumer spending declined. In that moment, insider deals were no longer experienced as relatively harmless accompaniments to economic growth. Instead, they started to look like the old patronage, but now, with much larger sums of money at stake (due to the greater borrowing capacity of states in the run-up to the crisis) and also, a much smaller circle of beneficiaries.[26]

In the UK and US, too, corruption was a common theme of UK Uncut and OWS.[27] However, in both countries, the demand to end corruption was not a matter of shady construction projects and political kickbacks. Instead, that demand was formulated in response to the gigantic corporate bailouts orchestrated in the aftermath of the collapse of Lehman Brothers and RBS. But the same rule holds here, as elsewhere: what made these bailouts "corrupt" was less the shady circumstances under which they were made, than the fact that they seemed to have nothing to do with restoring economic growth (that is, creating jobs, etc.).

In opposing these different manifestations of corruption, the occupiers of the squares seemed to be promoting two somewhat divergent ideas.

1) The rich should be made to feel the pain of the crisis, and of the austerity that followed. After all, neoliberal ideologues argued that everyone should take "personal responsibility" for themselves and their actions; in that sense, everyone should aspire to be petty bourgeois.

26 It is not only around the shores of the Mediterranean that anti-corruption demands circulated. Like Turkey, Brazil also witnessed a construction bonanza, putting money in the hands of stadium builders even as the cost of living was rising sharply for the urban poor. Added to that, a series of political scandals made it inevitable that denunciations of corrupt politicians would be a major theme of the riots that swept the country in June 2013.

27 *Adbusters* initially proposed that the 'one demand' of OWS be to get Obama to start a 'Presidential Commission tasked with ending the influence money has over our representatives in Washington.' In the end this demand was not taken up, but the one demand that was passed by an OWS general assembly, to support the Citizen's

The target of this discourse were the unions, as well as anyone drawing state benefits. As we saw above, however, the biggest handouts went not to the unions or the ultra-poor, but quite visibly to the ultra-rich. They made out like bandits, while everyone else suffered, through not only economic crisis, but also austerity. To get money out of politics would mean: to force the ultra-rich to take responsibility for their own actions.

2) At the same time, to the extent that venal politicians were cutting supports for the poor while handing out money to the rich, the occupiers demanded, not a levelling of the playing field, but rather, its tilting in their favour. State patronage should be directed away from fat cats and towards populist constituents ("the nation"). Occupiers thus demanded a popular bailout, both out of a sense of what is frequently called "social justice" and also because, like good Keynesian economists, they hoped that a popular bailout would restore the economy to health.

Behind this second demand rests a truth that has become increasingly obvious: a large portion of the population has been left out of the economic growth of the past few decades, and there is no plan to bring them back in. Throughout low-income countries, direct state patronage to the poor – a crucial foundation of the clientelist state – has gradually eroded, while privatisation deals benefit a slim layer of the elite. The limited partnership, in which the poor had been able to enjoy some of the gains of the nationalist project, is being dismantled.

It is worth noting that this dismantling has a generational aspect – particularly important in developing countries where population growth rates are high. Politicians know that populist measures cannot be wound down across the board without provoking mass anger and potentially mass rebellion. Instead, the state proceeds sector by sector. It begins by taking away the as yet unrealised privileges of the next generation. This process

United campaign against corporate personhood, was also centrally about the undue influence of corporations on the government. Such sentiments were constantly on view at occupy, e.g. 'I can't afford my own politician so I made this sign.'

is clearly at work in the shrinking urban formal sector in Egypt – now accounting for roughly ten percent of the workforce (including food processing, textiles, transport, cement, construction, and steel). Young people find themselves locked out of "good" jobs. Instead, they are confined to the non-agricultural informal sector, which absorbs over two-thirds of the workforce.

However, the state has not only retreated. When it can no longer afford to keep up its side of the patrimonial bargain, the state replaces handouts to the poor with police repression. The lines of patronage are thereby contracted and rearranged: the police and army benefit from an increased access to patronage, even as many other sectors lose such access. The police and army come to employ a fraction of those who would otherwise have found themselves on the outside of the new patronage system, but they employ that fraction only to keep the rest in line. Hence the potent symbolism of Bouazizi and Abdel Moneim. One body burnt to signal police repression, the other to signal a breakdown of popular state patronage. These two experiences are directly intertwined.[28]

It is for these reasons that the police have become the most potent manifestation, and the most hated symbol, of corruption. The expansion and militarisation of the police force seems to be the worst sign of the times. States everywhere are demonstrating that they are willing to spend huge amounts of money paying police, constructing prisons, and so on – even while they cut funding for schools and hospitals. States are no longer oriented, even superficially, towards treating their populations as ends in themselves. On the contrary, states now see their populations as security threats and are willing to pay to contain them.

Such containment is an everyday reality, especially for marginalised sections of the proletariat. Since the police are usually underpaid, they often supplement their incomes

[28] L.S. 'Hanging by a Thread: Class, Corruption and Precarity in Tunisia', *Mute,* January 2012 (metamute.org).

with bribes and kickbacks that are extracted from the poor. Daily interactions with the police thus reveal the latter to be some of the last remaining beneficiaries of the old corruption. At the same time, in squeezing the most vulnerable sections of the population, the police enforce the new corruption: they quash any resistance to an increasingly wealthy, neo-patrimonial elite.

The police do not only extract money from the poor; they are also out for blood. The overgrowth of police forces has everywhere been accompanied by a rise in arbitrary police violence and police killings, often the trigger for riots. Each time another body hits the ground, a section of the population receives the message loud and clear: "you no longer matter to us; be gone". This same message is on display, in a more punctuated way, in the anti-austerity protests. The police are there, on the front-lines of the conflict, making sure that the population stays in line and does not complain too much about the injustice of it all.

Opposition to corruption thus has a real basis in the immediate experience of the protestors. The fight against corruption registers a bitter experience of getting shut out, in a double sense. On the one hand, individuals are unable to enjoy the growing wealth of the new globalised economy, which is on display in the conspicuous consumption of the new rich. On the other hand, those same individuals find that they have been equally shut out of older systems of patronage – which were also systems of recognition (whether in its old regime or workerist form). Thus, to complain of corruption is not only to register the extremes to which inequality has risen, or the unfairness with which wealth is redistributed upwards in so many shady contracts. It is also about decrying a lack of recognition, or the fear of losing it: rampant corruption means that, at a basic level, one does not really count (or is in danger of not counting) as a member of the nation. What takes the place of a national community is only the police, as the arbiters

The Holding Pattern

of the shakeout. What would repair this situation, and restore the community? The occupations were themselves an attempt to answer this question.

5 THE PROBLEM OF COMPOSITION

The 2011 protesters put their bodies and their suffering on display, in public squares, in order to reveal the human consequences of an unrelenting social crisis. But they did not remain in that conceptual space for long. Occupiers spontaneously opted for direct democracy and mutual aid, in order to show the powers that be that another form of sociality is possible: it is possible to treat human beings as equal in terms of their right to speak and their right to be heard.

In the course of the occupations, horizontalist models of organisation tended to become ends in themselves. Faced with implacable and/or insolvent state-power, the occupiers turned inwards, to find within their self-activity a human community — one in which there was no longer a need for hierarchy, leadership or status differentiation. It was enough to be present in the squares, in order to be counted. No other affiliation or allegiance was necessary; indeed, other affiliations were often viewed with suspicion. In this way, anti-government protests — which took it as their goal to shoo the plutocrats out of office — became anti-government protests in another sense. They became anti-political. Of course, this transformation should not be seen solely as a progression: it marked an oscillation in the orientation of the protesters, from outwards to inwards and back out again.

Searching for precursors to this feature of the movement of squares has proven difficult. The movement's horizontalism was there in Argentina, in 2001. The movement also replicated the forms — consensus-based decision-making, above all — of the anti-globalisation protests (and before that, of the anti-nuclear protests).

But the movement of squares was different because the square occupations lasted for so long. For that reason, the occupiers were forced to take their own reproduction as an object.[29] The occupiers had to decide how to live together. Their ability to persist in the squares – to occupy for as long as it took to have an impact – was their only strength; their leverage was that they refused to leave. They adopted forms of governance that they claimed were better than the ones on offer in this broke and broken society.

It may be that the most relevant precursor to this feature of the movements is to be found in a previous square occupation, one that seems not to have been a direct reference for the 2011 protesters. That is Tiananmen Square. Despite his simplifications, Italian philosopher Giorgio Agamben captured something of the spirit of Tiananmen, in a way that is prescient of the 2011 protest movement. In *The Coming Community*, Agamben, speaking of "a herald from Beijing", characterises Tiananmen as a movement whose generic demands for freedom and democracy belie the fact that the real object of the movement was to *compose itself*.[30] The community that came together, in Tiananmen, was mediated "not by any condition of belonging" nor "by the simple absence of conditions", but rather, "by belonging itself".[31] The goal of the demonstrators was to "form a community without affirming an identity" where "humans co-belong without any representable condition of belonging".[32]

Agamben claims that, by disassociating themselves from all markers of identity, the occupiers of Tiananmen became "whatever singularities".[33] These whatever singularities remain precisely what they are, regardless of the qualities they happen to possess in any given moment. According to Agamben, in presenting themselves in this way, the occupiers necessarily ran aground on the representational logic of the state: the state sought to fix the occupiers into a specific identity, which could

[29] See Rust Bunnies & Co., 'Under the Riot Gear' in *SIC* 2, forthcoming.

[30] Giorgio Agamben, *The Coming Community* (University of Minnesota Press 1993), 85.

[31] Ibid., 85.

[32] Ibid., 86.

[33] Ibid., 85. The term is explained in the book's opening chapter.

The Holding Pattern

then be included or excluded as such. Thus, Agamben concludes: "wherever these singularities peacefully demonstrate their being-in-common, there will be a Tiananmen, and, sooner or later, the tanks will appear".[34]

[34] Ibid., 87.

To form a community mediated by belonging itself, in Agamben's sense, means the following: (1) The community is composed of all those who happen to be there; there are no other conditions of belonging. (2) The community does not mediate between pre-existing identities, in a coalitional politics; instead, it is born *ex nihilo*. (3) The community does not seek recognition by the state. It presents itself, at the limit, as an alternative to the state: real democracy, or even the overcoming of democracy. (4) The task of such a community is to encourage everyone else to desert their posts, in society, and to join the community, as "whatever singularities". This description matches the self-conception of the 2011 occupiers. They, too, wanted to be whatever singularities, even if they referred to themselves in a less philosophical fashion.

But we should be clear: for Agamben, Tiananmen *already consisted* of whatever singularities. The separation between students and workers that pervaded the square, down to the details of where one could sit, falls out of his account, entirely. Yet despite its failings as a description, Agamben's account captures something of the normative orientation of the movements. For it seems that in Tiananmen — as in the Plaza del Sol, Syntagma Square and Zucotti Park — the participants believed themselves to be beyond the determinations of the society in which they lived. The 2011 protesters certainly felt that way: they proposed to fight crony capitalism on that very basis.

The truth was, however, that the protesters remained firmly anchored to the society of which even their squares were a part. That was clear enough in the divisions between more "middle class" participants and the poor. But it wasn't only that: individuals with all sorts of pre-existing affinities tended to congregate in this or that corner of the square. They set up their tents in circles, with the open flaps facing inwards. More insidious divisions emerged along gender lines. The participation of women in the occupations took place under the threat of rape by some of the men; women were forced to organise for their self-defence.[35] Such divisions were not dissolvable into a unity that consisted only of consensus-based decision-making and collective cooking.

Here's the thing: the fact that the 2011 movements presented themselves as already unified, as already beyond the determinations of a horrible society, meant that their internal divisions were usually disavowed. Because they were disavowed, those divisions could only appear as threats to the movement. That is not to say that internal divisions were simply suppressed: it was rather that divisions could only be resolved – within the confines of the squares – by forming another committee or promulgating a new rule of action.[36]

The movement was forced to look inward, in this way, because it was barred from looking outward. Without the capacity to move out of the squares and into society – without beginning to dismantle society – there is no possibility of undoing the class relation on which the proletariat's internal divisions are based. The occupiers were thus contained within the squares, as in a pressure cooker. Class fractions that typically keep their distance from each other were forced to recognise one another and sometimes live together. In the tensions that resulted, the movement came up against what we call the problem of composition.

The composition problem names the problem of composing, coordinating or unifying proletarian fractions, in the course of their struggle. Unlike in the past – or at least, unlike in ideal-typical representations of the

[35] The best accounts of anti sexual harassment organising in Egypt can be found in the videos produced by the Mosireen collective (mosireen.org), and the testimonies translated on the facebook page of OPANTISH (OPeration ANTI-Sexual Harassment).

[36] Because it went so much further than all the other movements, Egypt was something of an exception in this respect. After the massacres of Mohamed Mahmoud St., the division between the Brotherhood and everyone else was clearly marked, with irreversible results.

The Holding Pattern

past — it is no longer possible to read class fractions as already composing themselves, as if their unity were somehow given "in-itself" (as the unity of the craft, mass or "social" worker). Today, no such unity exists; nor can it be expected to come into existence with further changes in the technical composition of production. In that sense, there is no predefined revolutionary subject. There is no "for-itself" class-consciousness, as the consciousness of a general interest, shared among all workers. Or rather, such consciousness can only be the consciousness of capital, of what unifies workers precisely by separating them.

The composition of the class thus appears, today, not as a pole of attraction within the class, but rather, as an unresolved problem: how can the class act against capital, in spite of its divisions? The movement of squares was — for a while — able to suspend this problem. The virtue of the occupations was to create a space between an impossible class struggle and a tepid populism, where protesters could momentarily unify, in spite of their divisions. That made for a qualitative leap in the intensity of the struggle. But at the same time, it meant that when the protesters came up against the composition problem, they found that problem impossible to solve.

For the occupiers came together by sidestepping the composition problem. They named their unity in the most abstract way: they were "indignant citizens" or "the 99 percent". It would have been unfashionable to say that they were the working class or the proletariat, but it would have made no difference: every universal is abstract when the unity it names has no concrete existence. For these reasons, the unity of the occupiers was necessarily a weak unity. It could hold together only so long as the occupiers could contain the divisions that reappeared inside the camps — divisions that were already present in everyday social relations: race, gender, nation, age, etc.[37] Is it possible to approach

[37] We should remember, however, that there are many divisions that escape these terms — or that are invented only in the course of concrete struggles. The proletariat is divided up in ways that cannot be named in advance. Thus, the point is not to name the terms of the composition problem, but only, to name the problem itself, as a key strategic question of our times.

the composition problem from the opposite angle, to begin from the divisions within the proletariat, and on that basis, to pose the question of unity?

Perhaps it is only by deferring unity, to make divisions appear as such, that proletarians will be forced to pose the question of their real unification, against their unity-in-separation for capital. In that case, in order to really unite, proletarians will have to become the beyond of this society – and not in an imagined way, but rather, by relating to one another, materially, outside of the terms of the class relation.

Why is the proletariat so hopelessly divided, today, as compared to the past? This question is more accurately posed as follows: why do divisions within the proletariat appear so clearly on the surface of society? How did identity politics come to replace class-based politics?

In the past, it seemed possible to disavow non-class identities, on the basis of an all-encompassing class identity. That disavowal was supported by ongoing transformations in the mode of production: capital had created the industrial working class; it seemed that it would now draw more and more workers into the factories (or else, that all work would be transformed after the fashion of the factories). As the industrial working class grew in size and strength, it was expected to become more homogeneous. The factory would render divisions of race, gender and religion inessential, as compared to class belonging – that was the sole identity that mattered, at least according to the workers' movement.

We would like to suggest that this vision of the future was possible only on the basis of a high demand for labour in industry. Of course, a high demand for labour has never really been a regular feature of capitalist societies (long booms are actually few and far between in capital's history). Nevertheless, it is possible to say that the demand for labour in industry was typically higher in the past than it has been since the 1970s. For, in the past, workers were drawn into the industrial sector, not completely, but tendentially. That had effects: when the demand for labour in industry is high, capital is forced to hire workers who are normally excluded from high value-added segments of production, on the basis of gender, race, religion, etc. A high demand for labour breaks down prejudices among *both* managers and workers, on that basis. What is supposed to follow is a material convergence of workers' interests.

That convergence did take place, at least to some extent, in the course of the workers' movement.[38] For example, in the US, agricultural mechanisation in the South displaced black sharecroppers, propelling their migration to booming Northern cities. There, blacks were absorbed into factories, and so also, into workers' unions. The integration of black workers into unions did not occur without a struggle, nor was it ever completed. Nevertheless, it was underway in the 1960s.

Then, this integration ran up against external limits. Just as the door to integration was beginning to open, it was suddenly slammed shut. The industrial demand for labour slackened, first in the late 1960s and then, again, in the crisis years of the early 1970s. The last hired were first fired. For black Americans, jails replaced jobs. The growth of the prison population corresponded closely to the decline in industrial employment.

A similar turn of events took place on the world-scale. During the postwar boom, low-income countries were tendentially integrated into the club of industrialised nations. But they were integrated only as the postwar boom was reaching its limits. Indeed, they were integrated precisely because it was reaching its limits: as competition intensified, firms were compelled to

[38] However, this process of unification was always incomplete. The workers' movement constituted itself as an attempt to force its completion (see 'A History of Separation', forthcoming in *Endnotes* 4).

Endnotes 3   **50**

scour the globe in search of cheap labour. Once the boom gave way to a long downturn, that integration broke down.

What has happened, since the 1970s, is that the surplus population has grown steadily. In essence, the growth of surplus populations put class integration into reverse; integration became fragmentation. That's because the industrial demand for labour is low. With many applications for each job, managers' prejudices (e.g certain "races" are lazy) have real effects, in determining who does or does not get a "good" job. As a result, some fractions of the class pool at the bottom of the labour market. What makes those fractions unattractive to certain employers then makes them very attractive to others – particularly in jobs where a high employee turnover is not really a cost to employers. The existence of a large surplus population creates the conditions for the separation out of a super-exploited segment of the class, which Marx called the stagnant surplus population. That separation reinforces prejudices among privileged workers, who know (on some level) that they got their "good" jobs based on employers' prejudice. It also reinforces non-class identities among the excluded, since those identities form the basis of their exclusion.

However, while capital is no longer overcoming divisions, the very scrambled nature of the new divisions seems to weaken them, in certain ways. Because it is an ongoing process, we can perhaps say that, tendentially, the unfolding of the general law of capital accumulation undermines stable identity formations in all segments of the labour market. More and more people are falling into the surplus population; anyone can, potentially. Increasingly, the stable-unstable distinction is the one that regulates all the other distinctions within the working class. That leads to a widespread sense that all identities are fundamentally *inessential*, in two senses:

The Holding Pattern

1) Not everyone, even within the most marginalised sections of the class, is excluded from stable jobs and public recognition. The present era has seen the rise of individuals from marginalised populations to the heights of power. That there are many women CEOs — and one black US president — gives everyone the impression that no stigma, no mark of abjection, is wholly insurmountable.

2) But also, the very nature of precarity is to dissolve fixed positions. Very few proletarians identify any of their qualifications or capacities as essential determinants of themselves. In a world without security there can be no pretence to normality, to identities that remain stable over time. Instead, lives are cobbled together, without a clear sense of progression. All lifestyles are commodified, their parts interchangeable. These features of a fragmented proletariat were present in the squares.

6 CONCLUSION: POINTS OF NO RETURN

What comes next? It is impossible to say in advance. What we know is that, at least for the moment, we live and fight within the holding pattern. The crisis has been stalled. In order to make the crisis stall, the state has been forced to undertake extraordinary actions. It is hard to deny that state interventions, over the past few years, have seemed like a last ditch effort. Interest rates are bottoming out at zero percent. The government is spending billions of dollars, every month, just in order to convince capital to invest in a trickle. For how long? And yet, for this long, at least, state interventions have worked. The crisis has been petrified. And its petrification has been the petrification of the struggle.

Indeed, since the crisis has been stalled, the class struggle remains that of the most eager and the worst off. Everyone else hopes that, if they keep their heads down, they will survive until the real recovery begins. Meanwhile, those engaged in struggle are themselves mostly lost in false hopes of their own: they hope that the state can be convinced to act rationally, to undertake a more radical Keynesian stimulus. The protesters hope that capitalism can be forced to rid itself of cronies and act in the interest of the nation. Unlikely to abandon this perspective – as long as it seems remotely plausible – anti-austerity struggles are themselves stuck in a holding pattern. They confront the objectivity of the crisis only in the state's impassiveness in response to their demands.

We see three scenarios, going forward:

1) The holding pattern could be maintained for a while longer, so that a second wave of struggle, like the 2011–13 wave, might emerge within its confines. That second wave may remain tepid, like its predecessor often was. But it is also possible that it could become stronger, on the basis of real bonds that have been created over the past few years. If that happens, we could see the resurgence of a radical democratic movement, more popular than that of the anti-globalisation era. This movement would not necessarily focus on square occupations; it may announce itself by means of some other tactic, impossible to foresee. Such a movement, were it able to find a leverage point, might be able to renegotiate the terms on which the crisis is being managed. For example, protesters may be able to foist the fallout of the crisis on to the super rich: with a new Tobin Tax, progressive income taxes, or limitations on CEO pay. Perhaps rioters will form substantial organisations, which are able to press for the end of arbitrary police violence and a partial de-militarisation of police forces. Maybe Arab states can be made to raise public employment levels, in order to absorb a backlog of unemployed university graduates. In any case, all of these demands, even if they were achieved, would be like forming a workers' council on the deck of the Titanic. They would be self-managing a sinking ship (though, admittedly, since the icebergs are melting, what that ship would hit is as yet unknown).

The Holding Pattern

2) The holding pattern could be maintained for a while longer, but the second wave of struggle, within its confines, could look radically different than the first one. Perhaps — taking their cue from the movement of squares — proletarians will see an opening for a new, more or less informal, rank-and-file unionism. This unionism, if it infected the huge mass of unorganised, private-sector service workers, could radically transform the terms within which the crisis is managed. It might be possible, on that basis, to approach the composition problem from the other way around. Fast food workers are currently striking in the United States, demanding a doubling of their wages. What if they succeed and that success acts as a signal for the rest of the class to pour out onto the streets? It is important to remember that a massive shift in the terms of the class struggle does not always correspond to a rise in the intensity of the crisis. The objective and subjective moments of the class relation do not necessarily move in sync.

3) Finally, there could be an intensification of the crisis, a global bottoming out, beginning with a deep downturn in India or China. Or else, the winding down of Quantitative Easing could spiral out of control. The end of the holding pattern would scramble all the terms of the era we have described. Ours would no longer be an austerity crisis, but rather, something else entirely, affecting much broader sections of the population. To blame corrupt politicians would no longer be possible, or at least, it would no longer be useful, since the possibility of a state management of the crisis would be foreclosed. That is not to say that revolution will suddenly appear on the table, as the only option left. To get worse is not necessarily to get better. The divisions within the proletariat run deep, and they only deepen with the further growth of the surplus population. It is entirely possible to imagine that class fractions will turn against each other, that hating one another, and ensuring that no one gets slightly better than anyone else, will take precedence over making the revolution.

THE LOGIC OF GENDER

On the separation of spheres
and the process of abjection

Within marxist feminism we encounter several sets of binary terms to analyse gendered forms of domination under capitalism.[1] These include: productive and reproductive, paid and unpaid, public and private, sex and gender. When considering the gender question, we found these categories imprecise, theoretically deficient and sometimes even misleading. This article is an attempt to propose categories which will give us a better grasp of the transformation of the gender relation since the 70s and, more importantly, since the recent crisis.

The account that follows is strongly influenced by systematic dialectics, a method that tries to understand social forms as interconnected moments of a totality.[2] We therefore move from the most abstract categories to the most concrete, tracing the unfolding of gender as a "real abstraction". We are only concerned with the form of gender specific to capitalism, and we assume from the outset that one can talk about gender without any reference to biology or prehistory. We begin by defining gender as a separation between spheres. Then, having done so, we specify the individuals assigned to those spheres. Importantly, we do not define spheres in spatial terms, but rather in the same way Marx spoke of the two separated spheres of production and circulation, as *concepts* that take on a materiality.

The binaries listed above appear to limit one's grasp of the ways in which these spheres function at present, as they lack historical specificity and promote a transhistorical understanding of gendered "domination", which takes patriarchy as a feature of capitalism *without making it historically specific to capitalism*. We hope to delineate categories that are as specific to capitalism as "capital" itself. We argue that these binaries depend on category errors whose faults become clear once we attempt to illuminate the transformations within capitalist society since the 70s. Forms of domestic and so-called "reproductive" activities have become

[1] In the broadest strokes, marxist feminism is a perspective which situates gender oppression in terms of social reproduction, and specifically the reproduction of labour-power. Often it considers the treatment of such topics in Marx and in subsequent marxist accounts of capitalism deficient, and in light of the 'unhappy marriage' and 'dual systems' debates, it generally supports a 'single system' thesis. It is also worth noting that this article is meant to continue a conversation from the 1970s, the 'domestic labour debate,' which turns on the relationship between value and reproduction, and which deploys Marxist categories in order to consider whether 'domestic' and 'reproductive' labour are productive.

[2] See 'Communisation and Value-Form Theory', *Endnotes* 2 (April 2010).

The Logic of Gender

increasingly marketised, and while these activities may occupy the "sphere" of the home, just as they did before, they no longer occupy the same structural positions within the capitalist totality, despite exhibiting the same concrete features. For this reason, we found ourselves forced to clarify, transform, and redefine the categories we received from marxist feminism, not for the sake of theory, but to understand why humanity is still powerfully inscribed with one or the other gender.

1 PRODUCTION/REPRODUCTION

> Whatever the form of the process of production in a society, it must be a continuous process, must continue to go periodically through the same phases. A society can no more cease to produce than it can cease to consume. When viewed, therefore, as a connected whole, and as flowing on with incessant renewal, every social process of production is, at the same time, a process of reproduction.[3]

3 Marx, *Capital*, vol.1 (MECW 35), 565.

When Marx speaks of reproduction he does not refer to the production and reproduction of any commodity in particular; rather, he is concerned with the reproduction of the social totality. However, when marxist feminists speak of reproduction, what they often aim to specify is the production and reproduction of the commodity labour-power. This is because, in Marx's critique, the relationship between the reproduction of labour-power and the reproduction of the capitalist totality is incomplete.

i When Marx speaks of labour-power, he claims it is a commodity with a distinctive character, unlike any other

Although Marx speaks of the specificities of the commodity labour-power,[4] there are some aspects of this specification which require more attention.

4 Marx, *Capital*, vol. 1 (MECW 35), chapter 6.

First, let us investigate the separation between labour-power and its bearer. The exchange of labour-power presupposes that this commodity is brought to the market by its bearer. However, in this particular case, labour-power and its bearer are one and the same living person. Labour-power is the living, labouring capacity of this person, and as such, it cannot be detached from the bearer. Thus the particularity of labour-power poses an ontological question.

Going back to *Capital*, at the outset of Chapter One we encounter the commodity, and it is only a few chapters later that we will fully discover its most peculiar manifestation, that is to say, labour-power. In accord with Marx, it is correct to begin with the naturalised and self-evident realm of commodity circulation, in order to render the commodity a curious and unnatural thing indeed. We will not, however, enquire only about what organises these "things", these objects; but rather – in terms of a gender analysis – we will enquire into these *other bodies*, human objects, which bumble about in their own "natural" way, and who, like the fetishised commodity, appear to have no history. Yet they surely do.

For at the heart of the commodity form is the dual character of labour – both abstract and concrete – and accordingly, Chapter One of *Capital* introduces the contradiction between use-value and (exchange) value. This is the contradiction which unfolds from the first pages of Marx's critique to the very end. Indeed, the split between these two irreconcilable aspects of the commodity form is the guiding thread that allows Marx to trace and disclose all the other contradictory forms that constitute the capitalist mode of production.

Let us summarise briefly this contradiction. On the one hand, the commodity in its aspect as use-value stands, in all its singularity, as a particular object differentiated from the next. It has a definite use which, as Marx claims, is necessary for its production as exchange-value. In addition, because it is singular, it is a single unit, one of many which add up to a sum, a quantity of individual things. It does not amount to a sum of homogeneous labour-time in the abstract, but a sum of concrete individual and separable labours. On the other hand, in its aspect as exchange-value, it represents an aliquot portion of the "total social labour" within society — a quantum of socially necessary labour time, or the average time required for its reproduction.

This contradiction, *the* contradiction — far from being specific only to "things" — is fundamentally the very condition of being in the world for a proletarian. From this standpoint, the proletarian confronts the world in which the capitalist mode of production prevails as an accumulation of commodities; the proletarian does this *as* a commodity — and therefore this confrontation is at once a chance meeting between one commodity and another, and at the same time an encounter between subject and object.

This ontological split exists because labour-power is neither a person nor *just* a commodity. As Marx tells us, the commodity labour-power is peculiar and unlike any other. The peculiarity of the commodity labour-power is what gives it a central place in a mode of production based on value, as the very use-value of labour-power (or living labour capacity) is *the* source of (exchange-) value. Furthermore, the contradiction between use-value and (exchange) value has additional implications, when we consider the very production and reproduction of labour-powers. This peculiar "production" is specific enough to deserve extra attention, for, as far as we know, *at no time does a labour-power roll off an assembly line*.

How then is labour-power produced and reproduced? Marx identifies the particularity of the use-value of labour-power. But does he adequately distinguish the production of labour-power from the production of other commodities? He writes:

the labour-time requisite for the production of labour-power reduces itself to that necessary for the production of [its] means of subsistence.[5]

[5] Marx, *Capital* vol. 1 (MECW 35), 181.

When raising the problem of the value of labour-power, Marx concludes that it is equal to the labour-time necessary for its production, as is the case for any other commodity. However, in this case, it is mysteriously reduced to the labour-time necessary for the production of the worker's means of subsistence. But a cart full of "means of subsistence" does not produce labour-power as a ready-made commodity.

If we were to compare the production of labour-power with the production of any other commodity, we would see that the "raw materials" used for this production process, i.e. the means of subsistence, transmit their value to the end product, while the new labour needed to turn these commodities into a functioning labour-power adds no value to this commodity. If we were to push this analogy further, we could say that – in terms of value – labour-power consists only of *dead labour*.

In the above quote, Marx reduces the necessary labour required to produce labour-power to the "raw materials" purchased in order to accomplish its (re)production. Any labour necessary to turn this raw material, this basket of goods, into the commodity labour-power, is therefore not considered living labour by Marx, and indeed, in the capitalist mode of production it is not deemed necessary labour at all. This means that however necessary these activities are for the production and reproduction of labour-power, *they are structurally made non-labour*. This necessary labour is not considered as such by Marx because the activity of turning the raw materials equivalent to the wage into labour-power takes place *in a separate sphere from the production and circulation of values*. These necessary non-labour activities do not produce value, not because of their concrete characteristics, but rather, because they take place in a sphere of the capitalist mode of production which is not directly mediated by the form of value.

There must be an exterior to value in order for value to exist. Similarly, for labour to exist and serve as the measure of value, there must be an exterior to labour (we will return to this in part two). While the autonomist feminists would conclude that every activity which reproduces labour-power produces value,[6] we would say that, for labour-power to have a value, some of these activities have to be cut off or dissociated from the sphere of value production.[7]

[6] Such as Leopoldina Fortunati: see *The Arcane of Reproduction* (Autonomedia 1981).

[7] On this point, we are very much influenced by Roswitha Scholz's value-dissociation theory, even if there remain major differences in our analyses, especially when it comes to the dynamics of gender. See Roswitha Scholz, *Das Geschlecht des Kapitalismus* (Horleman 2000).

ii Therefore, the reproduction of labour-power presupposes the separation of two different spheres

As articulated above, there is a sphere of non-labour or extra-necessary labour which envelops the process of transforming dead labour, that is commodities purchased with the wage, into the living labour capacity found on the market. We must now look at the specificities of this sphere.

Terms like the "reproductive sphere" are insufficient for identifying this sphere, because what we are trying to name cannot be defined as a specific set of activities according to their use-value or concrete character. Indeed, the same concrete activity, like cleaning or cooking, can take place in either sphere: it can be value-producing labour in one specific social context and non-labour in another. Reproductive tasks such as cleaning can be purchased as services, and prefab meals can be bought in place of time spent preparing meals. However, to fully appreciate how — beyond labour-power — gender is reproduced, it will be necessary to differentiate reproduction that is commodified, monetised, or mass produced from that which is not.

Because the existing concepts of production and reproduction are themselves limited, we need to find more precise terms to designate these two spheres. From now on we will use two very descriptive (and therefore rather clunky) terms to name them: (a) the *directly market-mediated* sphere (DMM); and (b) the *indirectly market-mediated* sphere (IMM). Rather than coming up with jargonistic neologisms, our aim is to use these as placeholders and to concentrate on the structural characteristics of these two spheres. In the course of our presentation (see Part 2) we will have to add another set of descriptive terms (waged/unwaged) to sufficiently elaborate the nuanced characteristics of these spheres.

The production and reproduction of labour-power necessitates a whole set of activities; some of them are performed in the directly market-mediated or DMM sphere (those that are bought as commodities, either as product or service), while others take place in that sphere which is not directly mediated by the market – the IMM sphere. The difference between these activities does not lie in their concrete characteristics. Each of these concrete activities – cooking, looking after children, washing/mending clothes – can sometimes produce value and sometimes not, depending upon the "sphere", rather than the actual place, in which it occurs. The sphere, therefore, is not necessarily the home. Nor is this sphere defined by whether or not the activities taking place within it consist of those that reproduce labour-power. It is defined by the relationship of these reproductive tasks to exchange, the market and the accumulation of capital.

This conceptual distinction has material consequences. Within the directly market-mediated sphere, reproductive tasks are performed under directly capitalist conditions, that is, with all the requirements of the market, whether they are performed within the manufacturing or the service sector. Under the constraints and command of capital and the market, the production of goods and services, regardless of their content, must be performed at competitive levels in terms of productivity, efficiency and product uniformity. The index of productivity is temporal, while that of efficiency pertains to the ways in which inputs are economically utilised. Furthermore, the uniformity of the product of labour requires the uniformity of the labouring process, and of the relationship of those who produce to what they produce.

One can immediately see the difference between tasks performed in this sphere, and that outside of it. In the DMM sphere, the rate of return on a capitalist investment is paramount and therefore all activities performed – even if they are "reproductive" in their use-value character – must meet or exceed the going rate of exploitation and/or profit. On the other hand, outside the DMM sphere, the ways in which the wage is utilised by those who reproduce the use-value labour-power (via the reproduction of its bearer) is not subject to the same requirements. If those ways are uniform at all, they are nevertheless highly variable in terms of the necessary utilisation of time, money and raw materials. Unlike in the DMM sphere, there is no direct market-determination of every aspect of the reproduction process. (In Part 2 we will address the indirectly market-mediated sphere of state-organised reproduction).

The indirectly market-mediated sphere has a different temporal character. The 24-hour day and 7-day week[8] still organise the activities within this sphere, but "socially necessary labour time" (SNLT) is never *directly* a factor in that organisation. SNLT applies to the process of abstraction occurring through the mediation of the market, which averages out the amount of time required within the labour process to competitively sell a product or service. Bankruptcy and the loss of profit are factors weighing on this process; likewise the innovative use of machinery in order to decrease the time required to produce goods. Thus, the increase of profit or market

[8] That is, homogeneous time. See Moishe Postone, *Time, Labour and Social Domination* (Cambridge University Press 1993), chapter 5, 'Abstract Time'.

share dominates the DMM sphere. Of course, mechanisation is also possible in the IMM sphere, and there have been many innovations of that sort. In this case, however, the aim is not to allow the production of more use-values in a given amount of time, but to reduce the time spent on a given activity, usually so that more time can be dedicated to another IMM activity. When it comes to the care of children, for example, even if some activities can be performed more quickly, they have to be looked after the *whole day*, and this amount of time is not flexible (we will return to this in part 5).

In addition, different forms of domination characterise these spheres respectively. Market dependency, or impersonal abstract domination, organises DMM relations of production and reproduction, through the mechanism of value-comparison in terms of socially necessary labour time. The kind of "direct market-mediation" within this sphere is abstract domination, and as such, it is a form of indirect compulsion determined on the market ("behind the backs of the producers"). Hence, there is no structural necessity toward direct violence, or planning, in order to allocate labour *per se*.

In contrast, there is no such mechanism comparing the various performances of the concrete activities occurring in the IMM sphere – which is to say, as being socially determined. They cannot be dictated by abstract market domination and the objective constraints of SNLT, except in an indirect way such that the requirements of production transform the requirements of labour-power's maintenance outside of the DMM sphere. Instead, other mechanisms and factors are involved in the division of IMM activities, from direct domination and violence to hierarchical forms of cooperation, or planned allocation at best.[9] There is no impersonal mechanism or way to objectively quantify, enforce or equalise "rationally" the time and energy spent in these activities or to whom they are allocated. When an "equal and just" sharing of these activities is

9 The gendered internalisation of this allocation of IMM activities, what we will call 'naturalisation', obviously plays a large role in this. We will look closer at this mechanism in Part 4.

The Logic of Gender

attempted, it must be constantly negotiated, since there is no way to quantify and equalise "rationally" the time or energy spent. What does it mean to clean the kitchen, what does it mean to look after a child for one hour: is your hour of childcare the same as my hour of childcare? This allocation cannot but remain a conflictual question.

2 PAID/UNPAID

Marxist feminists have often added to the distinction between production and reproduction another one: that between paid and unpaid labour. Like many before us, we find these categories imprecise and we prefer to use the waged/unwaged distinction. As we further explicate the spheres of DMM and IMM in relation to that which is waged or unwaged, we elucidate the overlapping of these spheres through the principle of *social validation*. En route we will explore the ways in which the activities in question can be called labour or not; that is, if they *qualify* as labour or not in this mode of production.

The difference between paid/unpaid on the one side, and waged/unwaged on the other is blurred by the form of the wage, by what we must name *the wage fetish*. The wage itself is not the monetary equivalent to the work performed by the worker who receives it, but rather the price for which a worker sells their labour-power, equivalent to a sum of value that goes one way or another into the process of their reproduction, as they must reappear the next day ready and able to work.[10] However, it appears that those who work for a wage have fulfilled their social responsibility for the day once the workday is over. What is *not* paid for by the wage appears to be a world of non-work. Therefore, all "work" appears to be paid tautologically as that which is work, since one does not appear to get paid for that which one does when not "at work". However, it is imperative to remember that Marx demonstrated that no actual living labour is ever paid for in the form of the wage.

[10] The fact that the wage itself does not come with a training manual is interesting. One may do with it 'as one pleases' – particularly those who are its direct recipients – and so it is not distributed according to the specificities of the IMM sphere, i.e. the size of one's family, standard of living or the responsible/economical use of a particular income stream. This point would require more attention, but for now it will suffice to say: it is just not the capitalist's responsibility.

Obviously, this does not mean that the question of whether an activity is waged or not is irrelevant. Indeed, she who does not go to work does not get a wage. Wage-labour is the only way the worker can have access to the means necessary for their own reproduction and that of their family. Moreover, validation by the wage qualitatively affects the activity itself. When an activity that was previously unwaged becomes waged, even when it is unproductive, it takes on some characteristics that resemble those of abstract labour. Indeed, the fact that labour-power is exchanged for a wage makes its performance open to rationalisations and comparisons. In return, what is expected from this labour-power is at least the socially-average performance – including all its characteristics and intensity – regulated and corresponding to the social average *for this kind of labour* (clearly the absence of value makes it impossible to compare it with any other kind of labour). An individual who cannot deliver a proper performance in the necessary amount of time will not be able to sell their labour-power in the future. Therefore, the wage validates the fact that labour-power has been employed adequately, whilst universally recognising it as social labour, whatever the concrete activity itself might have been, or whether it was "productively" consumed.

Now we must consider this distinction between the waged and unwaged, insofar as it intersects with that between the IMM and DMM spheres. When we consider those activities which are waged, we are referring to those which are social[11]; those which are unwaged are *the non-social of the social*: they are not socially validated but are nonetheless part of the capitalist mode of production. Importantly, however, these do not map directly onto the spheres of IMM and DMM.

We see that within the interplay of these four terms there are some waged activities which overlap with those of the IMM sphere: those organised by the state (the state

[11] Clearly, all activities taking place in the capitalist mode of production are social, but certain reproductive activities are rejected by its laws as non-social, as they form *an outside within the inside of the totality of the capitalist mode of production*. This is why we use the social/unsocial binary, sometimes found in feminist accounts, with caution. A problem with the term is that it can imply that 'reproductive labour' occurs in a 'non-social sphere' outside of the capitalist mode of production, in either a domestic mode of production (see Christine Delphy, *Close to Home: A Materialist Analysis of Women's Oppression* [Hutchinson 1984]), or as a vestige of a previous mode of production. It can even sometimes be used to argue that it is another mode of production left unsocial because of its lack of rationalisation and that

The Logic of Gender

sector). Within this imbricated set of categories, the sphere of IMM activities intersects with the sphere of waged labour. These waged and IMM activities are forms of state-organised reproduction that are not directly market-mediated (see figure 1 opposite). These activities reproduce the use-value of labour-power but are waged and thus socially validated. Nevertheless, these activities are not productive of value, nor are they subject to the same criteria of direct market-mediation (see above). They are social because they are remunerated through the social form of value. Because they are not productive of value, they are the forms of reproduction which are a collective cost to capital: they are paid indirectly through deductions from collective wages and surplus-value in the form of taxes.

Let us now turn things round one more time and look at what the wage *buys*; that is, what is an element of the wage, what constitutes the exchange-value of labour-power. The wage buys the commodities necessary for the reproduction of labour-power, and it also buys services which participate in this reproduction, whether directly (by paying a private nanny, for example) or indirectly (for example, by paying taxes for state-expenditure on education, which is part of the indirect wage). These services, whether they are productive of value or not,[12] have a cost that is reflected in the exchange-value of labour-power: they imply, in one way or another, a deduction from surplus-value.

What remains are the activities that are non-waged, and that therefore do not increase the exchange-value of labour-power. These are the non-social of the social, the non-labour of labour (see Addendum 1). They are cut off from social production; they must not only *appear as*, but also *be* non-labour, that is, they are *naturalised*.[13] They constitute a sphere whose dissociation is necessary to make the production of value possible: the *gendered sphere*.

what is needed is the socialisation of this sphere. We think it is less confusing, and far more telling, to focus on the process of social validation itself.

12 Services that are paid from revenue are unproductive, and, in this sense, are part of the waged IMM sphere.

13 Marx provides a useful insight into the process of naturalisation: 'Increase of population is a natural power of labour for which nothing is paid. From the present standpoint, we use the term *natural power* to refer to *social power*. All *natural powers of social labour* are themselves historical products.' Marx, *Grundrisse* (MECW 28), 327.

In the next part we will finally turn to the individuals who have been assigned to this sphere. However, we should first consider another binary: public/private.

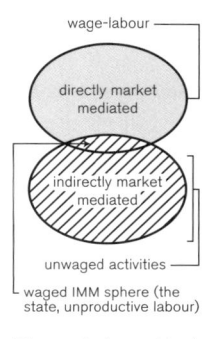

Figure 1. A graphical representation of the relation between the DMM/IMM and waged/unwaged spheres.

ADDENDUM 1: **ON LABOUR**

For us, labour will be defined, in its opposition to non-labour, as an activity that is socially validated as such, because of its specific function, its specific social character in a given mode of production. Other bases for definitions of labour are also possible, to cite a few: exchange between man and nature, expense of energy, distinction between pleasant/unpleasant activities. However, we think that none of these definitions can help us understand anything about the character of unwaged IMM activities. These definitions only take into account their concrete characteristics, and in the case of unwaged IMM activities, this leads to banal or absurd descriptions. Is comforting a child an exchange with nature? Is sleeping a labour that reproduces labour-power? Is brushing one's teeth labour? Brushing somebody else's teeth? We think that our definition of labour, while it may seem banal at first glance, is the only one capable of passing over these meaningless questions, and that it constitutes the right starting-point for research into the specific character of these activities.

The Logic of Gender

3 PUBLIC/PRIVATE

Many people use the category "public" to designate the state sector. And marxist feminists often use the concept of the "private" sphere to designate everything within the sphere of the home. We find it necessary to hold fast to the traditional dichotomy of private/public as that which separates the economic and the political, civil society and the state, bourgeois individual and citizen.[14] Prior to capitalism the term "private" referred to the household, or *oikos*, and it was considered *the* sphere of the economic. With the advent of the capitalist era the private sphere moved outward beyond the household itself.

Here we begin to see the inadequacy of the concept of "the private sphere" as a place outside of "the public sphere" that includes the economy, as for example in feminist theory. For the private is not merely that which is located in the domestic sphere, and associated with domestic activities. Rather, it is the totality of activities inside and outside of the home. As a result of the structural separation between the economic and the political (political economy) – corresponding to the spread of capitalist social (production) relations – the private sphere becomes increasingly diffuse, rendering the home only one amongst many moments of "the economic" or "the private". Therefore, contrary to most feminist accounts, it was *only* within the context of premodern relations – prior to the separation of the political and the economic under capitalism – that the private sphere constituted the household. In contrast, in the modern capitalist era, the scope of private exploitation spans the entire social landscape.

Where then is "the public" if the private is the totality of productive and reproductive activities? Marx claims that the public is an abstraction from society in the form of the state. This sphere of the political and the

[14] For Marx, civil society – or what in most political theory is considered 'natural' society – stands *opposed* to the state.

juridical is the real abstraction of *Right* separated from the actual divisions and differences constituting civil society. For Marx, this abstraction or separation must exist in order to attain and preserve the formal equality (accompanied, of course, by class inequality) necessary for self-interested private owners to accumulate capital in a manner uninhibited rather than controlled or dictated by the state. This is what distinguishes the modern state, which is adequate to capitalist property relations, from other state systems corresponding to other modes of production, whether monarchical or ancient democratic.

15 See Marx, *On the Jewish Question* (MECW 3).

This means that the modern capitalist state and its "public sphere" is not an actually existing place, but an abstract "community" of "equal citizens". Hence, the differentiation between the sphere of economic relations and that of the political — including relations between unequals mediated by relations between "abstract equal citizens" — renders "citizens" only *formally* equal according to the state and civil rights. As a result, these "individuals" appear as equals on the market — even though in "real life" (the private sphere of civil society) they are anything but.[15] This abstraction, "the public", must exist precisely because the directly market-mediated sphere is mediated by the market, a space of mediation between private labours, produced independently from one another in private firms owned and operated by private (self-interested) individuals.

What then is the relationship between on the one hand, the spheres of public/private, political/economic, state/civil society, and on the other hand, the spheres of direct and indirect market-mediation? The meeting-point of these spheres marks the moment of their constitutive separation, and defines those anchored to one as distinct from the other, as *different.* This difference is determined by whether those individuals defined by the state directly exchange the labour-power commodity

The Logic of Gender **71**

they bear within their person as their own property, or — if that exchange is mediated indirectly — through those with formal equality.

Now we are ready to look at the individuals who have been assigned to each sphere. What we see at first, when we look at the dawn of this mode of production, is individuals who have different rights, which are defined by the law as two different juridical beings: *men and women*. We will be able to see how this juridical difference was inscribed on the "biological" bodies of these individuals when we come to analyse the sex/gender binary. For now, we must see how the dichotomy between public and private does the initial work of anchoring individuals as men and women to the different spheres reproducing the capitalist totality through their differential right not merely to private property, but to *that property which individuals own in their persons*.

This peculiar form of property is necessary to generalised wage-relations because value presupposes formal equality between the owners of commodities so that "free" exchange (capital and labour-power) can occur despite the fact that there is a structural "real" inequality between two different classes: those possessing the means of production and those dispossessed of that form of property. However, "free exchange" can only occur through a disavowal of that class difference, through its deferral to another binary: *citizen* and *other*, not between members of opposed classes but between those within each class. In order to found the bourgeois mode of production, it was not necessary for all workers to be given equality under the sign of "the citizen". Historically, "citizen" only names a specific category to which both property owners and certain proletarians are able to belong. As capitalist juridical relations disavow class through the reconstitution of the difference between citizen and other, the historical conditions under which the bourgeois mode of production was itself constituted were various forms of unfreedom. For this reason we have citizen and other as mapping onto: *male (white)/ non-(white) male*.

For instance, under the conditions of slavery in North America, the classification of white was necessary to maintain the property of masters over slaves. Women were also classified as other, but for different reasons, as we shall see. One factor worth mentioning here is that within this relation of white/person of colour/woman, the preservation of the purity of the "white master", as opposed to the "black slave" is of the utmost importance — as well as the strict preservation of the dominant master signifier of equality ("white blood" and therefore "white mothers") across future generations of the bourgeoisie. Therefore the division between white and non-white women was also closely regulated in order to preserve such a taxonomy, within the mixed context of both plantation-based commodity production in the New World and the rise of industrial capitalism.[16]

However, what constitutes the citizen/other binary in this mode of production is not based upon a negative definition of slavery but rather upon "free" labour, consisting of those with, as opposed to without, the same formal freedom. "Free labour" as Marx identified it — that is, the technical definition of freedom for the wage labourer — requires what we might call "double freedom":

> For the conversion of his money into capital, therefore, the owner of money must meet in the market with the free labourer, free in the double sense, that as a free man he can dispose of his labour-power as his own commodity, and that on the other hand he has no other commodity for sale, is short of everything necessary for the realisation of his labour-power.[17]

Nevertheless, haven't women always been wage-labourers? Of course, since the origin of capitalism, women have

[16] See Chris Chen's 'The Limit Point of Capitalist Equality' in this issue.

[17] Marx, *Capital*, vol.1, (MECW 35), 179.

The Logic of Gender **73**

been bearers of labour-power, and their capacity to labour has been utilised by capital; but they have only quite recently become the *owners* of their labour-power, with "double freedom". Prior to the last quarter century, women were indeed free *from the means of production*, but they were not free to sell their labour-power *as their own*.[18] The freedom of ownership, which includes mobility between lines of work, was historically only for some at the expense of others. Those struggling for political and "public" freedom, or double freedom, were caught in a double-bind. They were forced to make arguments on behalf of their ("but-different") equality, while at the same time having interests in contradiction with those of others who identified with the same fight for equality on different terms.[19]

This is especially true in the case of women, who were caught between demanding freedom as the ideal, equal human, and freedom *as different.* This is because their "real difference" under capitalism is not ideal or ideological but embodied, and structurally reproduced through the practices which define women as different. This "real difference" is entangled within a web of mutually constitutive and reinforcing relations which necessarily presuppose the citizen, state and public sphere to which women might appeal for human and civil rights on the one hand, and reproductive rights on the other.

Therefore, even if it is true that formal freedom itself was a precondition for value production and exchange, nevertheless, what it organised—the civil society of bourgeois individuals—was necessary for the continuing reproduction of the public or legal sphere. The right to "be equal" and thus equally free, does not itself reorganise the distribution of property, nor as we shall see, the conditions of possibility for capital accumulation. These spheres work in concert. If this were not the case, it would be possible to abolish the actually existing forms of historically-specific "difference" through legal

18 In France, before 1965, women could not engage in wage-labour without the authorisation of their husband. In West Germany, that was not before 1977 — see Part 5 below.

19 We find the need for a class analysis which can cut through this thicket of intra-class disparities, while attending to the disparities of each with regard to their own particular and differential relation to capitalist domination. In short, proletarian identity, as an abstraction based upon a common form of unfreedom, was *never* going to account for everyone, even at the most abstract level. Another more nuanced analysis would be needed — one which would come up against the problematic of workers' identity itself.

and "political" actions, *within* the state. This would amount to the abolition of the private through the public sphere – a revolution through reform which is structurally impossible.

"Equality" as double-freedom is the freedom to be structurally dispossessed. This is not to say that it is not *worthwhile*. The question is, can it also become "worthwhile" to capital, the state and its attendant apparatuses of domination? As most of us will have experienced first-hand, the gender distinction has persisted long after differential freedom was abolished for the majority of women. If this differential freedom was in fact what anchored women to the indirectly market-mediated sphere, why did its abolition not "free" women from the category "woman" and the gendered sphere of reproduction?

Double-freedom and the sex-blind market

When looking at the history of the capitalist mode of production, it is striking that, in many cases, once inequalities have been secured by juridical mechanisms, they can take on a life of their own, making their own basis in law superfluous. As women in many countries slowly but surely received equal rights in the public sphere, the mechanism that reinforced this inequality in the "private sphere" of the economic – of the labour-market – was already so well established that it could appear as the enactment of some mysterious natural law.

Ironically, the reproduction of dual spheres of gender and the anchoring of women to one and not the other is perpetuated and constantly re-established by the very mechanism of the "sex-blind" labour-market, which obtains not for the man/woman distinction directly but rather for the price distinction, or the exchange-value of their labour-power. Indeed, labour markets, if they are to remain markets, must be "sex-blind". Markets, as the locus of exchanges of equivalents, are supposed to blur concrete differences in a pure comparison of abstract values. How then can this "sex-blind" market reproduce the gender difference?

Once a group of individuals, women, are defined as "those who have children" (see Addendum 2) and once this social activity, "having children", is structurally formed as constituting a handicap,[20] women are defined as *those who come to the labour-market with a potential disadvantage*. This systematic differentiation — through the market-determined risk identified as childbearing "potential" — keeps those who embody the signifier "woman" anchored to the IMM sphere. Therefore, because capital is a "sex-blind" abstraction, it concretely punishes women for having a sex, even though that "sexual difference" is produced by capitalist social relations, and absolutely necessary to the reproduction of capitalism itself. One could imagine a hypothetical situation in which employers did not enquire about the gender of an applicant, but only rewarded those who have "the most mobility" and those who are "the most reliable, 24/7"; even in this case gender bias would reappear as strong as ever. As an apparent contradiction, once sexual difference becomes structurally defined and reproduced, woman as a bearer of labour-power with a higher social cost becomes its opposite: the commodity labour-power with a cheaper price.

Indeed, the better-remunerated jobs — that is, those which can tendentially pay for more than the reproduction of a single person — are those for which a certain degree of skill is expected. In those skilled sectors, capitalists are ready to make an investment in the worker's skills, knowing that they will benefit from doing so in the long term. They will therefore privilege the labour-power that is likely to be the most reliable over a long period. If the worker is potentially going to leave, then she will not be as good an investment, and will get a lower price. This

[20] Because the creation of a future generation of workers who are for a period of their life non-workers is a cost to capital which it disavows, and because this activity is posited as a *non-labour that steals time away from labour*.

lower price tag, fixed to those who look like the kind of people who "have children", is not determined by the sorts of skills that are formed in the IMM sphere. Even though the sphere a woman is relegated to is full of activities which require lifelong training, this does not increase the price of her labour-power, because no employer has to pay for their acquisition. As a result, capital can use women's labour-power in short spurts at cheap prices.

In fact, the general tendency towards "feminisation" is not the gendering of the sex-blind market, but rather the movement by capital towards the utilisation of cheap short-term flexibilised labour-power under post-Fordist, globalised conditions of accumulation, increasingly deskilled and "just-in-time". We must take this definition of feminisation as primary, before we attend to the rise of the service sector and the increasing importance of care and affective labour, which is part and parcel of the "feminisation turn". This turn comes about through the dynamic unfolding of capitalist social relations historically, a process that we will see in the last two parts of the text. But first we must summarise what we have learned about gender until now, and attempt a definition. This requires analysis and criticism of another common binary: sex and gender.

[21] See Paola Tabet, 'Natural Fertility, Forced Reproduction', in Diana Leonard and Lisa Adkins, eds, *Sex in Question: French Materialist Feminism* (Taylor and Francis 1996).

ADDENDUM 2:   ON WOMEN, BIOLOGY AND CHILDREN

The definition of women as "those who have children" presupposes a necessary link between 1) the fact of having a biological organ, the uterus 2) the fact of bearing a child, of being pregnant 3) the fact of having a specific relation to the result of this pregnancy. Conflating the three obscures:

1) On the one side, the mechanisms that prevent, favour, or impose the fact that somebody with a uterus will go through pregnancy, and how often that will occur.[21]

The Logic of Gender

These mechanisms include: the institution of marriage, the availability of contraceptives, the mechanisms that enforce heterosexuality as a norm, and (at least for a long time and still in many places) the interdiction/shame associated with forms of sex that do not risk leading to pregnancy (oral/anal sex, etc.).

2) On the other side, the changing definition of what a child is and what level of care a child necessitates. While there was a period in which children were considered as half-animal, half-human creatures who only had to be cleaned and fed until they became small adults – that is, able to work – the modern reality of childhood and its requirements often make "having children" a never-ending business.

4 SEX/GENDER

We are now prepared to address the gender question. What then is gender? For us, it is the *anchoring* of a certain group of individuals in a specific sphere of social activities. The result of this anchoring process is at the same time the continuous reproduction of two separate genders.

These genders concretise themselves as an ensemble of ideal characteristics, defining either the "masculine" or the "feminine". However, these characteristics themselves, as a list of behavioural and psychological qualities, are subject to transformation over the course of the history of capitalism; they pertain to specific periods; they correspond to certain parts of the world; and even within what we might call the "West" they are not necessarily ascribed in the same way to all people. As a binary however, they exist in relation to one another, regardless of time and space, even if their mode of appearance is itself always in flux.

Sex is the flip side of gender. Following Judith Butler, we criticise the gender/sex binary as found in feminist literature before the 1990s. Butler demonstrates, correctly, that both sex and gender are socially constituted and furthermore, that it is the "socializing" or pairing of "gender" with culture, that has relegated sex to the "natural" pole of the binary nature/culture. We argue similarly that they are binary social categories which simultaneously de-naturalise gender while naturalising sex. For us, sex is the naturalisation of gender's dual projection upon bodies, aggregating biological differences into discrete naturalised semblances.

While Butler came to this conclusion through a critique of the existentialist ontology of the body,[22] we came to it through an analogy with another social form. Value, like gender, necessitates its other, "natural" pole (i.e. its concrete manifestation). Indeed, the dual relation between sex and gender as two sides of the same coin is analogous to the dual aspects of the commodity and the fetishism therein. As we explained above, every commodity, including labour-power, is both a use-value and an exchange-value. The relation between commodities is a social relation between things and a material relation between people.

Following this analogy, sex is the material body, which, as use-value to (exchange) value, attaches itself to gender. *The gender fetish* is a social relation which acts upon these bodies so that it appears as a natural characteristic of the bodies themselves. While gender is the abstraction of sexual difference from all of its concrete characteristics, that abstraction transforms and determines the body to which it is attached — just as the real abstraction of value transforms the material body of the commodity. Gender and sex combined give those inscribed within them a natural semblance ("with a phantomlike objectivity"), as if the social content of gender was "written upon the skin" of the concrete individuals.

[22] See her critique of Simone de Beauvoir's 'uncritical reproduction of the Cartesian distinction between freedom and the body.' Judith Butler, *Gender Trouble* (Routledge 1990), chapter 1: 'Subjects of Sex/Gender/Desire.'

The transhistoricisation of sex is homologous to a foreshortened critique of capital, which contends that use-value is transhistorical rather than historically specific to capitalism. Here, use-value is thought to be that which positively remains after revolution, which is seen as freeing use-value from the integument of exchange-value. In terms of our analogy with sex and gender, we would go one step further and say that both gender and sex are historically determined. Both are entirely social and can only be abolished together — just as exchange-value and use-value will both have to be abolished in the process of communisation. In this light, our feminist value-theoretical analysis mirrors Butler's critique in so far as we both view the sex/gender binary as being socially-determined and produced through social conditions specific to modernity.

The denaturalisation of gender

But gender is not a static social form. The abstraction of gender becomes increasingly denaturalised, making sex appear all the more concrete and biological. In other words, if sex and gender are two sides of the same coin, the relation between gender and its naturalised counterpart is not stable. There is a potential discrepancy between them, which some have called a "troubling", and we term "denaturalisation".

Over time gender is ever more abstracted, defining sexuality more and more arbitrarily. The marketisation and commodification of gender appears increasingly to *de-naturalise* gender from *naturalised* biological concerns. One might say that capitalism itself deconstructs gender and denaturalises it. Nature — whose increasing superfluity is in juxtaposition to gender's ongoing necessity — appears as the presupposition of gender rather than its effect. In more familiar terms, reflecting capital's "problem" with labour: "nature" (the "natural" side of the sex/gender binary) becomes increasingly superfluous to the generational reproduction of the proletariat, while the "cost" assigned to "female" bodies – or the counter-pole to sex – becomes increasingly imperative to capital accumulation as the tendency toward feminisation. Hence, the reproduction of gender is of utmost importance, as labour-power with a lower cost, while a reserve army of proletarians as surplus population is increasingly redundant.

What the female gender signifies – that which is socially inscribed upon "naturalised", "sexuated" bodies – is not only an array of "feminine" or gendered characteristics, but essentially a price tag. Biological reproduction has a social cost which is *exceptional* to average (male) labour-power; it becomes the burden of those whose cost it is assigned to – regardless of whether they can or will have children. It is in this sense that an abstraction, a *gendered average*, is reflected back upon the organisation of bodies in the same way exchange-value, a blind market average, is projected back upon production, molding and transforming the organisation of the character of social production and the division of labour. In this sense, the transformation of the condition of gender relations goes on behind the backs of those whom it defines. And in this sense, gender is constantly reimposed and *re-naturalised*.

5 THE HISTORY OF GENDER WITHIN CAPITALISM: from the creation of the IMM sphere to the commodification of gendered activities

To understand this dialectical process of de-naturalisation and re-naturalisation we first have to retrace the transformations within the gender relation over the course of the capitalist mode of production, and attempt a periodisation. At this more concrete level, there are many possible points of entry to take, and we opt for a periodisation of the family, since it is the economic unit that brings together the indirectly market-mediated (IMM) and the directly market-mediated (DMM) spheres which delimit the aspects of proletarian reproduction. We must try to figure out whether changes in the family form correspond to transformations in the process of labour's valorisation.

The Logic of Gender

i Primitive accumulation and the extended family

During the era of primitive accumulation, a major problem facing the capitalist class was how to perfectly calibrate the relationship between the IMM and DMM spheres such that workers would, on the one hand, be forced to survive only by selling their labour-power, and on the other, be allotted only enough personal property to continue self-provisioning without bringing up the cost of labour-power.[23] Indeed, at the moment when the IMM was constituted, it had to take on as much as possible of the reproduction of labour-power, to be as big as possible, but *just enough* so that the proportion of self-provisioning allowed nevertheless required the habitual re-emergence of labour-power on the market. Therefore, the sphere of IMM supplementing the wage was subordinated to the market as a necessary presupposition of wage-relations and capitalist exploitation, and as its immediate result.

In the course of the transition from the 18th to the 19th century, the family — centred in the home as a unit of production — became *the* economic unit mediating between the IMM and DMM spheres of labour-power's reproduction. However, for the first part of the 19th century, as long as no retirement benefits existed and as long as it was also the case that children were expected to go to work before they even reached puberty, the family comprised several generations residing in one home. In addition, the activities of the IMM sphere were not carried out by married women alone; indeed they were done with the participation of children, grandmothers and other female relatives, even lodgers. If it was the case that only the "singly free" adult male members of the family could legally be owners of the wage, this did not mean that adult women and young children did not also work outside the home.

[23] See Michael Perelman, *The Invention of Capitalism: Classical Political Economy and the Secret History of Primitive Accumulation* (Duke University Press 2000).

Indeed, at the beginning of industrialisation, women represented one third of the workforce. Like children, they did not decide if or where they would take employment, or which job they would perform; they were more or less subcontracted by their husbands or fathers. (Marx even compared it with some forms of the slave trade: the male head of the family bargained the price of the labour-power of his wife and children and chose to accept or decline. And let us not forget that in some countries, such as France and Germany, women only got the right to work without the authorisation of their husbands in the 1960s or 70s). Far from being a sign of the emancipation of women, or of the modern views of the husband, women working outside the home was a blatant indicator of poverty. Even if married women were generally expected to stay at home when the family could afford it (where they often did home-based production, especially for the textile industry), many women never married – for it was an expensive business – and some were not supposed to become pregnant, forming their own family. Younger daughters were often sent to become servants or helpers in other families, remaining "officially" single. Therefore, even if those responsible for the IMM sphere were always women, and those responsible for the wage were always men (one could say, by definition), the two genders and the two spheres did not map one to one in that period.

ii The nuclear family and Fordism

In the second part of the 19th century, what some call the second industrial revolution, there was a progressive move towards the nuclear family as we think of it today. First, after decades of labour struggles, the state stepped in to limit the employment of women and children, partly because it was faced with a crisis in the reproduction of the work force. Labour-power was expected to become more skilled (for example literacy increasingly became a skill required to access a job), and increasing attention was given to the education of children. A new category emerged, that of childhood, with its specific needs and phases of development. Looking after children became a complicated business, which could no longer be provided by elder siblings.[24]

This process culminated with Fordism, and its new standards of consumption and reproduction. With the generalisation of retirement benefits and retirement homes, generations came to be separated from each other in individual houses. The allocation of family responsibilities between husband and wife became strictly defined by the separation between the spheres. IMM activities that used to be carried out together with other women (such as washing clothes) became the individual responsibility of one adult woman per household. The married woman's life often came to be entirely confined to the IMM sphere. It became the fate of most women, and their entire lives (including their personality, desires, etc.) were shaped by this fate.

It was therefore with the nuclear family (in a specific period of capitalism, and importantly, in a specific area of the world) that gender became a rigid binary, mapping one to one with the spheres. It became a strict norm, which does not mean everyone fitted into it. Many feminists who refer to gender as a set of characteristics that define "femininity" and "masculinity" have the norms of that period in mind. From this point on, individuals identified as women were born with different life-destinies than individuals defined as men – they lived "on two different planets" (some on Mars…), and were socialised as two distinct kinds of subjects. This distinction cut across all classes.

No longer helped by other members of the family, doing the IMM activities isolated behind four walls, married women were made to bear the entire burden of IMM activities on their own. This isolation would not have

[24] For the effects of compulsory education on working-class families see Wally Seccombe, *Weathering the Storm: Working-Class Families from the Industrial Revolution to the Fertility Decline* (Verso 1993).

been possible without the introduction of household appliances turning the most extreme physical tasks into chores that could be carried out alone. The washing-machine, the indoor water-tap, the water heater – these helped to dramatically reduce the time spent on some IMM activities. But every minute gained was far from increasing the housewife's leisure time. Every spare moment had to be used to increase the standards of reproduction: clothes were washed more often, meals became ever more varied and healthy, and most importantly, childcare became an all-consuming IMM activity from infant care to the facilitation of children's leisure activities.

iii The 70s: real subsumption and the commodification of IMM activities

The commodification of IMM activities is clearly not a new phenomenon. From the beginning of capitalism it was possible to buy ready-made meals instead of cooking them, to buy new clothes instead of mending them, to pay a servant to look after the children or to do the housework. However, those were privileges of the middle and upper classes. Indeed, each time an IMM activity is turned into a commodity, it has to be paid for in the wage. Therefore, the mass-consumption of these commodities would only have been likely in periods of steady wage increases, since these services, as long as they were only formally subsumed, increased the exchange-value of necessary labour in an inverse ratio to surplus-value.

However, as a result of the possibilities opened by real subsumption, the value of some of these commodities can decrease at the same time as they are mass-produced. Advances in productivity make these commodities more and more affordable, and some of them – particularly ready-made meals and household appliances – slowly but surely became affordable with the wage. Nevertheless, some IMM activities are more difficult to commodify at a price low enough to be paid

The Logic of Gender

for by every wage. Indeed, even if it is possible to commodify childcare, it is not possible to make advances in productivity that would allow its cost to become ever cheaper. Even if the nourishing, washing of clothes, and so on, can be done more efficiently, the time for childcare is never reduced. You cannot look after children *more quickly*: they have to be attended to 24 hours a day.

What is possible is to rationalise childcare, for example, by having the state organise it and thereby reducing the adult-to-child ratio. However, there are limits to how many children one adult can possibly handle, especially if, in that process, this adult has to impart a specific standard of socialisation, knowledge and discipline. This work can also be performed by the cheapest labour possible; that is, by women whose wage will be lower than the wage of a working mother. But in this case, IMM activities are simply deferred to the lowest-paid strata of the total population. Therefore the problem is not reduced. Rather, its negative effects are redistributed, often to poor immigrants and women of colour.

So we see that all these possibilities are limited: there is always a remainder, which we will refer to as *the abject*,[25] that is, what cannot be subsumed or is not worth subsuming. It is obviously not abject *per se* — it exists as abject because of capital, and it is shaped by it. There is always this remainder that has to remain outside of market-relations, and the question of who has to perform it in the family will always be, to say the least, a conflictual matter.

6 CRISIS AND AUSTERITY MEASURES: THE RISE OF THE ABJECT

With the current crisis, all signs indicate that the state will be increasingly unwilling to organise IMM activities, since they are a mere cost. Expenses in childcare, elderly-care and healthcare are the first to be cut, not to mention education and after-school programs. These will

[25] We take this term in its etymological sense: *ab-ject*, that which is cast off, thrown away, but *from something that it is part of*.

become DMM for those who can afford it (privatisation), or lapse into the sphere of unwaged indirect market-mediation – therefore increasing the abject.

The extent of this remains to be seen, but the trend in countries affected by the crisis is already clear. In the US, and in most countries of the Eurozone (with the notable exception of Germany), governments are cutting their spending to reduce their debt-to-GDP ratios.[26] Countries like Greece, Portugal and Spain, but also the UK, are drastically scaling down their expenses in healthcare and childcare. In Greece and Portugal public kindergartens are closing down. Infringements on the rights of pregnant women to maternity leave and benefits, or to resume their jobs after maternity, have been reported in Greece, Portugal, Italy, and the Czech Republic.[27] In the UK, where state-run nurseries are closing one by one, the situation is described by an anti-capitalist feminist group involved in the Hackney nurseries campaign, Feminist Fight Back:

> All over the UK local authorities have begun to announce significant reductions of funding to social services, from libraries and healthcare to playgrounds and art groups, from rape crisis centres to domestic violence services. Of particular relevance to women are the profound effects that will be felt in children's services, both in council and community nurseries and in New Labour's flagship Sure Start Centres, which provide a variety of services to parents on a "one-stop" basis.[28]

In a country where the Prime Minister himself advocates the organisation of community services on a "voluntary basis", under the central policy idea of the "Big Society", a culture "where people, in their everyday lives, in their homes, in their neighbourhoods, in their workplace … feel both free and powerful enough to help themselves and their own communities",[29] anti-state feminists are faced with a dilemma:

[26] See the previous article in this issue, 'The Holding Pattern'.

[27] Francesca Bettio, 'Crisis and recovery in Europe: the labour market impact on men and women,' 2011.

[28] Feminist Fightback Collective, 'Cuts are a Feminist Issue'. *Soundings* 49 (Winter 2011).

[29] Speech by David Cameron on 'the Big Society', Liverpool, 19 July 2010.

Our aim is for provision "in and against the state". This raises a core question in the struggle over public goods and shared resources and labour: how are we to ensure that our autonomous efforts to reproduce our own communities do not simply create Cameron's Big Society for him? — thereby endorsing the logic that if the state will no longer provide for us we will have to do it ourselves?[30]

The struggle around kindergartens which took place in Poznan (Poland) in 2012 also reflects this dilemma. The municipality is slowly transferring all the public kindergartens to private institutions to save costs. When the workers of one of the nurseries protested with parents and activists, against privatisation, the local authorities came up with the option of letting the workers organise the nursery, but without providing them with any subsidies or guarantees. This made it a very dim option that was eventually rejected by the workers and parents.[31]

However, some marxist feminists seem to glorify the self-organisation of IMM activities by women as a necessary step in the creation of an alternative society. For example Silvia Federici, in her 2010 text "Feminism and the Politics of the Common in an Era of Primitive Accumulation":

> If the house is the *oikos* on which the economy is built, then it is women, historically the house-workers and house-prisoners, who must take the initiative to reclaim the house as a center of collective life, one traversed by multiple people and forms of cooperation, providing safety without isolation and fixation, allowing for the sharing and circulation of community possessions, and above all providing the foundation for collective forms of reproduction. […] It remains to clarify that assigning women this task of commoning/collectivizing reproduction is not to concede to a naturalistic conception of "femininity". Understandably,

[30] Feminist Fightback, 'Cuts are a Feminist Issue'.

[31] Women with Initiative (from Inicjatywa Pracownicza-Workers' Initiative), 'Women workers fight back against austerity in Poland', *Industrial Worker* 1743, March 2012.

many feminists would view this possibility as "a fate worse than death." [...] But, quoting Dolores Hayden, the reorganisation of reproductive work, and therefore the reorganisation of the structure of housing and public space is not a question of identity; it is a labour question and, we can add, a power and safety question.[32]

Silvia Federici is right — we do consider this possibility worse than death. And her answer to this objection, which quotes Dolores Hayden rather freely, misses the point: the labour question *is* an identity question.[33] Even if we might, in the crisis, have no choice but to self-organise these reproductive activities — and even though, most likely, abject reproduction will in the end mainly be foisted upon women — we must fight against this process which reinforces gender. We must treat it as it is: a self-organisation of the abject, of what no one else is willing to do.

It is important here to state that, even if unwaged IMM activities and the abject might refer to the same concrete activities, these two concepts must be differentiated. Indeed, the category of the abject refers specifically to activities that became waged at some point but are in the process of returning into the unwaged IMM sphere because they've become too costly for the state or capital. While IMM is a purely structural category, independent of any dynamic, the concept of the abject grasps the specificities of these activities and the process of their assignment in our current period. Indeed, we can say that, if many of our mothers and grandmothers were caught in the sphere of IMM activities, the problem we face today is different. It is not that we will have to "go back to the kitchen", if only because *we cannot afford it*. Our fate, rather, is *having to deal with the abject*. Contrary to the IMM activities of the past, this abject has already been to a large extent denaturalised. It does not appear to those performing

[32] Silvia Federici, *Revolution at Point Zero, Housework, Reproduction, and Feminist Struggle* (Common Notions 2012), 147.

[33] This is obviously not to say that we don't value the whole of Federici's contribution to the marxist feminist debate. Along with Dalla Costa and James's, *The Power of Women and the Subversion of the Community*, Silvia Federici's texts are surely the most interesting pieces from the 'domestic labour debate' of the 1970s. What we want to criticise here is a position that is currently influential within the 'commons' debate, and that we consider highly problematic.

The Logic of Gender

it as some unfortunate natural fate, but more like an extra burden that one must deal with alongside wage-labour.[34] Being left to deal with it is the ugly face of gender today, and this helps us to see gender as it is: a powerful constraint.[35]

Indeed, the process of de-naturalisation creates the possibility of gender appearing as *an external constraint.* This is not to say that the constraint of gender is less powerful than before, but that it can now be seen as a constraint, that is, as something outside oneself that it is possible to abolish.

A last thought, to conclude: if it happens to be true that the present moment allows us to see both our class-belonging and our gender-belonging as external constraints, this cannot be purely accidental. Or can it? This question is critical for an understanding of the struggle which leads to the abolition of gender, that is, to the reproduction by non-gendered individuals of a life in which all separate spheres of activity have been abolished.

[34] 'A massive and sudden emergence of uncanniness, which, familiar as it might have been in an opaque and forgotten life, now harries me as radically separate, *loathsome*. Not me. Not that. But not nothing, either. A "something" that I do not recognise as a thing. A weight of meaninglessness, about which there is nothing insignificant, and which curses me.' Julia Kristeva, *Power of Horrors: An Essay on Abjection* (Columbia University Press 1982), 2.

[35] Obviously there are nowadays some men, even if few, who do a considerable part of the abject. And they get to know what many women experience: *that the abject sticks to one's skin*. Many of these men, especially when they end up having to do most of the childcare, seem somehow to be undergoing a process of *social castration*.

A RISING TIDE LIFTS ALL BOATS

Crisis era struggles in Britain

MONDAY, 8 AUGUST 2011

Wandering north up Mare Street towards central Hackney helicopters throbbed in the air ahead, tightening an atmosphere already tense with August humidity and tales of riot.[1] The road was peculiarly desolate for evening rush hour, barren of the usual steady flow of traffic that trudges north–south along this inner-city artery. Remnants of some episode were visible: bins dismantled, turned over; rubbish sprawled, broken glass glittering on the open road; probably a confrontation with the cops. A fair few loitered, curious, oddly lacking intent – hipster riot tourists and other locals. A group of kids, mostly black, gathered nonchalantly about a pawn shop where a shutter and window were broken in, making a hole just big enough for a child or someone small to weasel through. A "gang" perhaps, or just some opportunists: were those casual figures playing lookout, while one or two went about stealing what they could? A few shopkeepers too, concerned for their property, milled about the street; a little further up, a smattering of police in fluorescent jackets.

Approaching the Narrowway, central Hackney's main shopping street, smoke billowed on the horizon in the direction of the helicopters, which seemed focused still a little further north, around Clarence Road. Half way up, the police had taped a cordon, preventing pedestrians from venturing further. On the corner a black couple stood resolute while a grizzled white drunk bawled, vitriolic into their faces. Routing around the cordon towards Dalston Lane a group of kids, scarves pulled over faces black-bloc style, glided past on bikes holding what might have been minor looted goods. Almost all the businesses were closed. A shop on Amhurst Road had its shutters full down, while dimly through the gaps the shapes of women could be seen avidly watching the news, probably scared to leave, either for their own safety or the shop's. At Clapton Square, an older Afro-Caribbean couple merrily

[1] For Siiri and Finn, whose entry into this world fired the starting pistol, and for their parents to whom we owed a gift.

Thanks to Larne, Chris, Richard and Sean for useful feedback.

A Rising Tide Lifts All Boats

joked with a TV news crew, "we're the parents – come interview *us*!" Entering this square, architectural relic of an old Hackney bourgeoisie, smoke hung in the air, acrid. Smouldering wheelie bin barricades lay in the street at the top. Turning into Clarence Road, a car was on fire.

Clarence Road runs down the Eastern flank of the Pembury Estate – one of Hackney's most stigmatised neighbourhoods, established by London County Council fiat in the era of interwar slum clearance, and now associated in the local press with salacious tales of turf war between the "Pembury Boys" and other local gangs; this is the Hackney sentimentalised in the months following the riots in *Top Boy*, a supposed British counterpart to *The Wire*. Through the late 1980s and early 1990s empty units on the Pembury were a magnet for squatters from Hackney's numerous anarcho and activist scene, who established convivial relations with the estate's tenants. And it was on Clarence Road that the Colin Roach Centre – named after a young black man shot dead in the notorious Stoke Newington Police Station in 1983 – was established with a remit of pursuing complaints about such things as police planting and dealing of drugs. The estate was cleared of squatters in 1993, just as the borough's long-term depopulation halted, though enough units remained empty for whole blocks to go derelict. After a gradual divestment under successive Tory and Labour governments, Hackney Council sold off the whole estate, with promises of improvements, to the Peabody Trust, a private housing association with a history of paternalistic involvement in housing London's poor dating back to Marx's day.[2] The Pembury's notoriety for "anti-social behaviour" subsequently legitimated Peabody's demolition of a large part of it to make way for "Pembury Circus", a large regeneration project that now aspires to bring more owner-occupiers into the neighbourhood. As well as crime, the Pembury has a reputation for tightly-knit community; something

[2] As a Peabody representative put it, in 1881: 'we house the deserving class… there are some people that are so low, that they could not live with our people'. Gareth Stedman Jones, *Outcast London* (Pantheon 1984), 185.

embodied in residents' organisations, and a sometimes vocal presence in the local media. On summer days like this strains of dancehall and reggae sometimes drift from the row of small shops that line one side of Clarence Road.

Now, diverse crowds of people milled about in the street, ranging from children to pensioners; asians, whites, slightly more blacks than others – unsurprising, given the demographics of the area. Overall probably only slightly more men than women, but the largest and most active contingent, young men, probably ranging later teens to thirty-somethings. Further down the street an abandoned black cab, door gaping open, windows smashed, rear bumper dangling off; a local convenience store offering Western Union money transfer, shutters broken through. A middle-aged black man setting out looted bottles on the pavement for people to take, finding this hilarious, shouting "free booze! free booze!" Tentatively, initially one by one, a little stream of people ducked through the broken shutters, then emerged again, clutching minor trophies: alcohol, Walkers crisps. Bedraggled-looking whites, perhaps alcoholics or homeless, took the opportunity; others just seemed to want to take part in the fun. All the while a police helicopter hovered close overhead, filling the air with tension, observing, yet the police did nothing. A gaggle of journalists, conspicuously large cameras surveilling those entering the shop, prompting cries of "no photos", "they're fucking feds"; then a momentary boiling over, threatening quite rationally to snatch or smash a camera. But they let him get away, under a barrage of curses. If they had known how the state would subsequently use images like that in their mass-prosecution…

There was little overt sense of "gangs" operating here, nor the simple opportunistic materialism of a "feral youth": the composition seemed to be something of a cross-section of the community, plus a smattering of riot

A Rising Tide Lifts All Boats

tourists and journalists, and the looting was perfunctory, a sideshow to the main event, which was about keeping the area cop-free. The mood was predominantly jovial, people revelling in the creation of a small liberated zone which the police seemed ill-equipped to quash. While the more "active" role tended to be played by the younger men, others offered a passively sympathetic presence, egging them on or making justifying arguments to onlookers. An older Afro-Caribbean man alternately giggled and shouted jokes across the street in the direction of the looted shop. A riot dynamic like this partly selects its own crowd: the terrified and the disapproving of course mostly vacate the scene once things get going, unless they have to stay to guard homes or property, leaving behind just those who want to make, support or observe the continuing riot. It was further up Clarence Road, on the periphery of the Pembury's rioting area and after this local riot's peak that Pauline Pearce – the nationally-celebrated "Heroine of Hackney"– gave her speech:

> Low up the fuckin' burning the property. Low up burning people's shop that they work hard to start their business. You understand? Poor [...]'s shop up there, she's working hard to make her business work and then you lot want to go and burn it up, for what? So that you can say you're "warring" and you're bad man. This is about a fuckin' man who got shot in Tottenham, its not about having fun on the road and busting up the place. Get it real black people, get real. We're here for a cause, and if we're fighting for a cause let's fight for a fuckin' cause. You lot piss me the fuck off. I'm ashamed to be a Hackney person coz we're not all gathering together and fighting for a cause, we're running down Foot Locker and thieving shoes. Dirty thief run off.[3]

On the corner next to the anarchist Pogo café a distressed woman lay on her back in the street, attended

3 Being a grandmother with a walking stick etc etc, and appearing to brave a feral mob mid-pillage to give it a good moral dressing-down, Pearce was easily canonised as one of the riot-wave's saints. It's worth noting though, that Pearce seems to have been responding as much to media coverage of riots elsewhere as to the activities of the crowd the viewer projects behind the camera: the Pembury Estate lacks anything like a Foot Locker store to loot. After the riots Pearce would be feted by senior politicians. Though it would emerge that she had served three years for smuggling cocaine from Jamaica, the Liberals employed her to give words of support to local businesses affected by the riots.

to by passers-by, including some black-clad types, presumably from Pogo, who brought water, trying to keep the atmosphere around her calm. Along the street were one smouldering car wreck after another, some on side streets. A motorbike had also been burned out, and more bins. Incongruously, amongst the wisps of smoke two priests in full robes were engaged in conversation with some locals; saintly nodding, downcast eyes; an older black man speaking of a need for black youth to stick up for themselves, finally. Others describing miserable conditions, the impossibility of finding jobs, feeling discriminated against by the "feds". Some red graffiti chorused: "fuck da feds"; further up, "fuck Cameron". The name Mark Duggan, and the police murder of a black man were on some lips, but not all; still, that event was clearly a symbol. The priests just listened. Debris indicated a pitched battle had taken place. A row of teenagers, some wearing the archetypal hoodies, on the front steps of a terraced house, consuming beer and crisps, probably looted from the convenience store; a foaming beer can lobbed at a friend.

Back down Clarence Road a new car was now in full blaze, worryingly close to a house. Residents leaned out of windows looking peculiarly calm, given the situation. Night was gradually falling, and the flames stood out in the dark. The crowd had parted around the car, worried about potential explosion. A stream of looters were still making off with items from the shop: crates of beer, bottles of Lambrini. We braved the flames to dash further up the street and into the crowd. Unprompted, a young black guy enthused to us "this is it! The fucking revolution! The people taking back the streets!" Another compared the events favourably to the student movement of 2010–11: this was "*real* protest". The owner of a wool shop stood in his doorway, protecting his business, and the cabbie whose vehicle had been half destroyed attempted to extricate what was left.

After a while the police helicopter flew in low for a bit, as if to intimidate the crowd, but the cops themselves were still bizarrely absent, perhaps content to leave the riot as long as it was contained in an area already deeply stigmatised. The sound of sirens and a stroll around the neighbourhood found them massed, inactive on Pembury Road, which cuts through the estate on the west side of the area of conflagration. Were they mustering forces, waiting for a strategic moment, or just observing from afar? At the bottom of Clarence Road, the crowd was now restive, uneasy about the long absence of a their main partner in riot. "There are no cops man!", someone shouted, "where the hell are the police!?" while the chopper just throbbed in the sky above – cataloguing, presumably, all of our faces, clothes, postures, interactions, ready for the systematic analysis that would later convict thousands.

It is a perversity of a riot like this, built entirely around liberation of territory from the cops, that the complete absence of this protagonist, while seemingly realising the riot's very aim, deprives it of the dynamic which enables it to develop. The police, in this sense, are not an external force of order applied by the state to an already rioting mass, but an integral part of the riot: not only its standard component spark-plug, acting via the usual death, at police hands, of some young black man, but also the necessary ongoing partner of the rioting crowd from whom the space must be liberated if this liberation is to mean anything at all; who must be attacked as an enemy if the crowd is to be unified in anything; who must be forced to *recognise* the agency of a habitually subjected group. Now, without direct confrontation in a number of hours, the riot was starting to sag. People seemed actually to be *willing* the cops to return, even perhaps to the point of self-destruction. A young white man dressed like an anarchist cried "MARE STREET!" repeatedly, gesturing for the crowd to follow him that way. We drifted along with the flow as it crossed the boundary of the estate to enter the Narrowway, with its greater supply of shopfronts.

Those massed troops we'd seen had evidently been primed to oblige the crowd in response to such provocation. Almost immediately a riot van screeched in, prompting a wave of heckling: "MURDERERS!". Some in the crowd, too, were prepared, immediately letting forth a quite intense volley of rocks, beer cans etc, which clattered into the van as it sped past. A can rebounded and thudded hard into my chest, spraying beer down my front. Some of the men started gathering around a bank on the Narrowway, smashing at its windows. A kid let off a fire extinguisher pointlessly into the street. As they penetrated the bank, a riot van sped into the crowd, forcing it to part back towards the Pembury, but suffering a broken window from one well-aimed brick as it slid by. Cops were now moving in from the south in full riot gear, at the bottom end of the Narrowway. At the end of Clarence Road a new convoy of riot vans rolled in. Again the crowd was well prepared, unleashing volleys of missiles. One flew straight for the head of a driver, shattering the window but not passing through. Kids kicked obstacles in front of the vans, trying to block their way, without success. Anything – tree branches were pulled down, rammed flailingly at the cop vehicles. Now an unfortunate bus rolled up behind the riot vans blocking Dalston Lane, its front windows already gaping – sign of an incident elsewhere in the city – and was forced to turn awkwardly around in the street, to avoid another riot that now filled the road ahead of it. Police charged. "Clear the area!" We ran, fearing a kettle.

Separated from the bulk of the crowd, we moved off. The road was clear but several shops had been hit: JD Sports, a posh sandwich shop, Ladbrokes. A gaggle of friendly alchies accosted us, an inebriated woman

A Rising Tide Lifts All Boats

grabbing and kissing us. "BOO!" she shouted at a passing hipster, tense from the goings-on: he jumped a mile before she headlocked him, declaring her love and showering him with the same kisses. Were they deliberately heading for the riot? Similar types had been present in the midst of the crowd: just those left when the streets cleared of the "respectable", perhaps, or looking for opportunities under cover of the riots? In more or less deserted streets, as we rambled through Hackney, we found only drunks and some Turkish guys – perhaps out to protect their businesses – hanging out with police. In a kebab shop we asked one cop if this was happening anywhere other than Hackney. He laughed: "Are you joking love? It's literally everywhere".

They were completely overwhelmed. Police organisational and communications structures seem to have more or less collapsed around this point, strained by the sheer numbers of police officers being drafted into the capital from elsewhere in the country. Individual officers were reduced to communicating horizontally with each other, using their personal mobile phones, while the backups did not have proper equipment or any instructions as to what they should do. Camden, Lewisham, Catford, Croydon, Kilburn, Peckham, Battersea, Balham, Barnet, Clapham Junction, Ealing, Barking, Enfield, Bromley, Chingford Mount, East Ham, Birmingham, Liverpool, Bristol, Nottingham, Woolwich and Bromwich were all now experiencing riots or related disturbances: the rioting had clearly spread far, far beyond its original trigger point – far even beyond Greater London's vast metropolitan sprawl; something missed in the frequent international naming of these as "London" or "Tottenham" riots. These were *England* riots: halting at the small market town of Gloucester, before the Welsh border, spreading a long way north to Manchester, but sparing the northernmost reaches of the country, and the whole of Scotland, perhaps due to the wet weather further north.[4]

[4] It should also be remembered that Scotland in general has experienced much less rioting than England over recent decades.

WHY RIOT

So who were these rioters, and why were they rioting? A certain explanatory, justificatory discourse was already present in the midst of the Pembury riot itself, uttered by rioters and especially by the older, more passive participants to anyone who cared to listen. These explanations were not the *post festum* fabrications of journalists or social scientists, eager to slot the events from afar into their own pre-formed narratives or theoretical contraptions, nor the retrospective rationalisations of kids who, in the spur of the moment, acted merely on impulse, or for the opportunity of getting some loot. They were an organic aspect of the riot itself, part of its general ambience, immediately perceptible to anyone present. Looting was in any case a marginal, tokenistic aspect of at least this particular moment in the national riot-wave; there were scant opportunities for effective looting on the Pembury Estate anyway, ruling out some immediate "consumerist greed" as a significant motivation. And the extended timespan of the Pembury riot, the crowd largely inactive, palpably *wondering what to do*, for long intervals while the cops gathered their forces nearby, undermines any appeal to "impulse" or the vagaries of mob irrationality. No: this riot came from the start with its own conscious justifications, and sustained them through the course of a primary conflict with the cops. The murder of a black man, poor conditions, unemployment: diverse explanations were given. And no doubt there were some people merely seizing an opportunity for some free booze. But, while various, there is an obvious coherence to this set of explanations, describing a world of condensed urban deprivation, and the need for revolt against it. What's more, one explanation in particular stood out in its frequency: the role of the police and the need for Pembury youth to stand up for themselves against the systemic harassment exemplified in generalised stop-and-search; the need to finally take a stand, to stage a *real* protest against such treatment.

Contrary both to the authoritarian refusal to allot any legitimate agency to rioting subjects, in order to condemn them as unworthy of recognition (and thus as worthy of exemplary punishment), and a radical reversal of signs on this reading which would like to hold up the riots as some pure space of lumpen negativity, devoid of any meaningful intention (for fear of the taint of "politics"), a coherent struggle was being waged here, with a definite and quite transparent content: to insist upon respect from the cops, force recognition of a subject where daily grind sees only an *abject*. The Pembury riot itself already carried this content; the verbalised justifications in its midst merely clarified something already evident. This riot *demanded* the presence of the police, as the immediate interlocutor for whom it was performed, whose recognition it insisted upon, whose presence and participation it invited, and through whose efforts it was constituted.

The building national riot wave which had been triggered a couple of days previously, just a few miles north in the adjacent borough — and the mounting social tensions of the years running up to it — supplied its broad conjunctural context; a deep neighbourhood history of abjection and stigmatisation, most directly at the hands of the cops, its local one. At four o'clock in the afternoon the police had supplied an additional proximate cause: manhandling two young black men in a stop-and-search at Hackney Town Hall, just a few minutes walk from the Pembury Estate, in an area already pumped for riot, and correspondingly swamped with expectant coppers ready-equipped with NATO-style helmets. The Pembury riot, that is to say, was before all else an anti-police riot. It would be a bitter experience for those involved that the direct outcome of such riots — of their fleeting rebellions against a disrespecting Police — was an extreme escalation of the social logic of abjection, in which they would be projected as little better than wild animals; yet, looking back from a year or two's hindsight, many of them would come to affirm the experience as something they'd happily do again.

MARGINS

Such riots are a habit of Britain's deprived estates, dating back to the area-based policing that developed following the Notting Hill Carnival riots of 1976 – the long, hot summer that also gave us punk. From the late 1960s, Enoch Powell's voice in the wilderness had helped to set the agenda of both the National Front's reborn, post-CND Mosleyism, and a nascent New Right within the Conservative Party that, in response to its defeat at the hands of the miners, would eventually push beyond the lingering one-nationism of the Heath Government to incarnate itself in an Iron Lady. Now, while a simmering monetarism, emanating from the Institute of Economic Affairs, made its way even into the ruling cabinet of "Labour Party Capitalist Britain", and while the struggles of the workers' movement reached their crest, a contested reconfiguration of class relations was already underway at the level of urban space, with "race" as mediation constituting the sharp edge. A metropolitan police force that had finally come round to the conclusion that black people actually were more likely to be criminals, after all; a far right eager to capitalise on this revelation through such traditional pursuits as the provocative march through minority neighbourhoods; urban communities increasingly resistant to such harassment; a rebellious punk youth who coveted the anti-authoritarian credentials of the riotous rastas: by these vectors there cohered a new politics of space in Britain, focused by – but not reducible to – race. Under the 1824 Vagrancy Act's "sus law", the police increasingly targeted residents of pre-identified and preeminently black "problem" areas for routine stop-and-search, now that residency in such places was considered enough in itself to provide grounds for suspicion. Thus the stigma already placed upon areas such as Brixton by their particular positions in the distribution of urban misery was given a reflexive reinforcement in the new style of policing aimed at their containment.

Defined as spaces on the margins of society, inherently lawless, to be managed under a regime of mere "social control", these stigmatised neighbourhoods came to represent the internal limits of the restructured capitalist state; enactments of a nasty, brutal state of nature which would provide exemplary justification for the consolidating Leviathan. Under this crystallising regime, the residents of such places are only representable as warning signs to the rest of the nation, the grab-bag of failed subjects who constitute what has recently come to be known as "broken Britain": the dole scroungers, hoodies, illegal immigrants, single mothers, chavs, drug dealers, fatherless blacks, gang members, *et cetera*. Yet this has never been the "ghetto" in anything other than a metaphorical sense: the symbolic exclusion represented by the marginal housing estate does not amount to a literal exclusion from economy or state, and such areas have always maintained some variety in terms of ethnic composition. And, while the development of these places cannot ultimately be separated from general global logics, the British case should be differentiated from others such as the US and France.[5] Shaped by the encounter of post-colonial immigrants with remnants of an "indigenous" working class, with the decayed remainder of a post-war social-democratic housing often providing the architectural setting, the poor urban neighbourhood in Britain shares certain characteristics with the French case. But, in Britain, it was never relegated to the periphery of the city. Rather, it has typically filled the spaces left by a particular mix of (1) interwar inner-city slum clearance, (2) the razing of large areas of working class habitation by the blitz — which left sizable bomb sites in London right up to the 1970s, and (3) post-war "white flight" to suburban developments. From these factors London's

[5] See Loïc Wacquant, *Urban Outcasts* (Polity 2008) for a comparative analysis of the American and French cases.

population was actually in decline for most of the 20th Century, after the peak of the Victorian slum; a tendency that only turned around in the 1990s.

The inner-urban and "white flight" connections here invite comparison with the American ghetto, but the latter is a much more pronounced structural aspect of a society forged directly in plantation slavery — as opposed to profiting off the latter from a distance before moralising about it when it suited. "Black" as a declared ethnicity is, of course, multiples higher as a percentage of the population in the United States, and the American ghetto is an expansive urban area, much larger than the marginal blocks and estates of British cities, and more a world unto itself.[6] In Britain, while these places do, of course, condense unemployment and other social "dysfunctions" relative to other zones in the urban geography, residents typically continue their existences as workers, consumers or students elsewhere, beyond the bounds of these merely residential areas. Nor does the state hold back from penetrating such spaces with its own institutions: youth services; social workers; one or another remedial neighbourhood scheme. If the state posits such places as its own internal limits, it is thus important not to take it too literally at its word, for while these developments reinforce real long-term deprivation, the most salient dimension on which this exclusion occurs is a social logic of abjection experienced first and foremost in the encounter with the repressive arm of the state. Everything else follows: mediatised victimisation of residents, unending chain of aspirant cabinet members feigning deep concern, think-tank concept creation, crypto-racist scandals about a feckless, parasitic underclass.

ANTI-COP

Faced with this dynamic, residents do not always remain passive. Indeed, the imposition of such policing can contribute to the formation of at least the *negative*

[6] Probably in part reflecting these spatial differences, according to census data intermarriage rates are significantly higher in England; a mixing that seems to find a cultural counterpart in the history of British pop music.

A Rising Tide Lifts All Boats

unity of a community self-organising against the cops: some neighbourhood "defence campaign", for example, oriented around retribution for the death in police custody of a community member, or the indifference of state and media to one or another racist tragedy. Such things have been a persistent, if often submerged, current in London life throughout the decades of capitalist restructuring — cecades in which hundreds of deaths in police custody, typically of blacks, have not resulted in a single convicted officer. Though it typically runs up against an impassive state, this sort of community self-organisation only rarely issues in a full-blown riot-wave: it is never on its own a sufficient condition. It does, however, provice a compact social measure of highly combustible material which, given a broader climate of social tension, risks setting the country at large ablaze. 1981, 1985, 2011: the pivotal riots of all these years have found their immediate causes in the deaths — real or perceived — cf black people at the hands of the cops, in marginal areas.[7] In this period, only the Poll Tax riot stands out as a major national example of a riot in which a different foundational logic was at play: that of the conventional central London demonstration which tips over into crowd violence.

And, on one level at least, such rioting *works*. As a Broadwater Farm resident told us: the nation will long remember the name of Cynthia Jarrett, whose death during a police raid of her house sparked the 1985 Tottenham riot in which police attending got what local leftist MP Bernie Grant described as "a bloody good hiding" — including the hacking to death of PC Keith Blakelock; "and it'll sure as hell remember Mark Duggan". But Joy Gardner, who suffocated to death when two cops and an immigration official wrapped thirteen feet of surgical tape around her head; Roger Sylvester, a mentally ill man they held in a restraining position that induced brain damage and cardiac arrest; Colin Roach, who died from a shotgun injury in the entrance of Stoke Newington

[7] In 1991 and 1995 there were also significant riots of this type in Meadow Well estate, Newcastle upon Tyne, and Brixton, respectively, but neither precipitated the sort of broader wave we find in 1981, 1985 and 2011. Displaying a curious periodicity, other significant riots also occurred in 2001 and 2005, though these — especially 2005 — were of different types: a confrontation with the far right, and an inter-communal 'race' riot.

[8] The Stephen Lawrence campaign is an exception. Lawrence was stabbed to death in a racist attack in 1993 at the age of 18. Though police have been implicated in various ways, the fact that the direct perpetrators here were not police but just a group of white

police station... these people enter the canon of martyrs for a minor genre of long-term single-issue community campaign that has left little lasting impression on the country at large.[8] Such campaigns run up against a wall of silence, obstruction and intimidation, and a media landscape that has typically been tilted against them from the very first police press statements – rushed out after the incident to provide a convenient frame for the subsequent discourses: the deceased was a gangster/ a drug dealer/ insane, or had assaulted a police officer. Delegitimised in advance, they then tend to be pushed towards an apologetic position, where the victim must be painted an "angel", a "peacemaker" etc, while the police just go about their business. The only sort of "justice" possible in such circumstances is obviously a retributive one, and with a complete shut-out from the state's legitimacy-generating organs, the logical place for the playing out of such retribution is in a public confrontation with the cops in which a crowd presence can generate a momentum not available to individual, orderly campaigners. Donald Douglas, whose brother Brian was beaten to death by two police when on a night out, regretted his efforts to defuse a riot situation when tensions mounted between a crowd of mourners and attending cops:

> In hindsight, because you haven't reached a kind of conclusion that you want to, you think "well I wonder, if I wasn't so disciplined and organised and just allowed people to go and tear up the situation..." probably in hindsight that's the best that could've been achieved, and at least it would've been a day to remember, if nothing else. And some property or whatever would've been destroyed and that would've represented the death of Brian...[9]

When a similar incident a few months later – the death of Wayne Douglas (no relation) – did erupt in the Brixton riots of 1995, Donald thought this probably a more fitting outcome:

racists probably explains the greater scope for success within the British state. The Lawrence campaign has even become a national *cause célèbre* with Lawrence's mother gaining an OBE, a life peerage, and a spot in the Olympic ceremony as emblem of a harmonious multicultural Britain (though the Tory far right 'Traditional Britain Group' continue to argue for her 'repatriation'). Similar campaigns where the police are the direct object typically run up against a wall of state obstruction; the anti-police riot then presents itself as an obvious tactic for *making them listen*. The Lawrence campaign is an exception that helpfully obscures a repressive rule.

9 From Ken Fero and Tariq Mehmood's film, *Injustice*, 2002.

A Rising Tide Lifts All Boats **107**

Obviously it led to a catastrophe really in terms of shops being broken, cars being broken, but it clearly got the message home… because, in a sense, none of our demonstrations hit the front page of the paper quite to that extent, so it almost seems that if you want to be listened to, you've got to go and break something or burn something down or something.

It is probably no coincidence that the death of Wayne Douglas — a Brixton resident — precipitated a riot, and that of Brian Douglas didn't. The precedent of a local history of rioting, active in the memories of residents, or persisting in the local folklore — plus a history of community identification against the cops — seems to play a significant part in precipitating riots in some places rather than others. Hence a particular set of names recurs in the history of neoliberal riots: Brixton, Broadwater Farm, Handsworth.

British race relations have changed significantly during the decades of capitalist restructuring, tendentially eroding the status of the black as what we might call "primary abject" of the neoliberal state — feared immigrant, "wide-grinning piccaninnie", mugger, yardie, rudeboy — in favour of a more diffuse and less explicitly racialised set of figures: asylum seeker, single mother, chav, hoodie, benefits cheat. Second and third generations have grown up less problematically "British", while the Right has turned instead to Islamic and European bogeymen to define its programmes. Nonetheless London's poor black neighbourhoods have been at the leading edge of the logics of abjection through which a punitive state has come into being, and indeed their struggles within this logic are organically related to the transformations of "race" itself. If the black of the late 1970s and early 1980s was, to state it crudely, the prototype for today's "feral underclass", the major linking thread here is not "race" as any essential trait, nor even any stable, coherent sociological category, but a social logic of abjection by which specific figures, associated primarily with poor urban neighbourhoods, are posited as the limit concepts of affirmable social class – just as the traditional lumpen was the necessary negative corollary to a positive working class identity. A result and constitutive moment of this logic is the riot as rebellion against the police.

RESTRUCTURING RIOT

Prior to the beginnings of capitalist restructuring in the mid-to-late 1970s, this sort of community anti-police riot did not occur; its relative frequency over the last three decades – occurring in about 1 of every 6 years – is a notable characteristic of the period. Probably due to the dominance of an orderly system of wage bargaining over other sources of social antagonism, the riot had largely faded out as a form of struggle during the era of the workers' movement. And where conflicts did erupt around immigrant communities, these were of a different character, such as the 1958 Notting Hill riots, when Teddy Boy racists attacked the houses of West Indian residents. The 1970s were a transitional phase in which police fears of leftist and black militancy, and tensions around the perceived hedonistic culture of blacks, underlay a ramping-up of tensions in some deprived inner city neighbourhoods, while the broader social crisis of that era set in. Immigrant workers of the 1970s entered a job market structured around a heavily corporatist and predominantly white, male labour movement that was coming up against its own limits at the intersection of the long secular decline of Britain's manufacturing base and the beginnings of a more global downturn in manufactures. While some immigrant workers fought hard for unionisation, such as the Asian women strikers in the famous Grunwick dispute, the labour movement was predominantly elsewhere, representing someone else, and fighting its own concluding battles. Thus the demands of these workers lacked the kind of systemic integration by which governments would be, as a matter of course, compelled to consult Jack Jones, General

Secretary of the Transport and General Workers Union, on matters of policy. And when unemployment hit, it of course tended to hit such workers harder.

At the same time, proliferating militancies, threads of rasta, black power and other positive identities, and elements of a certain "refusal of work" attitude, provided forms for the expression of an antagonistic culture, particularly for the young.[10] It was in this context that the police came to revise earlier assessments of blacks as a low-crime group, and to start showing frustration with a militant anti-police discourse that had developed in organic relation with a series of minor riots, raids and repressions from the early 1970s. A turning point here was the Notting Hill Carnival Riot of 1976, in which more than 100 officers were hospitalised after a conflict broke out between police and carnival-goers when a bunch of black youths tried to de-arrest an alleged pickpocket. White punks in the area — Notting Hill was still at that time associated with a certain squatty, radical milieu — rushed to the scene, hankering after the boldly anti-authoritarian credentials of black youth: an encounter famously encapsulated in The Clash's "White Riot". From this point on, police would establish a "containment policy" for black neighbourhoods in areas such as Brixton and Hackney, targeting youths in particular for stop-and-search under the sus law, and sending into these areas specialized units such as the notorious Special Patrol Group.[11] As a political actor, the Metropolitan Police now found in the emphasis on black crime an effective tool for enhancing its legitimacy amongst the population at large.[12] And it was in this period that "mugging" took off as a term[13], identifying particularly black street crime: a concept that would play a key role in justifying an escalating experimentation with punitive styles of policing that had not previously been used by the British police outside of Northern Ireland — perennial testing ground for the British state's mechanisms of repression. All of this was a convenient context for an ascendant National Front,

[10] Our overview of the racial politics of this period draws particularly on Paul Gilroy's classic, *There Ain't No Black in the Union Jack* (University of Chicago Press 1987), especially, 108-142.

[11] The London Metropolitan SPG had been set up in the early 1960s to deal with public disorder and to respond to terrorist threats. Its namesake and equivalent in Northern Ireland was associated with loyalist paramilitaries, and was the first section of the British police to be given training by the British Army in the anti-riot tactics developed there.

[12] Gilroy, *Ain't No Black*, 120.

[13] British usage of this term suddenly increased eight-fold between 1975 and 1980. In American English a similar rise began in 1960. Source: Google Ngrams.

proffering a neo-Nazi message which exchanged the East London Jews of the 1930s for the Afro-Caribbeans and Asians of the 1970s. The resulting conflicts with anti-fascists – emerging from the punk, student, and Trotskyist scenes of the moment – and black and Asian communities, when the NF would march through their neighbourhoods, provided further pretext for heavy police intervention into neighbourhoods which were sinking into deeper abjection as the social crisis of the late 1970s escalated.[14]

1979's Winter of Discontent, and the inability of Callaghan's Labour government to begin in earnest the capitalist restructuring that had been set at its place, brought a Tory New Right to power with a programme of inflation-busting monetary restraint. Unemployment, rising through the 1970s, now rocketed, undermining the bargaining power of an already-embattled labour movement and further reinforcing the marginal status of some urban communities. The 1980 riot in St Paul's, Bristol demonstrated to the authorities that it was not only the more enduringly troublesome black communities of London that could constitute a threat, and – anticipating historian David Starkey's racist comments three decades later – that even whites could evidently prove similarly disruptive when exposed to the morally corrosive example of their black neighbours, for they had constituted at least 50 percent of the crowd.[15] Exposing the constellations of a superstitious copper's cosmology, in which urban unrest was paired up not only with blackness but also literalistically with 1970s leftist militancy, some police apparently read the appearance of Tariq Ali in Bristol shortly before the riot as evidence that they must have been the work of that eternal agent of social disturbance: the outside agitator.

But the real epochal explosion was to come a year later. In early 1981 thirteen black teenagers died in an unexplained house fire in Deptford, South East London, with many suspecting a fascist attack. Indifference of state and

14 A key moment here was the 1977 'Battle of Lewisham', in which the National Front clashed with a newly consolidated anti-fascist movement, and the police used riot shields for the first time on mainland Britain. While the histories of the two forms are closely entwined, such encounters with the far right should be distinguished from the community anti-police riot that is a focus of this article.

15 Gilroy, *Ain't No Black*, 126. Starkey, casting around on national television for an explanation for the 2011 riot-wave, claimed that 'the whites have become black'. See BBC Newsnight, 12 August 2011.

A Rising Tide Lifts All Boats

media prompted a demonstration in central London led by the *Race Today* collective on 2 March, on which the police suffered a bloody defeat when attempting to cut it short. Shortly after, perhaps smarting from these events, the Metropolitan Police launched "Operation Swamp 81"[16], a "saturation policing" strategy that sent large numbers of plainclothes Special Patrol Group officers into the area around Brixton's Railton Road, notorious as a sort of lawless semi-liberated zone in which police were often reluctant to tread, thus making low-level crime such as street-level ganja-selling more viable. Just as in 2011, this escalating stop-and-search raised tensions in the area. Then, when a pool hall brawl spilled over into a stabbing on Friday 10 April, and police on the scene were suspected of preventing the victim from getting to hospital, a riot dynamic began to develop, with crowd attempts to intervene, and more police being drafted in. Overnight, rumours spread, the incident mutating into a case of death by police brutality, and cops were warned about the risks of further inciting an already restive neighbourhood. But, eager to play their hand, they decided to push on with the stop-and-search. The next day, working class youths from the surrounding area — black and white alike — flocked into Brixton, expecting some excitement. The second trigger-point came with the stop-and-search of a cabby on Railton Road. Plainclothes police on the scene were claimed to have been found wearing National Front badges. For the next several hours there ensued the worst bout of civil unrest seen in Britain in at least a century as looting and arson spread throughout the Brixton area, and the police completely lost control of the streets, under hails of bricks and molotov cocktails against which they were ill-defended, given the lack at this time of the standard tools of the riot cop.

Indeed, it was the 1981 Brixton riot and the "summer of a thousand Julys" which followed it — reverberations being heard around the country until late July, with another major peak in Toxteth, Liverpool, also triggered by racialised

[16] The name, presumably was not arbitrary: notions of an indigenous population being 'swamped' with threatening strangers have been a mainstay of British racism for decades.

stop-and-search – which really crystallised a new approach to policing. The friendly, bicycling community bobbies of yesteryear came to be replaced by something resembling a medieval army: helmeted, shielded foot-soldiers equipped with hand-held cudgels for cracking proletarian skulls, plus a cavalry of mounted officers capable of moving at speed and striking from above, and the ever-present threat of CS gas, water cannon, or plastic bullets, should this not prove to be enough. This repressive configuration – pioneered by an occupying army in Northern Ireland – was now imported into mainland Britain to deal with the enemies within. And it would see its first full deployments here with the breaking of the last holdouts of the workers' movement: the miners at the Battle of Orgreave in 1984, and the printers in Wapping in 1986–87. At the same time, the sus law – now widely perceived to be a contributory factor in the generation of riots – was scrapped, barely a month after the end of the riot wave, while the Scarman Report, commissioned in response to the riots, found some fault in the policing of black neighbourhoods, and contributed to a bureaucratic reconfiguration of policing in which the preservation of an image of race neutrality would be a priority. While mainstream media continued to deploy an animalising discourse about these neighbourhoods as social sinkholes brimming with rampant, asocial criminality – a sort of "heart of darkness" in the midst of the city – they remained home to multifarious cultures of militancy, mixing black nationalism, rastafarianism and varied leftisms into a campaigning culture of neighbourhood defence.

Local government in this era, especially in London, had been entered by leftists who set about promoting various anti-racist and positive discrimination policies, encouraging the flow of black workers into state institutions in particular. And in response there developed a neoliberal variant of anti-racism, against skin colour as identity-marker, against special treatment of particular groups as such, rather than as utility-maximising individuals.

Thus it was that the Thatcher government campaigned for re-election, at the height of nationalist jingoism after the Falklands War, boasting of scrapping the sus law, and arguing that if "Labour say he's black, Tories say he's British". Anti-racism of one type or another had become a matter of state policy, no matter how bigoted Thatcher and her ilk as individuals. Then, as the 1980s progressed, pushing for a more positive programme in comparison to the spasmodic activism of rioters, a generation of reformist black leftists such as Diane Abbot established footholds in a Labour Party now beginning to undergo its own restructuring beyond the politics of the labour movement.

If an anti-racist politics was on the political agenda in this period, and if certain militant identities were in the air in some of the communities that rioted, this does not make the 1981 riot wave as a whole immediately reducible to a demand of blacks to become "normal proletarians".[17] It is important to remember that black communities were here — as in 2011 — only detonation points for a riot-wave which brought in many others; even the Brixton riots didn't just involve the local black community. And while the self-organisation of such communities against the police of course expresses a certain demand to be treated another way, the immediate norm here is that of an equal subject before the law — more directly a matter of citizenship than of class belonging. While issues of marginality on the labour market no doubt contributed significantly to tensions, and the repressive role of the police cannot ultimately be extricated from a certain social imperative to keep the lid on such marginal strata, it is important to avoid collapsing mediations here which, in their distinction, constitute the only intelligible structure of such events. While they are certainly related — universal manhood suffrage was a major demand of the workers' movement — there's no law in capitalist society that automatically equates the normal proletarian with the full citizenship rights of

[17] For this claim, see Rocamadur, 'The Feral Underclass Hits the Streets', *SIC* 2, forthcoming.

the bourgeois subject. And, while the specific cultural embodiments of the politics of race which persisted in the Britain of the early 1980s have indeed faded, the same demands have persisted, for the cops have not ceased harassing black people in the street, beating them to death in cells, and attempting to smear their names when conflicts get out of control. Campaigns over deaths in police custody persist, now with a generational cross-section that leaves rastas and a certain residual rhetoric about "Africa" in the older brackets, alongside fully "naturalised" younger generations expressing similar demands in a language inflected more with grime or hip-hop; people unified thus in at least one negative sense – the conviction that police behaviour is *not fair*. And in this mix, the odd thread about police treatment of "working class" communities persists as a minor element, from those still attempting to conjure some broader solidarity.

If we are to periodise Britain's urban riots, the clearest rupture is not between some positive black identity in the early 1980s and a putative negativity that followed it, but between a more consensual mode of policing in the era of the post-war settlement – an era in which class compromise was embodied in a much less polarised urban geography – and the organically entwined development of a more repressive mode with an increasing abjection of particular urban neighbourhoods, as that settlement unravelled from the 1970s. In contrast to the vagaries of political identity formations there is a clear measure here for periodisation: the anti-police riots we find exemplified in 1981 and 2011 were a novelty when they emerged in the 1970s, and they have persisted since. The logic that compels these developments is not reducible to race, but it is not incidental that black neighbourhoods were at the leading edge: shut out of a corporatist white labourism that was already in crisis as industry wound down and unemployment mounted, anyone outside and demanding entry into that movement could only swim with the flow of this crisis. Black workers

A Rising Tide Lifts All Boats

would never come to be systematically incorporated into the labour movement, but black *people* could be formally incorporated into the one entity with which they increasingly came face-to-face as the workers' movement receded: the state. This has been the real development of "race" from the 1980s on. But while these are important transformations — particularly in institutionalising efforts to support force with consent — a social logic of race tends to persist in asserting itself through such formalisations. The structural locations of poor neighbourhoods within the economy, and the symbolic constructs by which black = street = crime, lingered on. Black deaths in police custody continued, and neighbourhoods such as Broadwater Farm remained marginal "no-go areas", off-limits enough to the police for them to preserve at times a certain nominal sense of autonomy, making them, for example, convenient places for the positioning of the pirate radio antennas which have played such an important role in the proliferation of London's urban cultures during the restructuring.

INSECURE

Meanwhile, with the complete defeat of the workers' movement and a breathtaking pace of deindustrialisation that outstripped anything seen elsewhere, the traditional working class that had been a central protagonist of British society since the industrial revolution, with its own peculiar corporatist culture and conservatism, found itself staring into the abyss.[18] In gestures of neoliberal populism, appealing to its industrious, liberal values, this class was invited to remake itself as a sort of pseudo-petit bourgeoisie: everyone a little entrepreneur, with their little stock of capital, their little stake in some ideal future catallaxy. Not only the famous flogging cheap of council housing stock, but also the inducement to take out shares in the privatising ex-state utilities, the "Big Bang" opening of the City to barrow-boy geezers, who would make a quick wad on some reckless speculation

18 While extreme waves of deindustrialisation also occurred elsewhere, such as the American mid-west, the national-level scuttling and sinking of industry in general was a peculiarly British phenomenon.

and end up a *parvenu* "loadsamoney", flashing cash in sprouting cocktail bars by the end of the 1980s... Those who were not in a position to make the necessary leap — especially those in the more emphatically industrial areas further north — got long-term unemployment, often masked as "incapacity". And they stayed there: UK unemployment didn't even get back to the level of the end of the turbulent, crisis-ridden 1970s until around the millennium, and it has only increased from there. If workers were lucky, they got absorbed into the burgeoning state sector that has remained by far the biggest employer in Britain to the present, or eventually made their way into one or another precarious service sector job. But either way, from here on, being "working class" was either an increasingly vague, nostalgic identity construct, tethered to Grim Up North/ Stuck-up South binaries and rosy Coronation Street images of a dead world, or something to be disavowed in favour of glib assertions that "we're all middle class now". Even appeals to a generic postindustrial wage-labour became increasingly tenuous evidence for a positive class identity, given the ubiquity of the wage-form in remunerating everyone from CEO to streetsweeper. While class, of course, persisted as a deep, structuring logic — and wealth polarised to an ever-greater extent — the British working class had been thoroughly decomposed, and this brute fact of polarisation translated less and less clearly into any straightforward sociological, political-economic, or even cultural schema.

The heightened structural role of unemployment in this era, mediating a broader global tendency towards the production of a surplus population through Britain's peculiarly dramatic post-industrialism, contributed to a generalised precarisation of the wage. The workers' movement already having been divided and defeated, at legal and policy levels employment rights were now curtailed in favour of an extreme flexibilisation. As these developments rippled through the economy, the key surface distinctions came increasingly to be between

A Rising Tide Lifts All Boats

those who were more successful in navigating the tides of an insecure labour market, and those who were less so. Thus a fundamentally relative, ambiguous mode of social distinction substituted itself for the faux ontology of corporatist class culture. On this shifting scale all positive positions are defined and structured against a negative *someone else*. There's "us", and there are those who've failed; who don't try hard enough; who are lazier than the rest of us; who parasitise the collective taxpayer; who don't even care for their own neighbourhoods. Thus a fractal logic by which white professionals — come round to anti-racism — measure themselves up against feckless chavs; poor whites against an immigrant bogeyman; South Asians against lazy Afro-Caribbeans; Afro-Caribbeans against Somali criminality, and so on.

Contrary to the pseudo-sociological taxonomies of media stereotypes, the "less so" here, the *someone else*, has never come to constitute any coherent "underclass", definable by its relation to welfare receipts, unemployment etc. Indeed, through this period the opposition of welfare and work came to be undermined by a proliferation of welfare untethered to unemployment, such as child benefit, or actually hinging directly on work, such as tax credits. At the same time, unemployment itself has been redefined as an ever-steeper chute back into the labour market; recent developments in "workfare" are only the latest extension of this longer term logic. Thus, while massive unemployment was the direct consequence of Thatcherite restructuring as whole major industries were demolished, this has given way to a regime of insecurity in which structural tends to segue into frictional unemployment, and worklessness appears as "jobseeking". On the other hand, employment itself has become increasingly unstable as a category, with rising temp work, short-term contracts, and most recently the "zero-hour contract", by which employees are guaranteed no minimum number of hours of actual work, but must simply hope for the best from one week to the next. In these senses, comparisons of actual employment levels with those of the 1970s can be deceptive, since the meaning of the work/unemployment distinction has changed so significantly over the period. If unemployment figures remain high compared to the years of the post-war settlement, employment itself is qualitatively less distinguishable from unemployment.

For these reasons it is important not to read the tendential precarisation of the wage as leading necessarily to the constitution of any neatly delimitable "surplus population", identified simplistically by a lack of formal employment or residency in some marginal zone: it was never directly "the surplus population" that took up residency in Britain's poor urban estates, nor was it in any immediate sociological sense a "surplus population" of unemployed that developed a propensity to riot over this period. Indeed, a majority of rioters in 2011 seem to have been either in full-time education or employed, and though unemployment remains of course higher in the marginal areas in which riots tend to generate – and was spiking significantly in the period leading up to the riots, making it legible, perhaps, as a significant contributing factor – it has remained markedly low in hyper-flexibilised Britain, compared to other European countries.[19] While the general law of capitalist accumulation is to produce a surplus population, and this is a central dynamic of this epoch, we should also be wary of identifying these developments with a clearly specified "precariat" class, for the erosion of the stability of the wage is something socially general, not neatly confinable to a specific part of the population: insecurity is everywhere, only with varying types and degrees of intensity. The production of a surplus population is a matter of the deep inner logic of the capital relation; its forms of appearance are mediated with too much complexity to be easily mapped "at the surface of society", equated simplistically with unemployment or marginality.

[19] Out of the 270 sample rioters interviewed in the *Reading the Riots* study, half were students and about a quarter were unemployed. Nevertheless, many rioters retrospectively cited a lack of job prospects, unemployment or the fear of unemployment as a reason for their rioting. *Reading the Riots* (Guardian and LSE 2011), 4.

If the "someone else" is identified by a different social logic, it is not however an unrelated one. With generalised precariousness and the erosion of the stability of the wage-form as the core integrative moment in social reproduction, those who navigate these turbulent waters with less success come to embody in themselves the insecurity of the entire social order. The security of everyone else is premised on a constant repetition of acts of social distinction which cast out and stigmatise the less successful. The state of insecurity that underpins the social whole demands management, containment in condensed areas; a perpetual making safe of society for capital. Along a shifting but constitutive perimeter, the Police establishes itself as a substitute integrative moment, defining the security of all those who are within, against the insecurity of those without; building consent from the former with force against the latter. The social logic at play here is what we've been calling "abjection".[20] By this logic, those expelled or abjected are not literally externalised, but rather remain in an internal, mutually-constitutive relation with that which abjects them. The restructured capitalist state is built upon its abjects, and can never expel them entirely, for the logic of abjection is an integral aspect of the general regime of labour insecurity. In place of a regulation of social reproduction by collective bargaining around the wage relation, as that reciprocal integration of capital and labour unravels, social order is maintained increasingly by a forced subordination of society to capital's rule, in the form of a hypertrophied repressive apparatus constantly re-applied to *those who fail*. Though at a very general level such stigmatising distinctions have a long and stubborn history, with even Beveridge's blueprint for the welfare state designed to exclude some set of sub-proletarian unworthies, this is not a return to a Victorian distinction of deserving and undeserving poor, as is often rhetorically claimed. What Beatrice Webb in 1886 called the "outcasting force" was a shaking-off of the disorderly from the rigours of growing productive industry, whence

20 Our usage of the concept of abjection here derives from Imogen Tyler, who in turn derives it from Kristeva. Tyler applies the concept to a set of case studies: travellers, women, 'chavs', illegal immigrants etc. In this usage the term has a certain descriptive value, but Tyler herself doesn't supply any real unified historical or material basis for the phenomena she describes. See Imogen Tyler, *Revolting Subjects: Social Abjection and Resistance in Neoliberal Britain* (Zed Books 2013).

they would trickle into dissolute pools of irregular employment in the East London slums of the time.[21] That world is, of course, long-gone. The precarious and the irregular are no longer peculiar to some residuum left by a growing industrial working class; as that class dwindles, these tendentially become universal. The current logic of abjection – the new outcasting force – is incomprehensible in abstraction from this broader restructuring of the capital relation since the 1970s.

The marginal urban neighbourhood of this period is the exemplary symbolic location for the playing out of this outcasting force, and the black immigrant its first exemplary subject – what we above called the "primary abject" of restructured capitalist society. But this logic does not limit itself simply to distinctions of "race". Over the last three and a half decades the urban abject has mutated to encompass a broader range of figures, while retaining an umbilical link to the immigrant communities of the 1970s. Thus the "chav", peculiar rendering of the new "residuum": the poor remainder of the white working class after its Thatcherite liquidation, *as if this class had become a race.*[22] The riotous inner-urban subjects of the late 1970s and early 1980s were never really any single mono-ethnic group; even then, the meaning of "race" was given less by any notional biological attribute than by the urban environment itself as a place of danger and criminality, calling for tougher law and order. And there were plenty of whites who wanted to riot in Notting Hill, St Paul's, Brixton. But over time the significations of the urban abject have shifted: the black militant is gone as a figure of fear, but the fatherless petty criminal remains, alongside the scandalously fertile mother. To the set has been added the *Eden Lake* image of the hoodied teenage chav, slouching along behind an aggressive little dog, and the multi-generational dole-scrounging family. By the social logic of abjection, those who fall foul of the regime of generalised insecurity tend to be constructed as one or another of these stigmatising

[21] Beatrice Webb, *My Apprenticeship* (1926), 166. Cited in Stedman Jones, *Outcast London*, 12.

[22] The term 'chav' reputedly has etymological associations with Romani gypsies – another permutation of the abject. It came into general use as a sort of pseudo-racialising term of class hatred in Britain in the early 2000s.

figures, especially where their marginality is mediated through a specific spatial configuration, tethering them to some notorious place in the urban geography. And as such they come directly face-to-face with the most punitive side of the state, worthy of suspicion by virtue of their clothes, their place of residence, their seemingly intentionless loitering in public places…

While deaths in police custody remain a particularly racialised affliction, a broader police harassment of the poor is of course much more widely experienced. The incomplete incorporation of blacks into the British state from the 1980s, and the reconfiguration of policing around a stronger bureaucratic neutrality, helped to de-centre race as a trigger-point for large-scale social unrest. Most significantly, perhaps, the scrapping of the sus law and thus a de-prioritising of stop-and-search tactics from the early 1980s, eroded one of the major bases of common anti-police sentiment, perhaps going some way to explaining why anti-police riots following the usual black deaths in 1991 and 1995 did not spill over into the kind of larger-scale conflagration seen in 1981 or 1985. But with the rash of anti-terrorism legislation in the 2000s, we have seen a return of generalised "sus law"-style policing, this time with the need for "reasonable suspicion" entirely dropped.[23] Once again the residents of poor urban neighbourhoods have been subjected to increasing levels of routine stop-and-search backed by legislation ostensibly intended for something entirely other. While, in this context, the Muslim has come to be identified as the major figure for racialised suspicion[24] – alongside the immigrant, of unspecified race – anti-terror legislation has been used for the persecution of blacks, chavs, travellers, activists etc. Other legislation too, such as the introduction of the ASBO (Anti-Social Behaviour Order) has helped to criminalise the urban proletariat (typically identified with its more disruptive, youthful embodiments).

23 The reintroduction of stop-and-search under Section 44 of the 2000 Terrorism Act removed the need for 'reasonable suspicion'. Though the conceptual and practical association for the state between terrorism and area-based crime is clear, in 2009, 100,000 stop-and-search procedures were recorded without a single terrorism conviction being made. The withdrawal of Section 44 in March 2011, and the reintroduction of 'reasonable suspicion' neither alleviates the tensions accrued over those 11 years, nor prevents Police continuing area-based stop-and-search.

24 The tie of such abjectifying processes to notions of race, even when the identifier in question is actually *a religion*, was on display in responses to the 22 May 2013 killing of

Of course, the social logic at play is never merely one-sided. The state does not merely *decide* to punish the poor, but rather evolves its tactics in organic relation to the practices of the communities in question, as well as broader social dynamics. No doubt certain modes of criminality and black market activity do become more pronounced in these areas as prospects for an orderly, stable incorporation into the labour market and broader society diminish. But the relation is a distinctly asymmetrical one, in which what are at play for the police are not only the direct law-and-order issues of particular neighbourhoods, but also their own legitimacy for capital, state, and a society at large whipped into ever greater levels of bigoted frenzy by a media that well knows how to sell stories. Indeed, like the Vietnam body-count, stop-and-search has been propelled over recent years by bureaucratically-driven quotas, in which individual officers are expected to conduct a specified number in a specified time, but must at the same time supposedly demonstrate that they are not doing this on the basis of any racial profiling – which is of course irrelevant if the area in question is predominantly black.

Nonetheless, as Britain paddled in the low waters of the "Clinton boom" and beyond, such ordnance lay mostly dormant, and the locus of what little rioting did occur shifted to Muslim communities with a partial 9/11-era redistribution of the abject. For a while asset bubbles, an ever-expanding higher education sector, the auratic qualities of new tech, and "cool Britannia" bullshit projected an optimistic future in which all might hope to have a role, no matter how encumbered in debt and degradation. As the systemic wage increases of the post-war settlement receded into the past and wealth continued to polarise, glimmers of hope came from other areas. The education sector – which had already grown dramatically in the mid-20th Century to pump out escalating quantities of white collar to fill the transformed business environment of that era – continued its ascent,

soldier Lee Rigby in Woolwich: Police apparently described the attackers as 'of Muslim appearance'.

A Rising Tide Lifts All Boats

while the actual economic opportunities dropped away. In place of the stable, pseudo-guild qualities of the old labour movement, the labour market of restructured capitalism would be a *meritocracy* in which it was simply a matter of demonstrating one's individual worth. Everyone could aspire to be, if not wealthier than their parents, then at least better educated. The gleam of qualifications would offer the semblance of class advancement, and further break the back of those recalcitrant old proletarian *ressentiments* which dictated that each should stick to their rightful place; that fancy words are *not for me*; that fine talk and poncing around are so much nothing compared to my callused, honest hands. New Labour made it policy to entice half of all school leavers into higher education, while it set about demolishing student grants. Even those young proletarians who wouldn't make it into the university system tended to do some other post-16 education, often backed by benefits, with the hope of securing a stable, well-paid job and aspiring ultimately to buy in to the ever-inflating property bubble.

All this vanished with the 2008 crisis. Saved from outright burst by one or another state endeavour, the housing bubble hovered, frozen in air, no longer presenting itself as a proxy pension fund, yet still freezing out most remaining aspirants. When the all-out crash did not come, it was only to be a long, slow deflation instead. The grade inflation–wage deflation couplet came quickly to show itself for what it was, with fees escalating and job prospects continuing to vanish. And, with the almost overnight doubling of unemployment and a rash of austerity measures which would directly impact standards of living, the "urban outcast" was left with little prospect but further punishment for their own predicament as the police tried to keep the lid on a society riven with rising tensions. The general horizon of immiseration and diminishing future where all this has taken place is one of fractal differentiations in which broader solidarities have been generally lacking – each reaching for their own little life-raft, kicking the others away. Distinct but downwardly-convergent trajectories, capable sometimes of unifying negatively into a fleeting movement of rage at this descent, only to disperse again, each to their own particularity. Despite this negativity, this decomposition, these were years in which a long-receding tide turned.

TURN

If the longer-term logics of abjection help us to identify the typical trigger-points of modern urban riots in Britain, with their focus on police, on stop-and-search, and their racial inflections, this cannot explain the specificity of the riot-wave of 2011 as a whole. The anti-police trigger-point is only that: beyond this, the wave overspills into a multitude of events and actors too great and too various to be legible in the same terms. At such point our object becomes a national phenomenon, combusting a large part of urban England and sending the major organs of a capitalist state into convulsions. We must then pose the question of why a conventional local anti-police riot should precipitate in so large-scale a conflagration at this particular time rather than another. There can be little doubt that the general answer to this question lies in crisis era sequences of struggle, and that the riots of 2011 must ultimately be viewed as a moment in the broader global upsurge now encapsulated by that year – an upsurge in which the form of the riot has played no small part. But while the general unifying context for all these struggles is of course that of economic crisis, it is difficult to identify with precision any direct articulations between the England riots of 2011 and other struggles on a world-level. What *is* clear is that it was no coincidence that the rapid contagion of this riot-wave occurred in a country that was already boiling from open struggles which had been building through years of social crisis. These struggles had come to a head in 2010–11 only to sense their own impossibility in the face of a state that would brook no demand, but the proliferation of riots within the student and trade union demonstrations of that period, and the shifting composition in these towards younger and more proletarian kids, had transformed the horizon of possibility, establishing new modes of violent excitement and contestation as an immediate precedent. If inner-city communities united against the police provide a compact measure of socially combustible material then, the sustained heat of the period, and the brittle dryness of the broader terrain, set the stage for Tottenham to become England.

The first sparks of accumulative unrest came with a scattering of strikes, occupations and walkouts between January and November 2009. The Lindsey Oil refinery saw wildcat actions that appeared as a throwback to a previous era of British class struggle, when workers occupied the site in response to the new Italian contractor IREM giving a high percentage of its new contracts to Italian and Portuguese workers. These strikes rapidly led to nationwide solidarity actions — illegal in the UK since the 1990 Employment Act — in other oil refineries, and later power plants. Though new jobs were created to appease demands for a 50/50 distribution of work, the subcontractors had to turn on their heels and make half of these workers redundant again in June, provoking a second wave. In March, Ford Visteon was declared insolvent and put into receivership, resulting in the closure of three of its factories. Around 610 workers were dismissed at the close of the day with no guarantee of redundancy or pension packages. A seven-week occupation of the Belfast factory won intense support from the nearby community, where workers lived. Workers at Basildon smashed up their site — which contained no real valuable machinery — and then held a 24-hour picket. Visteon workers also occupied a site in Enfield for nine days. And, in October and November, Royal Mail went out on strike over the "modernisation" of postal work. These actions were small, particularised and very limited, but occurring with the onset of major crisis, and against a sterile historical backdrop, they appeared as the first murmurings of an approaching period of contestation. Yet they were to prove atypical in relation to the coming wave, in which immediate workers' struggles were marginal at most: in Britain's peculiarly post-industrial economy even the problem of struggles breaching a "glass floor" into production seldom puts itself on the agenda.

Meanwhile, localised and largely independent university campus struggles had been bubbling away in the background. For some universities, detailed restructuring plans had been set firmly in place before the crisis had materialised, often with outside hit-men parachuted in to swiftly make drastic cuts and departmental rearrangements before getting out quick. Tendencies towards privatisation, modernisation and outsourcing which have accelerated in this crisis, were of course already proceeding apace in preceding years. But while these generalised conditions caused ripples of localised protest between 2007 and early 2009, only Israel's attacks on Gaza provoked a national wave of university occupations at this point. Though quite unrelated, these were the direct precursors for the anti-cuts occupations which followed. Campus-based anti-cuts groups emerged mostly in the second half of 2009 when Treasury figures revealed a £100 million cut in education funding scheduled for the following year – the first such cut since the 1980s. Students swiftly responded with counter-demands which were as impossible as they were predictable, the simple negation of the announcement itself: no redundancies, no increase in tuition fees, no funding cuts, reductions in executive pay, assurance of academic freedom.[25] Though the formulation of such demands in current conditions produces distinct cognitive dissonance, the gap opened up by this dissonance permitted analysis to begin to develop through a variety of protests, occupations, actions, discussion groups and collective texts. It was a

[25] Initial demands of the Sussex Stop the Cuts campaign after their first meeting in October 2009.

gap not merely between some "capitalist realism" and what this realism rules out of bounds, but between our capacity to revise long-held expectations downwards and the rate of acceleration at which prospects were really dropping away: the systemic logic by which both "stop the cuts" and the "graduate with no future" are placed on the agenda. These early localised campus struggles never began from an entirely positive, stable or homogenous identity or programme. As well as uttering the helpless pleas of anti-austerity, and reaching for the usual garb of 1960s slogans, they took up memes developed through the student movements in Austria and Germany, New York and California: "Demand Nothing, Occupy Everything" and "No Future".

TEETH

A shift came in December when New Labour let forth a "Christmas kick in the teeth", announcing further cuts in funding of £135 million, this time specifically to universities, and additional to the £600 million general "efficiency saving" cuts of the pre-budget report earlier that month. Festive inebriation temporarily dulled reflexes to the first real-term cuts to public spending per student in decades. But these localised struggles soon intensified within their own bounds, and *ad hoc* connections of solidarity with other campuses began to develop. Nevertheless, as individual departments in each university were left to creatively gloss and bind the budget cuts into their own personalised agendas, students remained largely locked into local and sectional battles over redundancies, cuts to union funding, eradication of services and the butchering of unprofitable Humanities departments. One by one, cuts hit universities across the country, resulting in a spontaneous proliferation of activities: gestures of solidarity, days of joint action, carnivals, parties and meetings. By spring 2010, a wave of occupations had occurred, the most prominent being Middlesex, whose left-leaning philosophy department – one of a handful in the UK – was threatened with closure. These occupations motivated greater movement between campuses, but with occupations also came property damage and greater levels of repression. When fifty Sussex students occupied the university's administrative building, six were suspended for trespassing and "holding staff hostage" in a protest that ended with riot police fighting students on university soil, while a tweeded Vice Chancellor surveyed the action from the hillside above.

The general election of May 2010 was a major turning point. With no political party managing to gain enough support to win outright, Gordon Brown – who, throughout his career in the Treasury, had claimed to have "put an end to boom and bust" – resigned, and the UK saw a coalition government of Conservatives and Liberal Democrats, the first true coalition since the Second World War. Many students had voted for Nick Clegg's Lib Dems, based on their pre-election promises not to raise tuition fees, on which they reneged almost instantly. Tory leadership in the midst of a severe economic crisis gave the moment resonances with the Thatcher era; combined with a "little liar" sidekick, this conjured sentiments of heightened contempt within the nascent student movement. The new coalition soon released their Spending Review, fixing the budgets for every governmental department until 2014–15, with the stated aim of eliminating the structural budget deficit through drastic cuts, over a five-year rolling horizon. The hole in education funding was to be filled through a major restructuring of the education system: the Browne Report, released at the same time, recommended removing the cap on tuition fees, which were to be paid for by committing undergraduate students to mortgage-sized debts.

The lashes dealt by the ruling cabinet's Old Etonians were not confined, though, to this fairly isolable tier. As if welcoming the broader conflict that could not but threaten to ensue, the state took on multiple other subjects simultaneously with a rash of austerity measures impacting diverse strata. Dramatic cuts in public spending led to the emergence or remobilisation of multiple groups who would change the dynamics of anti-austerity struggles. Before the election, the Save EMA Campaign, created the previous year, had made David Cameron promise to protect the EMA grant.[26] Even after the election, Education Secretary Michael Gove had officially stated his commitment to it. Nevertheless, the Coalition announced plans to cut EMA funding by 90%. A parliamentary vote was considered unnecessary due to it being departmental rather than governmental spending — signalling for many that the government did not even recognise them as subjects. The Save EMA Campaign held multiple protests all over the UK in 2010 and would later begin to filter into the central demonstrations of the student movement. At the same time, in Haringey — the London borough containing Tottenham — residents returned after the summer holidays to discover eight of thirteen youth clubs mysteriously closed. Save Haringey Youth Services, a local project of around 3000 members — 2000 of whom were young people — embroiled itself in a long and frustrating campaign not just to get their youth clubs back, but firstly to discover what had actually happened to them. On 10 November they were forced to raise a freedom of information request merely to obtain confirmation of the closure. On the same day, coincidentally, came the signal event in the radicalisation of the anti-cuts movement: though a range of university and other more general anti-cuts movements had been building increasing momentum throughout this period, the real qualitative shift came when the building housing the Tory HQ at Millbank was smashed into and occupied by a bunch of A-level students and young undergraduates during a union-led student demonstration.

26 EMA (Education Maintenance Allowance): a benefit payment of £10-30 a week for 16-19 year olds from low-income families towards travel and equipment expenses, enabling them to stay at school.

MILLBANK

A week earlier, David Willetts, Minister of State for Universities and Science, had accepted the Browne Review, but decided to cap tuition fees at £9,000, essentially tripling them overnight. In response, the University College Union (UCU) and the National Union of Students (NUS) – now coming round to a recognition of the spontaneous student struggles, and at least lending them a national frame – had called the demonstration, which attracted around 50,000 university, A-level and Further Education students, as well as lecturers, teachers and other staff. It was not simply to be about tuition fees, however; at stake were also the EMA grant, unemployment, generalised precariousness. The NUS and its then president Aaron Porter – soon to become a £125/hour education consultant – cooperated closely with the police in the build-up to the march, helping design the route, then acting as guard dogs on the day, guaranteeing protesters wouldn't stray from the righteous path. The march was to pass through Whitehall and Westminster and end at Tate Britain where Porter would give a speech. Thousands of people didn't get that far.

Outside Parliament, texts and tweets flew about how things were kicking off at Millbank – once home of New Labour, now home of the Tories – just down the road. About 100 people had charged into the building shouting "Tory scum, here we come!", while thousands – overwhelmingly school kids and undergraduate students – had flooded the courtyard and were cheering at the occupiers above. "Greece! France! Now here too!" When the Territorial Support Group[27] arrived they were attacked simultaneously at ground level by the crowd, and from those above with eggs, sticks, bottles and, in one case, a fire extinguisher. A row of nervous-looking NUS representatives linked arms in a chain, attempting to prevent more from getting inside, to heckles of "You're all Tories too! Shame on you for

[27] Territorial Support Group: launched in 1987 as a reincarnation of the notorious Special Patrol Group, whom we encountered earlier. One of the major aspects of the retooling of the British police force after the 1981 riots.

turning blue!" Angry and excited conversations in the crowd: the moribundity of the NUS, the potential toppling of the Coalition. Bonfires lit; effigies of Cameron and Clegg burned; people ecstatic; sound systems blasted — a big party that lasted for several hours. Many of the chants, banners and slogans were familiar from localised campus struggles of the preceding year; a simultaneous sense of continuity and discontinuity. This dramatically symbolic event had induced a shift in the horizon of possibilities: gone the inevitable boredom and futility of the conventional central London A–B demonstration, and in its place the possibility at least for some destructive and powerfully symbolic fun for a generation of kids born after the Poll Tax riots.

While the strike had declined over preceding decades as a major form of struggle, the demonstration had apparently grown as a means for the orderly expression of pious dissent.[28] The limitations of this form had been rammed home back in 2003 when the largest protest ever in the UK — against the Iraq War — failed to do more than help establish a national consensus of polite objection to the inevitable.[29] At most, the "violence of a tiny minority" on the fringes of such demonstrations could hope to create some media spectacle which would otherwise be entirely lacking in the trudge to Speaker's Corner or Trafalgar Square. Thus a certain rationality to an anti-globalisation-style "diversity of tactics", and a tedious ritual of dividing up "good" and "bad" protesters. The invasion of Millbank set in train a crisis in this construct. NUS, government and media sang initially, of course, from the same traditional hymn sheet, with Aaron Porter describing Millbank as the "despicable" work of a "tiny rogue minority", and offering that time-honoured weapon of struggle — the candlelit vigil — as alternative. Having crawled out of the shadows of the Blair years, the NUS thereby promptly confirmed its own illegitimacy in relation to a student movement that was elsewhere, doing something much more exciting. From here on, less

[28] See Adrian Cousins, 'The crisis of the British regime: democracy, protest and the unions', *Counterfire*, 27 November 2011. Cousins' findings are perhaps counter-intuitive, given the current relative lack of the sort of leftist demos that were a regular event in the 1970s and 1980s. The stats measure not demonstration size or frequency, but numbers of people declaring themselves to have taken part in such action. It may be that such participation has become more socially general while repeat participation from a core of 'usual suspects' has declined.

[29] It would take another decade for that consensus to actualise itself at the level of state, with the failure of the Tory government to gain adequate support for war on Syria.

polite tactics would proliferate – destruction of property, fighting cops, occupying buildings – and the swelling groups of masked-up schoolkids at the heart of much of this activity looked less and less like a minority of "professional anarchists". In these demonstrations we repeatedly witnessed arguments between people in the street over this spreading fractiousness, uncomfortable at the giving-way of conventional distinctions. Oxford Street; a wealthy-looking woman, bags of shopping; screaming at a group of masked-up and very young-looking teens: "Why must you cover your face?! Don't you realise that we are not your enemy? We *do* support you but don't cover your face!" The fear of a loss of order was palpable. A *Guardian* journalist registered surprise after talking to Millbank occupiers: "Those dressed in black were children too, and several fresh-faced excited students said this was their first demonstration."[30] Standard narratives of "outside agitators" and "militants" were now being forcibly displaced by one of "students radicalised by the cuts". Instead, a new distinction now came into play with the emergence of groups such as UK Uncut and Arts Against Cuts providing the figure of the "good" radicalised student, able to more eloquently articulate their radicality and transform acts of property damage and occupation into something more palatable, window-dressed with poetry readings and performance art.

[30] Patrick Smith, 'Student protest: the NUS lobby wasn't enough for us', *Guardian*, 10 November 2010.

MIDDLE-CLASS

It has been a trope of some interpretations of the student movement and riots to read their relation by analogy to the French *banlieue* riots and CPE movement of 2005–6, as another case of a middle-class student movement being troubled by more lumpen elements – sometimes with an implicit plotting of these terms on a traditional reform–revolution axis. It is a banal truth of that moment that the social distribution of misery tended to favour elements of the student movement who were not also present in the riots: one would be hard-pressed, of course, to find anywhere in the riots the sort of liberal-progressive sentiments of UCL students who knew perfectly well that there would be many graduates with rather less future than themselves.

But it would be a major distortion to grasp this as a matter of "middle-class" students having "their" movement invaded by some "underclass". Unsurprisingly, there were plenty of university students involved in these struggles who were rather less than middle-class: in 2011 the UK higher education participation rate was around 50 percent. Though participation is obviously distributed in favour of the better-off, it remains the case that going to university is a normal proletarian pursuit, and it is not at all unusual for kids from marginal estates to aspire to some academic achievement. One might even say that the polarisation in Britain is as much about which university you go to, and which subject you study, as it is about whether or not you get a degree — the Media student from London South Bank vs the PPE from Oxbridge or LSE; the call-centre Literature grad vs the unlettered worker with a *real* trade. And, with the general debasement of coinage in higher education, what might once rightly have been viewed a privilege has turned increasingly into a debt burden. By 2010 the British student already typically mixed studies with precarious part-time employment to supplement their student loan, or depended on welfare — conditions that were only worsening with the deepening of crisis. It was thus no accident, nor any entirely external intrusion, that shifted the student movement towards a more negative, rebellious composition as it felt the emptiness of its own demands.

The student movement was always in some sense a "proletarian" movement, albeit one in which some members were distinctly less proletarian than others. Convention dictates that one imagine the lumpen proletarian to be young, for the young tend to blend into the idle and feckless more or less by definition — sitting as they do at the frontier of the job market. But youth, of course, is not a class: it cannot be assumed that the younger participants and "EMA kids" who came into the movement from Millbank onwards, represented in any clear sense a class distinct from those already involved in the movement. While EMA might be needed to support post-16 vocational – rather than academic – training, it was at the same time not a fundamentally separate issue from university fees: both EMA cuts and fee-increases could potentially affect the same person, who might need financial support to continue education post-16, in order to then go to university. And the same person could simultaneously be affected by youth club closures – and even stop-and-search. But what can be said with certainty here is that the diminishing futures of that moment hit not only the poorer, but also the younger, harder: while those already at university might scrape through with moderate fees for their last year or two, those a couple of years below them would get the full £9000/year for their whole university education, if they made it that far, lose the state support for their pre-university studies, enter a tougher job market when they got there, and so on. And of course, the young tend to be less cowed in their relations with the cops, having not yet been fully schooled in such things…

OCCUPATION

Following the excitement of Millbank another huge national wave of occupations took place – around thirty-five in total – providing sites for the planning of further actions. Students were becoming increasingly combative in relation to policing; one occupation, for example, putting together a custom monitoring system for mapping police action during protests. Occupations set up websites and twitter accounts, Facebook pages and so on, communicating around the clock with each other and with a general public. They attracted a huge number of visitors – lecturers, intellectuals, activists, actors,

A Rising Tide Lifts All Boats

schoolkids. But they were fundamentally incapable of turning themselves into anything really confrontational: for the most part university administrations just tolerated them, and any attempts to intervene disruptively into the flows of everyday university life — such as that at Goldsmiths, where students occupied the library — tended to immediately delegitimise the occupations in the eyes of the broader student body. With these struggles ostensibly aiming to defend education, disruption of the university appeared an immediately self-contradictory tactic, leaving most of these occupations to subsist in uneasy cooperation with university authorities, working at most as bases for planning the larger demonstrations. Groups in Brighton, frustrated at the limits of their campus occupations, began making efforts to incorporate even younger kids, visiting schools to encourage walkouts and protests.

On 24 and 30 November the NCAFC and ULU,[31] both freshly mobilised after Millbank, called national walkouts and protests for students of all ages, encouraging a viral spreading of the word: "…chalk the details on the pavement outside your place of education… request that folk 'send the text viral' — i.e. text it to your own friends to text onto their friends… send texts to all your friends in different schools and different colleges telling them you've walked out."[32] Around this time a network of younger students emerged called "School and Further Education Students Against the Cuts" who were in constant communication with the university groups. There were noticeably much more young people at these demonstrations, and the atmosphere more like a big party. Like the riots that followed, the police had been completely unprepared for Millbank, drafting only 225 officers for a predicted crowd of 20,000 — there were actually 50,000. Consequently, later demos saw a heightened police presence, more violence and the implementation of kettling. This tactic seems to have first been used in London in 1995 against disabled people

[31] NCAFC: the National Campaign Against Fees and Cuts, self-described as a 'network of student and education worker activists', emerged from University College London in February 2010; ULU: University of London Union — by far the largest students' union in London, and often a central organisation in student demonstrations.

[32] This call appeared on the NCAFC website, anticuts.org.uk.

in a Disability Rights protest outside Parliament, before being fine-tuned in the 1999 WTO protests, and employed again at the 2001 May Day protests. But the bending of the judicial system towards the rapid and severe punishment of activists – sending them to the Crown Courts, where penalties are much harsher – had no such precursor.[33] This seems to have set a precedent for the punishment of rioters the following August. That Edward Woollard, the student who threw a fire extinguisher off the roof of Millbank, was arrested for attempted murder and later sentenced to two and a half years in jail for violent disorder, resulted in bays of approval from a large section of the public. Taking no chances, a Chief Superintendent for domestic extremism – appointed a week earlier – began an intelligence operation to monitor the dangerous incitement of "fringe elements", while on 24 November, the Met swamped central London with an extra thousand Greater London cops, both riot-geared and mounted. Blocking protesters from Parliament Square, their typical site of enforced containment, huge games of cat and mouse came to characterise these protests, with students running down back alleys, dodging and trying to outwit the cops, until eventually getting kettled. Initial atmospheres were festive, with dubstep and grime sound systems, lots of dancing and coloured flares being set off, but as hours passed the crowd became frustrated and started vandalising and setting fire to things. After several hours of dancing, interspersed with violent confrontations, they finally released everyone. Around the city, those not trapped in kettles were involved in a mass array of fleeting actions, and universities and schools nationwide were either in protest or occupation.

[33] Only 5 percent of 'suspected criminals' typically appear in the Crown Court.

STICK

Though violence had been building and proliferating throughout the protests, the day of the vote in December – when the fee-hikes would predictably be passed – was the pinnacle of heavy policing. The police response to Millbank was the blanket implementation of kettling, mounted charges on crowds and, increasingly, generalised attacks on protesters: the baton to the head. The fact that the composition of these protests now involved an infusion of younger students and more turbulent kids seemed to solicit ever heavier responses from the cops. On the day of the vote, field hospitals were set up to deal with the anticipated victims and an estimated thirty protesters were treated for head injuries, leading to over fifty recorded complaints to the IPCC. Middlesex student, Alfie Meadows was beaten with a truncheon as he tried to leave a kettle in Parliament Square, and had to be rushed to hospital for immediate life-saving brain surgery.[34] Another protester, Jodi McIntyre, was pulled from his wheelchair and dragged across the floor by cops. These were the stories that attracted the imagination of media and public, and were campaigned for by friends and support groups, but there were many more such cases.

The whole of Westminster was established as a series of mass kettles, some mobile, others compressed, which provoked frustrated bursts of fighting. In a hypersymbolic gesture, a masked-up protester managed to break free and scale Whitehall, before smashing the windows of the Treasury, and people set fire to whatever they could find, including the giant Christmas tree on Parliament Square, to keep warm in icy temperatures. We received a text to say that the National Gallery was in flash-mob occupation. Meanwhile, on Regent Street, another highly symbolic attack occurred, this time against a caricatural British institution, when a car carrying Prince Charles and Camilla to the London Palladium for a Royal Variety Performance was attacked by protesters shouting "off with their heads!" That one protester had managed to poke the Consort of the Heir Apparent with a stick, through the car's open window, apparently sent chills down authority spines over the proximity of the "mob". But a large group was contained

[34] Much like a death in police custody, the police inverted the story and charged Alfie and his friend Zak King with violent disorder, a charge they have only recently succeeded in having dropped.

in a tight kettle on Westminster Bridge without food, water or toilet facilities for hours in the freezing cold, some needing treatment for respiratory problems, chest pains or bruised ribs after severe crushing.

In January, as eyes turned to another wave of struggle now picking up in the Arab world, parliament inevitably voted to cut the EMA grant. While the presence of younger and more turbulent kids had lent dynamism and kick before the December tuition fee vote to an otherwise more limited student movement, there was a relative lack of reciprocal participation from university students on the day of the EMA. In the same month the press informed Haringey residents that the council had officially agreed to cut youth services by 75%. A councillor had erroneously claimed that the community had already been consulted and all was fine, as there were a plethora of voluntary organisations ready and willing to step in to pick up the extra work. The council then warned that if the community did not cooperate over the cuts, it would be at the expense of "disabled and abused" children,[35] but it would happily compromise and offer a consultation over the remaining 25%. Youth workers across London soon noticed the mounting tension around these issues, and some began predicting riots.[36]

With the tuition fee and EMA votes both lost and nothing comparably concrete on the horizon, the subsequent protests became chaotic, theatrical, fun and frustrated. The TUC (Trades Union Congress) "March for the Alternative" in March 2011 was the second biggest demonstration ever on British soil, bringing out onto London streets much of the remnant workers' movement, and providing another organisational skeleton for the heterogeneous and more chaotic elements that had emerged through the student movement. The point of destination for all union-led marches is Hyde Park, once the site of the 1855 Sunday Trading Bill riots (considered by Marx at the time to herald the coming English

[35] 'Our Story So Far', Save Haringey Youth Service website.

[36] It is woth noting that at least some cuts-driven restructuring of youth services had an overtly punitive focus, prioritising the jobs of those specialising in youth crime. See Alex Newman, 'Hackney Council Youth Services Job Cuts Slammed', *Hackney Citizen*, 4 April 2011.

A Rising Tide Lifts All Boats   **139**

Revolution[37]), the main assembly point for the Chartist movement and the Reform League; long a standard arena for the performance of political gestures, at a safe distance from the institutions and shopfronts of central London. A good chunk of the estimated quarter of a million people present that day trudged the weary old track to Hyde Park, to be reassured by Labour Party Leader, Ed Miliband, tottering on a plinth, that they could relax, for they had arrived at "the alternative": the deficit need not be reduced by quite such nasty means. Through the unfolding of the student movement, building numbers had reached their limits of tolerance for such forms, preferring to hang back and preserve energy for more organic and spontaneous break-off activities, starting from one or another of the various feeder marches.

At Oxford Circus, UK Uncut were conducting a day of action against tax-avoiding corporations, and the police protectively swarmed the largest and most expensive. Riot vans surrounded the Apple Store entirely, which was nevertheless brimming with shoppers; Topshop, drenched in paint and graffiti, with several broken windows, was now fortified with layers of riot cops. Nearby, Scientologists handed out pamphlets mimicking the aesthetic of a socialist newspaper. Our day consisted of arriving at the fresh destruction of a recently expired action or event, having been directed to the scene by tweet or SMS. Everything felt more fleeting and mobile than the previous events leading up to the vote, and you could bounce from pocket to pocket of actions or interventions; some real, some performance. BHS occupied by poets; a suited woman chasing a human £20 note; a gang of Robin Hoods riding, for hours, on imaginary horses. Again a mixture of students, school kids, artists, anarchists; small, diverse groups in a large, mobile flow; a swarming mass on a tangent to the main union march, but still managing to occupy large areas of central London. Piccadilly was now under siege, and the Ritz had been smashed into. A sharper spatial

[37] Marx, 'Anti-Church Movement Demonstration in Hyde Park', *Neue Oder-Zeitung*, 28 June 1855 (MECW 14), 303.

distinction into divergent forms of action seemed indicative of a reduced concentration and widened scope, in comparison to the kettled concentrations of preceding demonstrations. UK Uncut had occupied Fortnum and Mason – the Queen's favourite grocery shop – and some occupiers were on the balcony, glugging bottles of champagne swiped on the way through. The atmosphere outside grew tense as riot police were pumped into the area and began lining every side street. It seemed a conscious tactic that day to avoid the need to kettle by simply indicating it as a threat. Following those violent long hours of containment in December, the fear of kettling was explosive, and any signal sent huge booing crowds launching towards the cops until they backed off. A group of protesters momentarily surrounded the police, chanting "kettle the cops!"; a woman posed for a photo, holding a kettle and with a sign saying "Cameron, don't put the bloody kettle on"; a severely injured man stumbled around, blood gushing down his face, reeling in shock and pumped with adrenalin: "they're crazy!" Concerned for his life, we pleaded with cops for paramedics or an ambulance: "no, that ain't my job love". The bleeding man ran off into the crowd, to haunt the rest of the day. As a kettle began, the crowd went mad, frantically trying to break through police lines, and violent fights broke out, distracted eventually by an attempted break-in of a bank. The streets were brimming until late, and as we wandered the city that evening to get a sense of the damage, almost every bank we came across had been smashed in. Forensic teams on their hands and knees dusted for fingerprints. And as that day drew to a close some activists made an abstract first stab at establishing a resonance with the Arab Spring: Trafalgar was to become Tahrir. The cops had little difficulty moving them on, and it was not to be until after Britain's own wave had crashed in August that a more self-consciously international squares movement would sprout in the alluvium...

A Rising Tide Lifts All Boats

In April 2011, reggae star and DJ, Smiley Culture – key emblem of a naturalised London Afro-Caribbean culture ever since his 1980s tracks Cockney Translation and Police Officer – died from a single stab wound to the heart during a police raid on his home, in advance of his upcoming trial on a drug-related charge. The IPCC report – which was kept from both the public and his own family – predictably dismissed the incident, concluding that there had been no criminal conduct…[38] That same month, as the cuts to the benefits system came into effect, unemployment started to mount again – especially, as always, for the young – from the altiplano it had reached back in 2009 after the first outbreak of the crisis… But, briefly, the nation was tickled into stupefaction by the royal wedding. Over the days before this event, the police made a series of pre-emptive interventions, sending warning letters, making arrests of suspected activists and prominent student protesters, as well as conducting blanket stop-and-searches all over London. Sixty people arrested during the previous student march had bail terms that disallowed entry into central London the week of the wedding, and a series of raids were carried out on well-known squats to scavenge for DNA samples and other identity clues, under the pretext of searching for stolen bike parts. Crudely profiled "troublemakers" were detained in custody, apparently not being signalled for release until the newlyweds had safely sealed it with the public "balcony kiss". On the day of the wedding, central London became a free-for-all stop-and-search zone with face masks, fancy dress, drunkenness – even singing – incurring a possible charge of incitement to violence.[39] Such moves towards zero-tolerance and pre-emptive action had been developed through the course of student struggles, with students being arrested for such things as "failure to comply with a direction to leave when the police have reasonable belief that you may commit aggravated trespass".[40] This set the scene for the "total policing" strategies that would cohere and consolidate during and after the riots.

[38] IPCC: Independent Police Complaints Commission, a major part of the bureaucratic apparatus developed in this period to underwrite the nominal neutrality of the police. The IPCC is the latest in a series of acronyms performing the same basic function, dating back to the beginnings of current policing styles in the late 1970s, before which complaints had been handled directly by local forces. These structures were significantly reworked in response to the 1981 riots on the basis of recommendations in the Scarman Report.

Endnotes 3 **142**

The student movement had rapidly come up against its limits and frothed over into a fissiparous, disorderly state, with no real positive horizon but a bit of fun at the expense of the cops. Where there had been vague semblances of a positive programme at moments in this movement, this had always seemed dubious, half-hearted, tinted with the baseline cynicism of a certain "capitalist realism". All that was available as a framework for unity was a bland set of negative, umbrella demands: stop the cuts. And even this seemed – and ultimately proved – impossible. What else to do then but raise some hell? At least it would mean that there had been a fight. And what response could this invite but a further ramping-up of policing? That, ultimately, was the "meaning" of Millbank. Just as the sinister grin of the Cheshire Cat intensifies as its more seemingly contingent parts dissolve, through the development of these protests the police had increasingly appeared as the visceral presence of the state in the face of its supposed retreat or rollback. Yet somehow the consolidation of an abstract enemy into a single tangible one meant that the city – which hides itself behind the police – felt, for fleeting moments at least, more open and vulnerable, more reachable and breakable.

39 Four people were arrested in Starbucks for being dressed as zombies. As Amy Cutler explained: 'we were just dressing up as zombies. It's nice to dress up as zombies'.

40 Steph Pike of UK Uncut was arrested on this charge at a tax avoidance demonstration.

SWARMING

A short documentary published by the *Guardian* in late July presented Haringey teenagers discussing the impact of youth club closures. Chavez Campbell, a local teenager from Wood Green – which borders Tottenham – noted that the loss of a fixed and protected space "cuts kids' roots off and links, and then they don't really have anywhere to go".[41] Thrown out onto the streets, kids were both more prone to get caught up with gangs and more vulnerable to police harassment. Campbell concluded the documentary with a famous prediction:

41 Chavez Campbell, interviewed in Alexandra Topping and Cameron Robertson, 'Haringey youth club closures: There'll be riots', *Guardian*, 31 July 2011.

> I think it's gonna be swarming, I think people are gonna be trying to find things to do, people are gonna

A Rising Tide Lifts All Boats

want jobs, and that's going to be frustrating… There's going to be a riot, there'll be riots, there'll be riots.

This was the climate in which Mark Duggan was shot in Ferry Lane, Tottenham, at about 6:15pm on Thursday 4 August 2011. Officers from Operation Trident — a specialist unit within the Metropolitan Police which focuses on gun crime in predominantly black areas had been following his taxi. It has never been clear exactly what happened, but we know that they shot Duggan in the chest. Attempts to resuscitate him failed, and paramedics who rushed to the scene swiftly turned to walk away, heads bowed. The usual gears went swiftly into motion: an investigation initiated by the IPCC, and the scene cordoned off. As is often the case, the IPCC seems to have first engaged in some public relations damage-limitation on behalf of the police, communicating to the media the claim that there had been an exchange of fire between Duggan and Trident officers — a claim that would be discredited just days later, in the midst of a national riot-wave initiated in Duggan's name, when it would be shown that the only piece of evidence — a bullet lodged in a police radio — had actually been fired from a police gun. Police did not inform Duggan's family of his death, and when they pushed for information on where he was — having heard via the media that he had been involved in an incident — they were simply told to follow an air ambulance from Tottenham. Trailing this helicopter a few miles south to Whitechapel Hospital, they found only the police officer who had been injured at the scene.

In the absence of any official communication from the police, rumours quickly began circulating in the neighbourhood that Duggan had been deliberately executed, with some evidently worried about possible consequences: by the next morning David Lammy, the local MP, was already calling for calm in the face of community "anxiety". That there was a typical riot dynamic forming here is obvious in retrospect, and indeed it was probably obvious at the time to anyone present who had the slightest acquaintance with the recent history of urban unrest: cops had not only killed a young black man, but also a resident of the Broadwater Farm estate, with its long and dramatic history of antagonistic relations with the police; and now they were again failing to supply any information to family or community. After years of building tension on an estate already considered a serious problem area by the early 1970s, Cynthia Jarrett's death at police hands in October 1985 had precipitated an extraordinarily violent riot in which police came under armed attack, culminating in the killing of PC Keith Blakelock.[42] In the 2000s, with regeneration projects and declining crime statistics for the neighbourhood, those events might have seemed consigned to the past. But police still considered Tottenham in general a hotspot for (black) gun crime, drug-dealing and gang-related violence, and punitive policing had been stepped up over recent years around "The Farm", as it had in other such neighbourhoods. At least a day before rioting actually broke out, John Blake, who had grown up here with Duggan, saw it coming:

> There's hostility here, there might even be an uprising here, you don't know. Mark held Broadwater Farm together.

As night fell on Friday 5 August about 400 people gathered at Duggan's parents' home on the estate to pay their respects, in an already tightening atmosphere. But it was not until 1pm the following day that police summoned community representatives to a meeting. At this point they were warned clearly about the potential for unrest, but deferred to the IPCC, and still failed to send anyone to discuss matters with the family or community—perhaps the example of Keith Blakelock lingered here for police, just as that of Cynthia Jarrett did for Broadwater Farm residents. At about 5:30pm,

42 These events are still playing through the British legal system to this day, with a new arrest—28 years later—timed conveniently to correspond to the second anniversary of Mark Duggan's death and the beginning of an inquest into its circumstances.

A Rising Tide Lifts All Boats

under the watchful eyes of The Farm's CCTV cameras, a small demonstration crowd gathered and left the estate for the police station, lead by the prominent Broadwater Farm activist Stafford Scott, to demand some address. But the junior officers who were left at the station could only defer to the IPCC and Operation Trident, who were based elsewhere. Demands for dialogue with a senior officer were thus not met, with the crowd growing — and growing increasingly frustrated.

Anyone who, for political reasons, wants to hold that "The Riots" were entirely "demand"-free, a mere matter of the "negative language of vandalism" etc, will at minimum need to offer some explanation as to how they would separate these events, at which clear demands — on banners, in chants, in attempts to negotiate with cops — were present, can be separated from the riot-wave in which they issued, and which would not have occurred in their absence. Other key moments of the riot-wave in which comparable anti-police dynamics were dominant, such as Hackney, Salford, and probably Brixton, would also seem to require such explanation: for sure, in all of these cases a negative, violent mode of behaviour was prominent, rather than some orderly bargaining, but then demanding is not politely asking.

CONTAGION

As the evening pressed on, the composition changed, with mothers and children heading home, an infusion of football supporters, a larger quotient of young men, and a significant ethnic diversity — apart from the local black community, also Turkish, Polish, white British etc. At 8pm riot police turned up to protect the station from a rowdy but still non-violent crowd. A 16-year-old girl came forward to again press the demands, perhaps throwing something, and in response the cops moved forwards, shoving her, and probably attacking with riot shields and batons. This seems to have been the moment at which the emergent logic of crowd action kicked in, and community demonstration tipped over into riot. Even for a crowd that knows full well in advance what may be coming there is a first-mover problem which prevents the riot itself from being a straightforwardly intentional act; no individual or group can simply *decide* unilaterally to riot, unless the riot is already in process. This is why the immediate trigger very often appears as some relatively minor act of the police which unites a crowd in indignation against them; but such tipping-points do not come out of the blue – rather, they are themselves produced from some escalating dynamic, in which a crowd can certainly play an active role. By 8:20pm the crowd was attacking nearby police cars, setting them on fire, and pushing one out into Tottenham High Road as a sort of burning barricade. It then broke through police lines to attack the police station, throwing bricks, bottles, eggs. Unrest was now spreading throughout the area. At around 10.15pm, Tottenham post office was set alight and within half an hour, more police cars and a double decker bus. The Aldi supermarket and the now famous Carpetright store too were soon burnt down – and with the latter went a number of people's homes. More police were drafted in, including specialists from the Territorial Support Group, armed and with dogs and horses, with reinforcements from City of London Police. These arrived to jeering and chants: "we want answers"/ "no justice, no peace"/ "rest in peace Mark Duggan"/ "whose streets, our streets". They attempted to seal off the side streets to prevent the riot from spreading, while the usual helicopters throbbed overhead. But they had already definitively lost control of events.

During the night the windows of the local courthouse were smashed, and the probation service next door was set on fire, while the Opera House club in which Mark Duggan apparently used to rave was left untouched – a pointed selection of targets, as opposed to the sort of random mob irrationality which the scared and the

A Rising Tide Lifts All Boats

unsympathetic have traditionally perceived in rioting crowds since Gustav Le Bon and beyond. In the first clear example of the sort of mass-looting which would come to be associated with the riot-wave as a whole, rioting spread overnight to the nearby Tottenham Hale Retail Park where almost every single shop was looted and a supermarket set on fire. At around 3am in Wood Green – another nearby neighbourhood – some fires were started, and many shops looted. But again, some discrimination was in evidence: they apparently spared a clothes shop named "Loot", and the pound shop. By most accounts, there was little violence in these places, the activity being mostly focused on the beginnings of the largest bout of focused "proletarian shopping" the country has ever seen.

The rapid tip-over of an anti-police riot in the centre of Tottenham into this widespread looting was nothing particularly surprising: when a large anti-police conflagration provides cover enough, it is entirely typical for the next step to involve looting, whether as a seizing of opportunities, or as another disorderly gesture to capital or state.[43] Where shops are available to a rioting crowd, they will typically be looted. Appeals to factors like "consumerism" are entirely superfluous here – as if the desire to appropriate material goods needed an ideology to explain it! And loot itself aside, when shops are at hand they constitute one of the obvious objects for crowd violence, along with the premises of one or another hated institution, and things readily available in the street which will burn spectacularly and obstructively, such as motor vehicles. Brixton 1981, too, quickly crossed over into looting, once the cops had been driven from the area by swelling, aggressive crowds; also, Brixton and Handsworth 1985, Meadow Well 1991, Brixton 1995 – but not Broadwater Farm 1985, where most shops had long closed down. A distinction of 2011 was perhaps the rapidity with which ubiquitous means of instantaneous communication

43 Nor is it unusual for responses to such riots to involve attempts to appeal to looting as evidence that nothing else was at stake. In 1985, for example, Home Secretary Douglas Hurd claimed that the Handsworth riots had not been 'a cry for help', but 'a cry for loot'.

enabled the word to spread that police were on the back foot, opening up snowballing opportunities to take advantage of this, for straightforwardly instrumental reasons or with some other aim – such as revenge against shops that had rejected job applications, as one looter would retrospectively claim. Thus the famous Blackberry messenger communiqué that circulated widely as the disorder spread into Sunday 7 August, exhorting potential rioters to abandon the more destructive actions and enjoy the commodity free-for-all:

> Everyone in edmonton enfield woodgreen everywhere in north link up at enfield town station 4 o clock sharp!!!! Start leaving ur yards n linking up with you niggas. Guck da feds, bring your ballys and your bags trollys, cars vans, hammers the lot!! Keep sending this around to bare man, make sure no snitch boys get dis!!! What ever ends your from put your ballys on link up and cause havic, just rob everything. Police can't stop it. Dead the fires though!! Rebroadcast!!!!!

It is worth remembering though, that the contemporary state of means of communication is often appealed to in explaining the proliferation of riots: the pagers and "portable telephones" of the 1990s, CB radio in 1981... Any spontaneous unfolding of social unrest like this of course takes place in a context significantly shaped by the "affordances" of current communications technologies – technologies whose rapid development and proliferation has been one of the salient dynamics of the era. But these can only ever contribute a weak form of causality, shaping possibilities rather than driving things forward.

And while these actions should certainly be taken seriously as one of the most prominent aspects of the wave as a whole, we should avoid modes of explanation which project such things as some essential indicator of "what the riots were about", as if national riot-waves were a sort of vessel which could contain a singular, unproblematically identifiable content. No large-scale social event, no uprising like this, can straightforwardly be read as the simple expression of an inner content, for the actors and circumstances involved are too vastly heterogeneous to be susceptible to the kind of reduction that would be required. Everyone has their own reasons – many of them no doubt held in common – but it would be a fallacy to think that one could abstract from this mess some sort of singular social meta-intention without doing significant theoretical violence to the object. Better to focus on mapping the objective and subjective contingencies of which the riot wave was a precipitate, and tracing its unfolding logic. And in this logic, it is clear that the looting, dramatic as it was, kicked off only in the space already opened by an anti-police riot, before developing its own logic of contagion.

By Sunday morning, as riots continued in the Tottenham area, eight police officers were being treated in hospital, and there were reports of bystanders getting attacked. At 7am the police convened the first of a series of crisis meetings, drafting thousands of reinforcements into London from other regions. Standard official condemnations began to issue from the usual locations: Prime Minister's Office, local MP, commander of the Metropolitan Police. As social media – the encrypted Blackberry messenger service in particular – buzzed with speculation and incitements, police took notice that Enfield – an area quite close to Tottenham – was prominent as a possible point of eruption. Hackney carnival was preventively cancelled last minute, though this didn't stop rioting spreading into Dalston in the evening, with several shops and the Kingsland shopping centre looted. Brixton's carnival went ahead as planned, but as the sound systems were turned off and a noticeable tension filled the evening air, a young man was chased, dragged to the ground and bundled into a police van. A few hundred mostly masked youths gathered, and began to attack. Chain stores such as Vodafone, H&M, Footlocker, WH Smith, Currys and JD Sports were looted; KFC and McDonalds had their windows smashed; Footlocker and Nando's were set on fire after a till was stolen. But, in another show of crowd discernment, the highly central Ritzy cinema – with its many windows – was left untouched.

As anticipated, hundreds of youths gathered with the onset of evening in Enfield centre, at an apparently pre-planned destination. And of course, plenty of cops were there to meet them. Rioting erupted sporadically, and in a very mobile manner – presumably of necessity, in direct response to the police presence – rioters generally evading them to attack shops, vehicles, etc. At 9:30pm police tried to turn Enfield into a "sterile area", bringing in hundreds of riot cops, dogs etc. Dispersed, the crowd ran off to attack and loot a retail park, stealing televisions and alcohol as they went. Around 12:45am 3 officers were taken to hospital after being run over by a fast-moving vehicle. Then, during the night, the riot-wave spread to many other parts of London: Denmark Hill, Streatham, Islington, Leyton, Shepherd's Bush, Walthamstow; even Oxford Circus saw some disturbances. Crowds of young people gathered in streets around London, expecting local riots to trigger. Stand-offs between restless, expectant crowds and the police sometimes occurred without a full-blown riot breaking out – a negative demonstration that the riot is an emergent social event, rather than something produced by a singular decision, some linear intentionality.

MEDIATION

Sporadic looting; smashed shop windows; arson: a welter of the standard particulars of riot. We here find that any attempt at a singular narrative of the events necessarily begins to break down, due to their vast spread and proliferation into a multiplicity of local incidents. Thus the riot-wave becomes a different object for us, one necessitating a different kind of abstraction or summary. Something far beyond its roots in a few particular local histories of abjection and anti-police struggle, and something necessarily more "theoretical". At the same time we pass definitively from particular immediate struggles to a national mediatic event, in which practices are spread not only laterally and locally by word of mouth or by social media but by a growing awareness, crystallised in mainstream media coverage and official press releases, that much of the country is rising in some sort of revolt. And it is largely from this vantage point that we are constrained to track events the best we can. Rioters themselves are of course not constrained to the level of immediate struggles, but relate to these as they are mediated socially, not only on a level of lateral contagion via social media, word of mouth and SMS, but also by cohering national representations via mainstream media. With the inherently mimetic way in which such struggles proliferate too, a discussion of this mediation becomes unavoidable.

On Monday morning, as the rioting continued, doubts first emerged about the claim that there had been an exchange of fire between Duggan and the police. At 12:30pm Scotland Yard announced a quadrupling of police numbers in the capital. Meanwhile the Metropolitan Police finally offered an apology for their handling of the death to Duggan's family; the IPCC, on the other hand, blamed police for the lack of contact. In the early afternoon, shops began to shut in areas expecting unrest as rumours circulated on social media about further targets. It was at this point that central Hackney emerged as the Monday flashpoint with which we began this article. While rioting spread out from Hackney Town Hall to the Pembury Estate, down Well Street and to other areas of Hackney, 15 miles south, in Croydon, crowds of youths gathered to attack shops, buses, and bystanders. Around 7pm 200–300 ran through outlying neighbourhoods looting and setting small fires.

Around 9pm events spread to the town centre, where several large and very severe fires were started, including the Reeves Furniture shop – now famous as photogenic emblem of the most destructive aspects of the riots. One man was shot; a white middle-class guy was chased, tripped and beaten; another man pulled off his scooter and also beaten.

Simultaneously, in Ealing, crowds who again seemed to have been organised through social media moved to attack rich areas – cars, cafés, boutiques and commercial properties – apparently without interest in looting. Bystanders were assaulted. A 68-year-old man was attacked when trying to put out a fire in a dustbin, and later died. In Birmingham around 200 rioters set fire to an unmanned police station in an inner city area, and tried to attack the city centre. Police fended them off with extra officers, but later in the night kids returned to loot many shops. In Battersea bystanders identified rioters as "blues, yellows and reds" – members of local gangs who had apparently called a truce for the evening. In Camden some shops were attacked and confrontations with riot cops drifted up to Kentish Town and Chalk Farm. In Peckham a hundred-strong group cheered as a shop was set on fire, shouting "the West End is going down next". Cyclists and motorcyclists were violently dismounted with rocks, their bikes taken. With this litany of chaotic and often dark events coming to form a carousel of lumpen depravity, rotated on barely changing loops to ever-more plaintive, moralising tones, the authorised version of the riots began to consolidate: this couldn't all be "about" Mark Duggan; no, it was the work of a deranged, feral underclass[44], out to get whatever they could, at best because of some misguided "consumerism", at worst because they came from the work-shy urban cesspits of "broken Britain", lacking the authority of proper father figures who would have soon set them right, with a good old paternal clip round the ear. "Immorality" or "criminality"

44 This choice term seems to have skulked in the annals of criminal justice policy for some years before emerging as a synonym for 'chav' in the late 2000s, and finally gaining general currency as an abjectifying keyword in the midst of the riots, being bandied around by government figures like Ken Clarke.

A Rising Tide Lifts All Boats

had somehow become independent variables, spiking from out of nowhere, anthropomorphising themselves into a monstrous lumpen subject out to terrorise the great and good of the nation.

SCUM

Passing over into Tuesday 9 August, as the national "disgust consensus"[45] consolidated, the major inner-London generation points of the riot wave, with their longer local histories of anti-police antagonism — Tottenham, Brixton, Hackney — were now quietening down; inner London boroughs were now flooded with police from around the country. But the unrest persisted in the outer London boroughs, and had now spread West and North far beyond London. Now came the various community responses, starting with the self-righteous clean-up squads of the morning, and ending with armed Turkish and Kurdish shopkeepers and far right vigilante groups in the evening. The clean-up squad — a new type of what we might call "anti-abject" community self-organisation — played a convenient role here as the positive pole in a developing manichaeism, projected as everything the rioters were not. The blitz-spirited neighbourliness and social responsibility with which these people came together, symbolised by their brooms and rubber gloves — which were for the most part merely symbolic, since state-employed street-sweepers had already done the job earlier in the morning — stood in supposed contrast to the atomised, bestial *anomie* of the rioters: mere vandals, absent of all community, citizens who had failed and thus justly been cast into the state of nature *there below*. As one of these "riot wombles" penned across her vested torso: "looters are scum". In the discourses that now unfolded, the positive subjectivities constituted in local rebellions against this logic were definitively erased. No agency here; no reason; no intention; no grievance; no cause; no will; no morality; no

[45] For this concept see Tyler, *Revolting Subjects*, 23-24.

community: just a big hole in society into which the bad ones fall. Politicians, of course, took care to be photographed amidst this smug convulsion; "Boris! Boris! Boris!" cried the broom-brigade, as the tousle-haired Tory buffoon turned up to ensconce himself in the collective anti-chav backslap.

The gears of political reaction were now engaged. At 11am David Cameron made his first statement outside Number 10, after cutting short his holiday to return to London. He announced the recall of Parliament, and that there would be 16,000 police officers on London streets from that evening. Further north, in Birmingham, Nick Clegg was booed and heckled as he tried to assess the damage. During the day, special measures were introduced to enable the processing of the vast numbers of people who had already been arrested, and who were now apparently herded into overcrowded, unsanitary cells, lacking in food and water. Meanwhile, on the international level, an Iranian foreign ministry spokesperson called for British police to "exercise restraint", and for human rights organisations to investigate the shooting of Mark Duggan; Syrian media covered the riots in depth, focusing on the possibility that the military might be brought in; the Libyan state described the riots as a "popular uprising". In Egypt, social media buzzed with debates as to whether the riots should be seen as the Arab Spring come to England. The Metropolitan Police described Monday night's events as "the worst the [Met] has seen in current memory", and stated that they would now use plastic bullets if necessary. This would be the first time on mainland Britain (Northern Ireland having already, of course, had its share). Hoping to stem the tide of youths entering onto the streets to take part in the events, local councils now started sending out email and SMS warnings to parents, advising them to keep children inside. Even the online world now saw its own manifestations of riot-related behaviour. Amazon's top-selling sport and leisure items now included police-style

A Rising Tide Lifts All Boats

telescopic batons and baseball bats, sales of which had increased by 5000% in the previous 24 hours. And at around 3:30pm hackers defaced the website of Research in Motion in retaliation for the suggestion that Blackberry users' data would be released to the police.

As afternoon wore on towards evening, and many began to expect the return of the riots, shops closed early. In some areas — especially heavily Turkish and Kurdish areas such as Dalston and Walthamstow — they remained open, but guarded by large groups of vigilantes. At 5:25pm the IPCC announced that no shot had been fired by Mark Duggan before he was shot dead by a police firearms officer. It seemed bizarre at the time — indeed it still does now — that they would release such potentially explosive information at this point. Having no food at home, and with shops all shuttered, we headed for the only area where anything seemed open — the stretch of Turkish restaurants on Kingsland Road which had their own protection. A few shops and banks had been smashed in the night before, but the normally traffic-clogged area was now a ghost town. At Dalston Junction a lonely little Christian group sang hymns tunelessly in the dusk. Reaching the restaurant stretch, hundreds of Turkish people stood out in the street, jovial but ready for trouble: mostly young men, but also middle-aged guys and young girls, even entire families. But in the restaurant we were the only customers, alone with the Muzak. Staff were in good spirits; a sense of community solidarity palpable. Outside some dudes hauled bundles of baseball bats; the odd siren blaring; cops doing a route up and down the street seemingly more to announce their presence than anything else. We hung out in the crowd for a while. A gaggle formed in front of the Efes pool hall, with one man clearly in charge, giving orders in Turkish to the footsoldiers, but nothing came of it. This crowd was as pumped as the Pembury rioters of the previous evening, glorying in its sense of collective strength. At one point a few mostly white and hoodied teenagers hurried through the congregation, visibly on guard. A mob of Turkish men started following them down the street, turning and whistling for back-up, bristling for a fight, but it came to nothing. A little later a black couple showed up further down the street and the crowd bristled once more... but they were just there, like us, to get food.

We ducked into a half-shuttered convenience store. Showing off pepper spray and an old extendible police truncheon, the young Turk at the counter bragged: "bruv, I ain't never been so tooled up as this!" His mate brandished a heavy length of stiff wire — a makeshift bludgeon. "We got no choice, you know, these is our livelihoods; if we lost this business that would be everything gone." Outside, the crowd occasionally parted for police vehicles; those brutal-looking black armoured vans trundling up the road in convoy. We spied people inside. 7 or 8 of these, followed by a similar number of normal white riot vans. As this long convoy made its way through the crowd, many whistled and cheered raucously at the sign of mass arrests, treating the cops like heroes. A young copper in a soft hat wandered along the street, channelling the national consensus: "it's not political; it's just mindless violence now — these people are just going around smashing things up and looting — it's got nothing to do with that shooting." On our way home we passed two police officers stopping and searching three black teenagers, talking tensely; it wasn't because they were black.

Ten miles to the southeast, in racist old Eltham, community self-organisation against the riots had some different nuances. A vigilante crowd of around 200–300 people gathered in the street with the stated aim of protecting their community: mostly men, some claiming EDL (English Defence League) membership, fans of the Charlton Athletic and Millwall football clubs — the latter long associated with far right hooliganism. EDL leader Stephen Lennon: "We're going to stop the riots; police obviously can't handle it." Reported threats in the air that a "nigger"

A Rising Tide Lifts All Boats

would "get it tonight". Similar vigilante crowds gathered in Enfield, and Sikhs with sheathed swords and hockey sticks came out in Southall. Ominous signs of what might be in store – visions of building inter-communal strife – but little more: it all passed with little event since, while widespread conflagrations continued elsewhere the country, London had already quietened significantly – in response to such communal self-defence perhaps, or to the deployment of 16,000 police. Vigilante crowds would persist in coming out in Eltham even on Thursday – a day after the national riot wave had crashed, and two days after it had ebbed in London – still with the stated aim of protecting their communities from rioters, only to break into their own anti-police riot when cops came to clear the area. Thus the political ambivalence of communities organising in self-defence – whether against police or another community – came starkly into focus. By a perverse social logic, the mobilisation of a few territorially-defined inner-London communities against processes of abjection and police racism, its side-effects rippling out across the social fabric, had precipitated in further territorial self-organisations that were often racist, and that understood their role as one of policing; expelling the abject from the community. It is unsurprising which mode was preferred in the gathering national consensus. Many in the traditionally leftist Kurdish and Turkish community would come to distance themselves from the ways in which their pragmatic self-organisation had been incorporated into this discourse, expressing a qualified solidarity with the rioters of Tottenham in a march north from Kingsland Road to the area of the original trigger-point, a couple of weeks later.

On Tuesday night rioting continued in Birmingham, Bristol and Nottingham, and spread to Manchester, Salford, Bury, West Bromwich, Leicester, Gloucester, Wirral, Sefton and Wolverhampton. Though police claimed otherwise, it is tempting to wonder whether the massive reallocation of police to London gave rioters more opportunities elsewhere. However one explains it, Tuesday night was the night on which the country beyond London really burned: in Nottingham, at around 10.30pm, 30–40 men firebombed a police station; in Liverpool a crowd of youths assembled at 11:30pm, throwing missiles at police and attacking shops; at Birmingham's New Street station, police fought up to 200 looters who had attacked shops and set fire to cars – shots were fired at police, including at a helicopter, and petrol bombs thrown; from 11pm in Gloucester – a small provincial market town, which had nonetheless seen rioting before – rioting and looting took place; in Manchester, though the third largest force in the country, police lost control of the city centre as looting and arson kicked off in the shopping area. But the most dramatic events were probably in Salford, a city of about 250,000 in the Manchester area, where another anti-police riot ignited.

Salford: predominantly white; above average unemployment; 15th most deprived area in the country. At around 3pm on Tuesday rumours started circulating there about the possibility of riots, and "threatening behaviour" was reported on the main shopping street. In response, police descended en masse. Around the corner on the Brydon Estate they filmed hundreds of youths stockpiling broken-up breezeblocks. Riot police were deployed, but were immediately ambushed with intense levels of violence and much larger crowds than they had anticipated. While fires burned and a shopping centre was looted, outnumbered and overwhelmed, they persisted in trying to disperse the crowd. At one point, 600–800 rioters were attacking a group of 30 cops with rocks, and at 7.40pm the police were ordered to pull out of Salford, during which time Lidl supermarket was looted and set on fire, along with several cars in the car park. The office of a local housing association was set on fire, as well as a looted shop, burning out the family home above it. From 10.45pm the local police were bolstered by officers from 10 other forces, and re-entered Salford to gradually regain control. While looting, as ever, had occurred, what was notable about Salford was the violently anti-police focus of the events. Another deprived area subject to increasing stop-and-search, Salford's youth had followed the example of rioters elsewhere in the country and used the riot-wave as an opportunity to take some revenge.

DISGUST

As the riots continued overnight into Wednesday, at around 1am a fatal hit-and-run incident occurred in the Winson Green area of Birmingham. In another example of community self-defence, around 80 British Asian people had been guarding local businesses when a car hit some people in the crowd at high speed, killing two men and critically injuring a third who later died in hospital. This depressing event came to supply the icing on the cake of the national "disgust consensus", with media endlessly re-rolling the pleas of Tariq Jahan, father of one of those killed, for inter-communal solidarity, and for people to "calm down and go home". Winson Green borders the Handsworth and Lozells areas, which both have recent histories of rioting. In 2005 these areas had erupted into inter-communal race riots between Afro-Caribbeans and Asians, after rumours had spread about the gang-rape of a black girl. Now, with rumours circulating that the driver of the car had been black – and that the hit-and-run had been a deliberately orchestrated murder, with one car somehow allegedly being used to "lure" the men into the road before they were hit with another vehicle – the spectre of full-blown race riot reared its head, with members of the surrounding Muslim community apparently readying themselves for the exaction of reprisals. Jahan's speech was a direct intervention into this local situation, telling the angry young men around him to "grow up" and avoid escalating existing tensions. But, decontextualised as flagship video clip in the national media spectacle, Jahan's speech came to stand for the sane, moral voice of the nation at large, against the madness of rioters in general. Disembedded from its local referent, it came to imply that those around the country who continued to riot were now complicit in violence which, among other things, had cost a father his son. And as such, it seemed to work.

It would later emerge that the incident had been an accident, that some of those implicated had actually known the victims, and that a cop involved in the case had lied under oath; all of the 8 accused of murder were acquitted, and an IPCC investigation was launched into the conduct of the police. Many of those involved also turned out to be white. Associations of the incident with the riotous behaviour or anti-Asian violence of local blacks thus unravelled, leaving it an unfortunate but highly contingent event. Indeed, the more terrifying social dynamics that were at play in this case were less a matter of rioting in itself, than of a potential inter-communal strife emerging as racially and territorially-defined communities self-organised *against* the spread of the riots, and against looting in particular. Tuesday had put this prospect on the table, from broom-brigades to baseball-batted Turks, from Birmingham's Asian community to the EDL. But: nowhere the blacks. Out of this ambivalent social logic a distorted national consensus forged a blitz-spirited smugness against the asociality of the rioter, as the gallery of riot horrors rotated endlessly on our screens: the burning of a carpet warehouse and all the flats above it; the burning of a longstanding family furniture business; the mugging of a bewildered Malaysian student; and finally, poor, noble Tariq Jahan.[46]

Distinctly different types of incident were being aggregated here: on the one hand the arson that comes as a standard practice of rioting crowds; on the other, crimes contingent to the riots themselves, merely occurring amidst the general social chaos. Muggings, of

46 Jahan himself would later explicitly distance himself from the demonisation of rioters and the punitive escalations against them, acknowledging the problem of stop-and-search. See Jahan interviewed by Mehdi Hasan, 'I don't see a broken society', *New Statesman*, 24 August 2011.

A Rising Tide Lifts All Boats

course, occur all the time in London; hit-and-runs are not unusual either—though they seem to have a habit of occurring amidst the frenzied action of a riot.[47] Lumped together as aspects of "The Riots"—a strange synthetic object—it perhaps really did look like there had been some sort of *ex nihilo* upsurge of "criminality pure and simple", an inexplicable irruption of unadulterated immorality into British society, as authoritarian discourses from state, media and beyond were by now insisting.[48] Unless this object is decomposed into its constitutive events and dynamics, unless we contest the coherence of this object, "The Riots", we end up confined to spinning one or another alternative interpretation of the same set of incidents according to our more or less "radical" political persuasions: Cameron says The Riots are about "criminality"/I say they're about "politics"; state and media see a lack of community-spiritedness underlying The Riots/I say "fuck off with your community—I'm with the rioters"; Cameron says The Riots are about criminality/I say "great!" What ensues can only be a sort of weak rhetorical mud-wrestling match to which the opponent doesn't even show up. And however impressive a fight we might still put up, most of the ground is already conceded in the acceptance of a fundamentally spurious object. We cannot respond to the question of what "The Riots" were "about" with any singular, univocal answer, because they were not, and could not be, *about* anything, in the sense of expressing some essential, singular, unified intentionality, grievance, desire etc. As emergent social events, riots—and even more, riot-waves—abstract themselves from the contexts from which they precipitate to unfold in forms and patterns entirely irreducible to any single factor, subjective or objective.[49]

Much better instead then, to break them down into the chain of events and highly overdetermined social logics that they are. When we do that, what is left is not merely some empiricist chaos of facts and incidents,

47 As we've already noted, at least one other hit-and-run occurred in this midst of this wave—of police, in Enfield. Hit-and-runs have occurred in other modern urban riots, such as in 1981, when a disabled man was killed by police chasing stone-throwing youths.

48 'Criminality pure and simple': a phrase rolled out by David Cameron and others supposedly to identify the singularly negative, loot-centric focus of the 2011 riots. This stock phrase, however, is a recurrent meme in the history of British urban riots. Douglas Hurd used it to describe the Handsworth Riots of 1985, and the same phrase seems to have occurred in 1981. Interestingly, this term—the function of which is to posit criminality as an essential trait of the individual, ruling out any further-reaching but a rising tide of spontaneously unfolding actions, a perceptible mechanics of social upheaval by which a fairly standard community anti-police demonstration spills over into riot; by which this creates cop-free space for the usual looting; by which this looting then spreads at a startling rate, afforded firstly by the scale of the initial conflagration, and secondly by the ubiquity of lateral means of communication; by which other communities who recognise a common cause with the rioters of Tottenham then come out to wage their own anti-police riots, amidst the generalising disorder; by which this growing contagion precipitates a broader national crisis of law and order as the police struggle to respond; in which context there proliferates a chaotic mass of behaviours normally kept somewhat at bay in the "social peace", and in response to which other communities feel compelled to self-organise against the breakdown of order; which self-organisation then threatens to erupt into inter-communal strife; which all compels the formation of a national consensus of disgust at the whole unfolding thing, before it all dies down, we all go home, and the mass-incarceration begins. The last embers of the fire faded in Liverpool and Manchester that Wednesday, with only the English Defence League still carrying the torch, in Eltham, of a riot-wave that had its clearest roots in anti-racism.

explanation – seems to have some historical association with the anti-semitic figure of the Jew as physical embodiment of *crime itself*.

49 It is surely this quality of the riot-wave as emergent social event that makes it such a seductive, enigmatic object for philosophers and pundits, who readily queue up to scrutinise this charmingly inscrutable thing, in whose depths, it is supposed, there must be hidden some secret.

PUNISHMENT

The precedent established by the end of the student struggles for pre-emption, technological surveillance and increasingly severe punitive response, was consolidated in the state's handling of the riots. And the country was exceptionally well equipped for it too, having sleepwalked its way into being one of the most spied-upon nations in the world, with an estimated one CCTV camera for every 11–14 people. What followed was one of the biggest investigations in the history of the police force, Operation VERA, in which hundreds of specialists

A Rising Tide Lifts All Boats **163**

trawled through video footage in a race to identify the thousands of faces caught on camera. And though a new generation of student protesters had felt they had learnt their first crucial lesson in adopting black-bloc tactics, having your face covered seemed to offer no guarantee of protection in the case of the riots. The sheer extent of CCTV coverage — in designated "problem" areas especially — provided the technological capacity for resolute detectives to trail individuals over a series of hours, or even days, trying to catch just one glimpse of their unmasked faces, and assembling, in the process, incriminating montages of each one, their successive actions and, importantly, their networks. Within weeks of the riots, 4000 people had been arrested, mostly male and mostly between the ages of 18–24. That the very first batches of suspects to be rounded up were those easiest to identify — whose data tethered them firmly to the cops — allowed the government to confidently assure the nation that the riots were not the work of any average person, your normal British citizen, but that of "known criminals". Effectively, the police had initially identified and then recalled those people most familiar to it, most close-to-hand, those so candidly referred to by ex-Metropolitan Police Commissioner Ian Blair as "police property".[50] Why would the police refer to such people as their property? Because in some sense they do own them: their solid criminal records justify that they be constantly accessible, pulled into the station at will. As police property, they are defined, somewhat tautologically, by criminality — akin to a character trait. And as we have repeatedly been reminded, the acts of rioters are not just simple crimes like any other, but *criminality* per se; criminality *pure and simple*. That the only content to be found in the riots — and, by implication, the rioters — is criminality itself, exemplifies the logic of abjection at work here, turning those who rioted into mere "property"; a homogenous, illegitimate lump that can be separated out and cut off at will, like dead wood, from an otherwise functioning social whole.

[50] Ian Blair on *Newsnight*, 5 December, 2011.

This perceived homogeneity would appear in the blanket sentencing of vastly different acts according to norms completely other than those which would apply in normal, non-riot circumstances. In its generalised exemplary sentencing of rioters, the state seems to implicitly recognise the riot's real character as an emergent social event. Unlike individual crimes, as a socially generalising logic the riot implicitly puts society itself at stake; rather than the riot being a sum of the particular acts of rioters, these acts then become instances of this general logic. Each can thus be judged as such – as the putting at stake, ultimately, of society as a whole. The response of the Chief Constable of the Greater Manchester Police was clear:

> If you as an individual go out and shoplift, that's bad, but if you go out in a mob, that is something far more serious… because it threatens society itself. It threatens society itself. You know, we have to be honest, we're a thin blue line out there as police officers… the system will only work if the vast majority of people observe the law.[51]

The necessary size of this majority has yet to be definitively established. But that the thin blue line suffered at least a drastic stretching, that the city was rendered fleetingly, yet palpably, vulnerable and breakable, meant that every event and action was potentially explosive. This point had become clear in the student protests, but even clearer in the riots, and their respective repressions in part reflected this.

An onslaught of attention-grabbing sentences followed: 16 months for snatching an ice-cream, 6 for a bottle of water and 5 for receiving a pair of stolen shorts. The newspapers abounded with such tragi-comic examples. Disorder and the threat of disorder became blurred in convictions, sometimes even being treated equally. The 18 year-old Amed Pelle got almost two years in jail for

[51] Chief Constable Peter Fahy in Panorama, 'Inside the Riots', BBC One, 22 November 2011.

posting messages on Facebook, including one perceived to be inciting riots in Nottingham, "Nottz Riot, whose onit?", and one with a clear anti-police message "kill one black youth, we kill a million fedz, riot until we own cities". The same sentence was given to Dwaine Spence, who apparently led a 40-strong young, angry crowd on the "rampage" through Wolverhampton, attacking the police. But while Amed Pelle's case involved utterances, suggesting intent and motivation, other social media activities that led to convictions were more ambiguous. And severe punishment for such intent did not require that there had been any actual consequence. Though nobody showed up at McDonald's, the meeting point for the Facebook event "Smash Down in Northwich Town" — except the police — its creator received four years in jail. The same sentence was given to the poor youngster who drunkenly set up a website called "The Warrington Riots", despite no resulting event. And this, of course, constitutes the dark side of social media, the contents of which can first be seized by the police, and then treated, at will, as though already constitutive of reality.

Spectacular examples aside, the majority of charges were for burglary, property damage and the vague but — by this point in the wave of struggles, ubiquitous — category of "violent disorder". By mid-October, out of the 2000 people who appeared before the magistrates' court on more minor charges, 40% had received immediate custodial sentences, compared to 12% in 2010. But, as in the case of the student unrest before it, many minor incidents had been sent straight to the Crown Courts (where over 90% of cases end in jail terms), whose sentencing of the rioters were an estimated 18–25% higher than in non-riot conditions. Certain London courts in particular became industrial-style justice mills, staying open 24 hours a day, to rapidly churn through thousands of rioters, who, in the face of the temporarily-implemented quadruple custody rate, had been left to wait in cells below the courtroom, often crammed to their maximum capacity. The spectrum of candidates in the 2012 London mayoral election would propose the standardisation of this industrious spectacle for the city as a whole on their glossy campaign flyers. And if this display was not enough to appease a nation hungry for "justice", the Prime Minister would soon advise local councils that they should consider withholding the shrinking welfare cheques of all those families harbouring a rioter, or even, perhaps, evicting them – signalling to a mass of panicked parents that they should shop in their delinquent kids, to save their homes. As Nick Clegg echoed:

> If you go out and trash other people's houses, you burn cars, you loot and smash up shops – in other words, if you show absolutely no sense of respect to your own community – then, of course, questions need to be asked, whether the community should support you in living in that community... the principle that if you are getting some support from the community, you are going to have to show some support for that community, is a really, really important one.[52]

Community, community, community. Who's in and who's out? Clegg evidently understands the logic very well. A community without qualities, entirely negatively defined – the agglomerated mass of all those who do not trash other people's houses, burn cars, smash up shops etc. What does this community hold in common? Only the fact of not rioting, and only this insofar as someone else can perform that role. Rioting produces the community that abjects the rioter who riots against this abjection. The community produces the abjects who riot against this abjection to make it a community. Sentencing closes the circle of abjection, seals the bounds of community in law, and – just in case we hadn't noticed – prominent politicians step in to lard the whole thing in extra added legitimacy. Just as well, for the

[52] Nick Clegg, speaking in Manchester to businesses affected by the riots: *Guardian* News Blog, 13 August 2011.

bounds of that community – marked out by a thin blue line – had started to look pretty dodgy. Just the line of a tense and faltering smile without a face.

The social logic of abjection doesn't let up. After the riots, radicalisation of the endless restructuring under the current Con–Dem coalition proceeded at a startling place. While talking tough, the state began to make a wary few adjustments aimed at staving off similar upheavals. Every whiff of protest for a while met complete police lock-down. In the alluvium left by the crashed wave there sprouted Occupy, but in this context at least, somehow sadder, even more defeated than what had preceded it. The country had been stunned into silence by the riots; the mass of people involved in anti-austerity struggles largely put on pause; muted, mouths gaping open, heads turned, left to watch the spectacle of the riots burn themselves out. The first few attempts at post-riot protest signalled complete deflation. The march against pension reform on 30 November 2011 in central London resembled a state funeral procession, with approximately one police officer for every two protesters, and ten-foot-tall solid steel crowd-control fencing to funnel us along in a reduced and hyper-controlled version of that already-limited trudge. While the kettling of the student movement had provided the intense physical proximity, the compression to generate heat and escalate tension, the steel cordon left us utterly cold; this was autumn, turning into winter. Not only had the crisis struggles weakened, first in the face of the complete illegitimacy of their demands, second through the sheer magnitude of the systematic repression that followed the riots – the riots had also unified the country at large against the enemies within, the scum who had saddled an already crisis-ridden country with a whopping extra bill, estimated at around half a billion pounds.[53] And we would surely sink from the weight of it too, perhaps like those poor Greeks!

[53] Riots Communities and Victims Panel, *After the Riots*, 3.

In an Olympic opening ceremony a couple of miles from the sites of Hackney's riots, while order is ensured with paramilitary-style policing, a patriotic spectacle is summoned from Britain's disorderly history, throwing white punks and black grime kids from the nearby district of Bow against top-hatted Industrial Revolution bourgeois; an anarchic multicultural explosion about which we are to feel proud, included. A year after Smiley Culture's death, Dizzee Rascal decants the last of London's autonomous black subcultures onto the stage. Doreen Lawrence carries the torch through the South East London that lit the fuse of 1981; that murdered her son in 1993; where the EDL concluded the riot-wave in 2011. Just outside, a Critical Mass demonstration – ordinarily tolerated by the cops – is stamped on hard. Young black men continue to be stopped and searched multiples of times more than any other group, while a muted recognition that there may be problems with this approach slowly seeps through the post-riot political landscape, just as it did in the early 1980s. And in this sense at least, these riots may be said to have "worked". Persecution of the supposed feckless again ramps up, with the state-managed class-cleansing of London estates. Thatcher's long-awaited death lets loose a national outburst of schadenfreude as the survivors of the 1980s pour into central London to drunkenly celebrate something that feels vaguely like a victory: at least we outlived her.

It would take quite an optimist to find in all this any literal harbingers of revolution or of building class struggle. At most, for a few exhilarating moments, some had at last stood up – and it was exciting while it lasted. And the imprint of that exhilaration perhaps will persist in the political memory of a generation. But let's not imagine this wave could, of itself, have done anything other than crash and leave a long ebb tide behind. The anti-austerity struggles had nowhere to go, no real sense of possibilities but a gleeful breaking-through into some newly raucous situation, always without aim or positive

A Rising Tide Lifts All Boats

horizon; all demands impossible; the only meaningful modes of struggle – to at least give cops and Con–Dems a hard time – ruled by definition out of bounds. As such they could only invite an escalating punishment. The broader wave of struggles had crested and threatened to break as it came up against this impossibility. It would have needed some dramatic exogenous event to drive it further – another deep-sea earthquake, perhaps, from the juddering plates of the global economy, or some major harmonic resonance from global convergences of struggle. But such did not come, and here the wave intersected with the longer-term social dynamics of abjection which would make its inevitable crash all the more sudden and catastrophic.

Anti-police rioters too had been bound at best to rail in their illegitimacy against a police logic that makes them so. In themselves such riots will, of course, never constitute a significant challenge to a capitalist state whose vastly hypertrophied repressive apparatus is only the outer ring around deep social structures of consent which solidify all the more as their abjects struggle against them, even reproducing the function of police at the level of community self-organisation. Still, they can give us a good impression of what the "thin blue line" in crisis looks like. And let's not moralise about these riots after the fashion of a venerable leftism which once could have taken them as a throwback to the past – before the workers matured and *really started organising to win*; for the workers' movement is all out of actuality, long defunct as such a normative measure. And in recognising the sadness, the catastrophe of this wave, let's not pretend there was some other obvious way it could have gone, if we had only had the right X – for if X had really been on the cards it would almost certainly have been taken up. Past waves of struggle don't need armchair generals. But if we can scrape away the bullshit in which these things get caked, and look at them honestly, we can at least hope to figure out where we are now. Stuck in modes of struggle that rebound upon us. Residue of positive class belonging only at someone else's expense. And for *them*: class branded onto their very being as mere objects of disgust. Class declared by rule of law, enforced by police patrol. Thus class, at least, put at stake.

LOGISTICS, COUNTERLOGISTICS AND THE COMMUNIST PROSPECT

Jasper Bernes

What is theory for? What good is it, in the fight against capital and state? For much of the left, the Marxist left in particular, the answer is obvious: theory tells us what to do, or *what is to be done*, in the strangely passive formula often used here. Theory is the pedagogue of practice. Thus, the essential link between Comrade Lenin and his putative enemy, the Renegade Kautsky, the master thinkers of the Third and Second Internationals: despite their storied disagreements, both believed that without the special, scientific knowledge dispensed by intellectuals and dedicated revolutionaries, the working class was doomed to a degraded consciousness, incapable of making revolution or, at any rate, making it successfully. The task of theory, therefore, is to weaponise proletarian consciousness, to turn it toward right action. This didactic view of theory extends across the entire range of Marxist intellectual work in the 20th century, from the comparatively crude Bolshevist programmatics of Lenin and Trotsky to the sophisticated variants offered by Antonio Gramsci and Louis Althusser.

1 Karl Marx, 'Letter to Arnold Ruge', September 1843 (MECW 3), 144.

There are other, non-didactic theories of theory, however. We might look, for instance, to Marx's own very early reflection on such matters. There is no need to play teacher to the working class, Marx tells his friend Arnold Ruge: "We shall not say, Abandon your struggles, they are mere folly; let us provide you with the true campaign-slogans. Instead we shall simply show the world why it is struggling, and consciousness of this is a thing it will acquire whether it wishes or not."[1] The final turn in this formulation is crucial, since it implies that the knowledge theory provides already abounds in the world; theory simply reflects, synthesizes and perhaps accelerates the "self-clarification…of the struggles and wishes of an age". Theory is a moment in the self-education of the proletariat, whose curriculum involves inflammatory pamphlets and beer-hall oratory as much as barricades and streetfighting.

Logistics, Counterlogistics and the Communist Prospect

In this regard, theory is more a map than a set of directions: a survey of the terrain in which we find ourselves, a way of getting our bearings in advance of any risky course of action. I am thinking here of Fredric Jameson's essay on the "cultural logic of late capitalism", and his call for "cognitive maps" that can orient us within the new spaces of the postindustrial world. Though Jameson must surely count as an exponent of the pedagogical view of theory — calling for cognitive maps by way of a defense of didacticism in art — part of the appeal of this essay is the way his call for maps emerges from a vividly narrated disorientation, from a phenomenology of the bewildered and lost. Describing the involuted voids of the Bonaventure hotel, Jameson situates the reader within a spatial allegory for the abstract structures of late capitalism and the "incapacity of our minds…to map the great global multinational and decentered communication network in which we find ourselves caught as individual subjects".[2] Theory is a map produced by the lost themselves, offering us the difficult view from within rather than the clarity of the Olympian view from above.

Languishing in the shadow of its dominant counterpart, antididactic theory has often remained a bitter inversion of the intellectualist presumptions of the Leninist or Gramscian view. Whereas the didactic view tells us that revolution fails for lack of theory, or for lack of the right theory — fails because the correct consciousness was not cultivated — the communist ultra-left that inherits the antididactic view offers instead a theory of intellectual betrayal, a theory of militant theory as the corruption of the organic intelligence of the working class.[3] The role of theorists, then, is to prevent these corrupting interventions by intellectuals, in order to allow for the spontaneous self-organisation of the working class. As a consequence, the historical ultra-left, congealing in the wake of the failure of the revolutionary wave of the early 20th century and the victory of a distinctly counter-revolutionary Marxism, adopts a reflective and

[2] Fredric Jameson, 'Postmodernism, or the Cultural Logic of Late Capitalism', *New Left Review* 146 (July-August 1984), 84.

[3] See the forthcoming 'A History of Separation' in *Endnotes* 4 for a full exposition of the betrayal thematic within the ultraleft.

contemplative (if not fatalist) orientation to the unfolding of struggles, offering diagnosis at most but never any strategic reflection, lest it commit the cardinal sin of "intervention", playing the pedagogue to the masses. The result is a perversely unhappy consciousness who both knows better and yet, at the same time, feels that such knowing is at best useless and at worst harmful. This guilty self-consciousness plagues even those important theories — by Gilles Dauvé and Théorie Communiste, for instance — which emerge after 1968 as critiques of the historical ultra-left.

But if we really believe that theory emerges as part of the self-clarification of struggles, then there is no reason to fear intervention, or strategic thought. Any perspective militants and intellectuals might bring to a struggle is either already represented within it or, on the contrary, capable of being confronted as one of many obstacles and impasses antagonists encounter in their self-education. Strategic thought is not external to struggles, but native to them, and every set of victories or failures opens up new strategic prospects — possible futures — which must be examined and whose effects in the present can be accounted for. In describing these prospects, theory inevitably takes sides among them. This is not to issue orders to struggles, but to be ordered by them.

THEORY FROM THE GROUND

The following essay is an experiment in theory writing. It attempts to render explicit the link between theory as it unfolds in the pages of communist journals and theory as it unfolds in the conduct of struggles, demonstrating how reflections about the restructuring of capitalism emerge as the consequence of particular moments of struggle. From these theoretical horizons, specific strategic prospects also emerge, and inasmuch as they are discussed on the ground and affect what happens there, we can only with great effort avoid them.

We can (and perhaps should) always ask of the theories we encounter, *Where are we? In response to which practical experience has this theory emerged?* In what follows we are, for the most part, in the port of Oakland, California, beneath the shadows of cyclopean gantry cranes and container ships, pacing around anxiously with the 20,000 other people who have entered the port in order to blockade it, as part of the so-called "General Strike" called for by Occupy Oakland on November 2, 2011. Every participant in the blockade that day surely had some intuitive sense of the port's centrality to the northern Californian economy, and it is with this intuitive orientation that theory begins. If asked, they would tell you that a sizeable fraction of what they consumed originated overseas, got put onto ships, and passed through ports like Oakland's en route to its final destination. As an interface between production and consumption, between the US and its overseas trading partners, between hundreds of thousands of workers and the various forms of circulating capital they engage, the quieted machinery of the port quickly became an emblem for the complex totality of capitalist production it seemed both to eclipse and to reveal.

For our blockaders, then, all manner of questions unfolded directly from their encounter with the space of the port and its machinery. How might we produce a map of the various companies — the flows of capital and labour — directly or indirectly affected by a blockade of the port, by a blockade of particular terminals? Who sits at one remove? At two removes or three? Additionally, questions emerged about the relationship between the blockade tactic and the grievances of those who took part. Though organised in collaboration with the local section of the ILWU (the dockworker's union), in solidarity with the threatened workers in Longview, Washington, few people who came to the blockade knew anything about Longview. They were there in response to the police eviction of Occupy Oakland's camp and in solidarity with whatever they understood as the chief grievances of the Occupy movement. How, then, to characterise the relationship between the blockaders, many of whom were unemployed or marginally employed, and the highly organised port workers? Who was affected by such a blockade? What is the relationship between the blockade and the strike tactic? Once asked, these questions linked the moment of the blockade to related mobilisations: the *piqueteros* of the Argentine uprisings of the late 1990s and early 2000s, unemployed workers who, absent any other way of prosecuting their demands for government assistance, took to blockading roads in small, dispersed bands; the *piquets volants* of the 2010 French strikes against proposed changes in pension law, bands of dispersed picketers who supported blockades by workers but also engaged in their own blockades, independent of strike activity; the recent strikes by workers in IKEA's and Wal-Mart's supply chains; and everywhere, in the season of political tumult that follows on the crisis of 2008, a proliferation of the blockade and a waning of the strike as such (with the exception of the industrial "BRICS", where a renegade labour formation has initiated a new strike wave).

4 For an example, see 'Blockading the Port Is Only the First of Many Last Resorts' (bayofrage.com), a text that addresses many of the questions outlined above, and which was distributed within Occupy Oakland after the first blockade and before the second, multi-city blockade. In many regards, the essay here is a formalisation and refinement of a process of discussion, reflection and critique initiated by that text.

LOGISTICS AND HYDRAULIC CAPITALISM

These are not questions that belong solely to formal theory. They were debated immediately by those who participated in the blockade and who planned for a second blockade a month later.[4] Some of these debates invoked the concept of "globalisation" to make sense of the increasing centrality of the port and international trade within capitalism, in an echo of the alter-globalisation movement of the early 2000s. But it has always been unclear what the term "globalisation" is supposed to mean, as marker for a new historical phase. Capitalism has been global from the very start, emerging from within the blood-soaked matrix of the mercantile expansion of the early modern period. Later on, its factories and mills were fed by planetary flows of raw material, and produce for a market which is likewise international. The real question, then, is what kind of globalisation we have today. What is the *differentia specifica* of today's globalisation? What is the precise relationship between production and circulation?

Today's supply chains are distinguished not just by their planetary extension and incredible speed but by their direct integration of manufacture and retail, their harmonisation of the rhythms of production and consumption. Since the 1980s, business writers have touted the value of "lean" and "flexible" production models, in which suppliers maintain the capacity to expand and contract production, as well as change the types of commodities produced, by relying on a network of subcontractors, temporary workers, and mutable organisational structures, adaptations that require precise control over the flow of goods and information between units.[5] Originally associated with the Toyota Production System, and Japanese manufacturers in general, these corporate forms are now frequently identified with the loose moniker Just In Time (JIT), which refers in the specific sense to a form of inventory management and in general to a production philosophy in which firms aim to eliminate standing inventory (whether produced in-house or received from suppliers). Derived in part from the Japanese and in part from Anglo-American cybernetics, JIT is a circulationist production philosophy, oriented around a concept of "continuous flow" that views everything not in motion as a form of waste (*muda*), a drag on profits. JIT aims to submit all production to the condition of circulation, pushing its velocity as far toward the light-speed of information transmission as possible. From the perspective of our blockaders, this emphasis on the quick and continuous flow of commodities multiplies the power of the blockade. In the absence of standing inventories, a blockade of just a few days could effectively paralyse many manufacturers and retailers.[6]

[5] 'Lean manufacturing' begins as a formalisation of the principles behind the Toyota Production System, seen during the 1980s as a solution to the ailments of American manufacturing firms. See James P. Womack et al., *The Machine That Changed the World* (Rawson Associates 1990). The concept of 'flexibility' emerges from debates in the late 1970s about the possibility of an alternate manufacturing system based on 'flexible specialisation' rather than Fordist economies of scale, a system thought to be enabled by highly-adjustable Computer Numerical Control (CNC) machines. Michael J. Piore and Charles F. Sabel, *The Second Industrial Divide: Possibilities For Prosperity* (Basic Books 1984).

[6] Business writer Barry Lynn's *End of the Line* is devoted to

In JIT systems, manufacturers must coordinate upstream suppliers with downstream buyers, so speed alone is insufficient. Timing is crucial. Through precise coordination, firms can invert the traditional buyer-seller relationship in which goods are first produced and then sold to a consumer. By replenishing goods at the exact moment they are sold, with no build-up of stocks along the way, JIT firms perform a weird sort of time-travel, making it seem as if they only make products that have already been sold to the end-consumer. As opposed to the older, "push production" model, in which factories generated massive stockpiles of goods that retailers would clear from the market with promotions and coupons, in today's "pull" production system "retailers share POS [point-of-sale] information with their vendors who can then rapidly replenish the retailers' stock".[7] This has lead to the functional integration of suppliers and retailers, under terms in which the retailers often have the upper hand. Massive buyers like Wal-Mart reduce their suppliers to mere vassals, directly controlling product design and pricing while still retaining the flexibility to terminate a contract if needed. They gain the benefits of vertical integration without the liability that comes from formal ownership. Whereas in the early 1980s some thought that the emphasis on flexibility and dynamism would shift the balance of power from big, inflexible multinationals to small, agile firms, lean production has instead only meant a phase change rather than a weakening of the power of multinational firms. The new arrangement features what Bennett Harrison has called the "concentration without centralisation" of corporate authority.[8]

Lean manufacturing, flexibility, just-in-time inventory systems, "pull" production: each one of these innovations now forms a component part of the so-called "logistics revolution", and the corresponding "logistics industry", which consists of in-house and third-party specialists in supply-chain design and management. Enabled by the technical transformations of the shipping and transport

demonstrating the dangerous fragility of today's distributed production system, where a 'breakdown anywhere increasingly means a breakdown everywhere, much in the way that a small perturbation in the electricity grid in Ohio tripped the great North American blackout of August 2003'. Barry C Lynn, *End of the Line: The Rise and Coming Fall of the Global Corporation* (Doubleday 2005), 3.

7 Edna Bonacich and Jake B Wilson, *Getting the Goods: Ports, Labor, and the Logistics Revolution* (Cornell University Press 2008), 5.

8 Bennett Harrison, *Lean and Mean: The Changing Landscape of Corporate Power in the Age of Flexibility* (Guilford Press 1997), 8-12.

industry, containerisation in particular, as well as the possibilities afforded by information and communications technology, logistics workers now coordinate different productive moments and circulatory flows across vast international distances, ensuring that the where and when of the commodity obtains to the precision and speed of data. Confirming the veracity of the oft-quoted passage from Marx's *Grundrisse* about the tendential development of the world market, through logistics, capital "strives simultaneously for a greater extension of the market and for greater annihilation of space by time".[9] But logistics is more than the extension of the world market in space and the acceleration of commodital flows: it is the active power to coordinate and choreograph, the power to conjoin and split flows; to speed up and slow down; to change the type of commodity produced and its origin and destination point; and, finally, to collect and distribute knowledge about the production, movement and sale of commodities as they stream across the grid.

Logistics is a multivalent term. It names an industry in its own right, composed of firms that handle the administration of shipping and receiving for other corporations, as well as an activity that many businesses handle internally. But it also refers, metonymically, to a transformation of capitalist production overall: the "logistics revolution". In this latter sense, logistics indexes the subordination of production to the conditions of circulation, the becoming-hegemonic of those aspects of the production process that involve circulation. In the idealised world-picture of logistics, manufacture is merely one moment in a continuous, Heraclitean flux; the factory dissolves into planetary flows, chopped up into modular, component processes which, separated by thousands of miles, combine and recombine according to the changing whims of capital. Logistics aims to transmute all fixed capital into circulating capital, the better to imitate and conform to the purest and most

[9] Marx, *Grundrisse* (MECW 28), 448 (Nicolaus trans.).

liquid of forms capital takes: money. This is impossible, of course, since the valorisation process requires fixed capital outlays at some point along the circuits of reproduction, and therefore someone somewhere will have to shoulder the risk that comes with investing in immobile plant and machinery. But logistics is about mitigating this risk, it is about transforming a mode of production into a mode of circulation, in which the frequencies and channel capacities of the circuits of capital are what matters. In this the logistics revolution conforms to the hydraulic conception of capitalism outlined by Deleuze and Guattari in the 1970s, in which surplus value results not so much from the irreversible transformation of worked matter but from the conjunction of one flow (money) with another (labour).[10] In this account, influenced by Fernand Braudel's description of the origins of capitalism, and its revision by world-systems theory, capital is nothing so much as the commander of flows, breaking and conjoining various currents in order to create a vast irrigation and drainage of social power. Logistics turns solids into liquids – or at its extreme, into electrical fields – taking the movement of discrete elements and treating them as if they were oil in a pipeline, flowing continuously at precisely adjustable pressures.[11]

THE USE-VALUE OF LOGISTICS

So far our project of cognitive mapping has successfully situated our blockaders within a vast spatial horizon, a network of reticulated flows, against the backdrop of which even the gargantuan containerships, even the teeming thousands of blockaders, are mere flyspecks. But the picture we have given is without depth, without history; it is, in other words, a picture, and we might wonder whether some of the disorientation to which the concept of the cognitive map responds is aggravated by the spatial (and visual) approach. Perhaps "map" functions as metaphor more than anything else, referring to an elaboration of concepts and categories in

[10] Gilles Deleuze and Felix Guattari, *Anti-Oedipus: Capitalism and Schizophrenia* (University of Minnesota Press 1983), 227-228.

[11] Braudel, notably, treats capitalism as the intervention onto a pre-existing plane of market transactions by powerful actors who are able to suspend the rules of fair play for their own benefit. Capital is, fundamentally, a manipulation of circulation and the flows of a market economy. Fernand Braudel, *The Wheels of Commerce*, (University of California Press 1992), 22.

both spatial and temporal dimensions. A map, but also a story, chart, and diagram, because once we adopt the view *from* somewhere, the view *for* somebody, we place ourselves between a past and a future, at the leading edge of a chain of causes that are as much in need of mapping as the spatial arrangement of the supply chain, especially if we want to have any sense of what might happen next.

In other words, we will want to know why capital turned to logistics. Why did capital reorganise in this manner? In pursuit of which advantages and in response to which impasses? One answer, hinted at above, is that logistics is a simple accelerator of commodity flows. Logistics is a method to decrease the turnover time of capital, and thereby raise total profits. Short turnover times and quick production cycles can produce very high total profits with even the very low rates of profit (per turnover) which capitalists encountered in the 1970s. Logistics was one solution, then, to "the long downturn" that emerged in the 1970s and the general crisis it ushered in, as opportunities for profit-taking through investment in the productive apparatus (in new plant and machinery) began to vanish. As we know from numerous accounts, one result is that capital flowed into financial assets, real estate, and the like, amplifying the velocity and bandwidth of the money supply and the credit market, and concocting novel forms of finance capital. But this well-documented process of financialisation had as its hidden counterpart a massive investment of capital in the complementary sphere of commodity (rather than money) circulation, increasing the throughput of the transportation system and accelerating the velocity of commodity capital through a buildout in the form of tankers, port complexes, railyards, robotically-controlled distribution centers, and the digital and network technology needed to manage the increased volume and complexity of trade. The shipping container and the commodity future were thus

12 In Marxist value theory, circulation is often treated as an 'unproductive' sphere separate from the value-generating activities of the sphere of production. Because no surplus value can be added through 'acts of buying or selling', which involve only the 'conversion of the same value from one form into another', the costs associated with these activities (bookkeeping, inventory, retailing, administration) are *faux frais* pure and simple, deductions from the total surplus value (Marx, *Capital* Vol. 2 (MECW 36), 133). However, Marx argues that certain activities associated with circulation – transport, in particular – are value-generating, for the persuasive reason that it would be inconsistent to treat the transport of coal from the bottom of the mine to the top as productive but its transport from the mine to a power plant as unproductive.

complementary technical innovations, streamlining and supercharging different segments of the total circuit of reproduction. The ever-faster rotations of credit and commodities around the globe are mutually enabling relays. However, investment in these areas is not just about brute velocity; it also aims at reducing the associated costs of circulation and thereby increasing the total load of the transport systems. Alongside the obvious economies of scale and mechanisation afforded by container technology, integrated information systems vastly reduce the administrative costs associated with circulation, freeing up more money for direct investment in production.[12]

But these developments cannot be understood in terms of quantitative increase and decrease alone: increase in speed and volume of commodital flows, decrease in overhead. There is an important qualitative goal here as well, described by logistics as "agility"—that is, the power to change, as quickly as possible, the speed, location, origin and destination of products, as well as product type, in order to meet volatile market conditions. Corporations aim for "responsive supply chains", as the chapter title of one popular logistics handbook has it, "such that [they] can respond in shorter time-frames both in terms of volume change and variety changes".[13] In their interventive role, logistics experts might seek to identify and remedy bottlenecks in order to maintain agility. But as a matter of preventive design, specialists will strive to synchronise and distribute information across the entire supply chain so that suppliers can take appropriate action *before* intervention becomes necessary. This distributed information is referred to as a "virtual supply chain", a chain of transmitted symbolic representations that flows opposite to the physical movement of commodities. Entirely separate firms might use distributed data of this sort to coordinate their activities. The result, as Bonacich and Wilson note, is that "competition ... shift[s] from the firm level to the

Circulation, then, refers to two different processes that are conceptually distinct but in practice almost always intertwined. First, there is a metamorphosis in the form of the commodity, as commodities change into money and vice versa. This is 'circulation' not in actual space but in the ideal phase-space of the commodity-form. As Marx notes, 'movable commodity values, such as cotton or pig iron, can remain in the same warehouse while they undergo dozens of circulation processes, and are bought and resold by speculators'. We need to distinguish this type of properly unproductive circulation – 'where it is the property title to the thing and not the thing itself' that moves – from the physical circulation of the object in space, which might be thought of as an extension of the value-generating activities of the productive sphere (ibid., 153).

supply chain level".[14] But transparency of data does not level the playing field at all; typically, one of the actors in the supply-chain network will retain dominance, without necessarily placing itself at the centre of operations — Wal-Mart, for instance, has insisted its suppliers place Radio Frequency Identification (RFID) tags on pallets and containers, allowing it to manage its inventory much more effectively, at considerable cost to the suppliers.[15]

Before we consider the final reason for the logistics revolution, a brief historical note is in order. Until WWII, the field of corporate or business logistics did not exist at all. Instead, logistics was a purely military affair, referring to the methods that armies used to provision themselves, moving supplies from the rear to the front line, a mundane but fundamental enterprise which military historians since Thucydides have acknowledged as a key determinant of the success of expeditionary wars. Business logistics as a distinct field evolved in the 1950s, building upon innovations in military logistics, and drawing upon the interchange of personnel between the military, industry and the academy so characteristic of the postwar period, interchanges superintended by the fields of cybernetics, information theory and operations research. The connection between military and corporate logistics remained intimate. For instance, though Malcolm McLean introduced stackable shipping containers in the 1950s, and had already managed to containerise some domestic transport lines, it was his Sea-Land Service's container-based solution to the logistics crisis of the Vietnam War that generalised the technology and demonstrated its effectiveness for international trade.[16] Likewise, RFID technology was first deployed by the US military in Iraq and Afghanistan, at which point Wal-Mart begin exploring its use. Shortly afterwards, the Department of Defense and Wal-Mart issued mandates to their largest suppliers, requiring them to use RFID tags on their merchandise. The link

[13] Martin Christopher, *Logistics and Supply Chain Management* (FT Press 2011), 99.

[14] Bonacich and Wilson, *Getting the Goods*, 5.

[15] Erick C. Jones and Christopher A. Chung, *RFID in Logistics* (CRC Press 2010), 87.

[16] The story of Malcolm McLean and Sea-Land is narrated in Marc Levinson, *The Box* (Princeton 2010), 36–75, 171–178.

between corporate logistics and military logistics is so strong that the many of Wal-Mart's managers and executives – who set the standard for the industry as a whole – come from the military.[17]

Logistics, we might say, is war by other means, war by means of trade. A war of supply chains that conquers new territories by suffusing them with capillarial distributions, ensuring that commodities flow with ease to the farthest extremities. From this martial perspective, we might usefully distinguish, however, between an offensive and a defensive logistics. The offensive forms we have already described above: logistics seeks to saturate markets, reduce costs and outproduce competitors, maintain maximum throughput and maximum product variety. In this offensive aspect, logistics emphasises flexibility, plasticity, permutability, dynamism, and morphogenesis. But it finds its complement in a series of protocols which are fundamentally defensive, mitigating supply chain risk from blockades and earthquakes, strikes and supplier shortages. If "agility" is the watchword of offensive logistics, defensive logistics aims for "resilience" and emphasises the values of elasticity, homeostasis, stability, and longevity. But resilience is only ostensibly a conservative principle; it finds stability not in inflexibility but in constant, self-stabilising adaptivity.[18] In this sense, the defensive and the offensive forms of logistics are really impossible to disentangle, since one firm's agility is another's volatility, and the more flexible and dynamic a firm becomes the more it "exports" uncertainty to the system as a whole, requiring other firms to become more resilient. In any case, we can expect that, in the context of the economic crisis and the looming environmental collapse, logistics will become more and more the science of risk management and crisis mitigation.

Logistics is capital's art of war, a series of techniques for intercapitalist and interstate competition. But such wars are, at the same time, always fought through and

[17] Walmart CEO Bill Simon, a former Navy officer, initiated programs which recruit managers and executives from the military. Michael Bergdahl, *What I Learned From Sam Walton* (John Wiley 2004), 155. He has also established 'leadership' programs modeled on military academies.

[18] Christopher, *Logistics and Supply Chain Management*, 189-210.

against workers. One of the most significant reasons for the extension, complication and lubrication of these planetary supply chains is that they allow for arbitrage of the labour market. The sophisticated, permutable supply chains of the contemporary world make it possible for capital to seek out the lowest wages anywhere in the world and to play proletarians off of each other. Logistics was therefore one of the key weapons in a decades-long global offensive against labour. The planetary supply chains enabled by containerisation effectively encircled labour, laying siege to its defensive emplacements such as unions and, eventually, over the course of the 1980s and 1990s, completely crushing them. From there, with labour on the run, logistics has enabled capital to quickly neutralise and outmanoeuvre whatever feeble resistance workers mount. Although capital must deal with the problem of sunk investments in immovable buildings, machines, and other infrastructures, reconfigurable supply chains allow it unprecedented power to route around, and starve, troublesome labour forces. By splitting workers into a "core" composed of permanent workers (often conservative and loyal) and a periphery of casualised, outsourced and fragmented workers, who may or may not work for the same firm, capital has dispersed proletarian resistance quite effectively. But these organisational structures require systems of coordination, communication and transport, opening capital up to the danger of disruption in the space of circulation, whether by workers charged with circulating commodities or by others, as with the port blockade, who choose circulation as their space of effective action, for the simple reason that capital has already made this choice as well. The actions of the participants in the port blockade are, in this regard, doubly determined by the restructuring of capital. They are there not only because the restructuring of capital has either left them with no jobs at all or placed them into jobs where action as workers according to the classical tactics of the worker's movement has been proscribed, but also because capital itself has increasingly taken the sphere of circulation as the object of its own interventions. In this regard, theory provides us not only with the *why* of capital's restructuring but the *why* of a new cycle of struggles.

VISIBILITY AND PRAXIS

It should be obvious by now that logistics is capital's own project of cognitive mapping. Hence, the prominence of "visibility" among the watchwords of the logistics industry. To manage a supply chain means to render it transparent. The flows of commodities in which we locate our blockaders are doubled by flows of information, by a signifying chain that superintends the commodity chain, sometimes without human intervention at all. Alongside the predictive models of finance, which aim to represent and control the chaotic fluctuations of the credit system and money, logistics likewise manages the complex flows of the commodity system through structures of representation. We might imagine, then, a logistics against logistics, a counter-logistics which employs the conceptual and technical equipment of the industry in order to identify and exploit bottlenecks, to give our blockaders a sense of where they stand within the flows of capital. This counter-logistics might be a proletarian art of war to match capital's own *ars belli*. Imagine if our blockaders knew exactly which commodities the containers at particular berths, or on particular ships, contained; imagine if they could learn about the origin and destination of these commodities and calculate the possible effects — functionally and in dollars — of delays or interruptions in particular flows. Possession of such a counterlogistical system, which might be as crude as a written inventory, would allow antagonists to focus their attention where it would be most effective. Taking, for example, the situation of the French pension law struggles of 2010, in which mobile blockades in groups of twenty to a hundred moved throughout French cities, supporting the picket lines of striking workers but also blockading key sites independently, the powers of coordination and concentration permitted by such a system are immediately apparent.[19] This is one example of the strategic horizons which unfold from within struggles, even if most discussions of such counterlogistics will have to be conducted with particular occasions in mind.

But beyond the practical value of counterlogistic information, there is what we might call its *existential* value: the way in which being able to see one's own actions alongside the actions of others, and being able to see as well the effects of such concerted action, imbues those actions with a meaning they might have otherwise lacked. The contagiousness of the Arab Spring – for example – arises in part from the affirmative effect of transmitted images of struggle. Being able to see one's own action in the face of state violence reflected in and even enlarged by the actions of others can be profoundly galvanising. This is another one of the values of theory with regard to praxis – the ability to place struggles side by side, to render struggles visible to each other and to themselves.

This importance of visibility – or legibility, as he calls it – is essential to one of the best discussions of the restructuring of labour in late capitalism, Richard Sennett's *The Corrosion of Character*. Sennett suggests that the "weak work identity" of contemporary workplaces – distinguished mainly by computerisation, in his treatment – results from the utter illegibility of the work processes to the workers themselves. Visiting a bakery which he had studied decades earlier for his first book, *The Hidden Injuries of Class*, Sennett finds that, in place of the physically challenging processes of the 1960s bakery, workers now used computer-controlled machines which can produce any kind of bread according to changing market conditions, simply by pressing a few buttons. As a result, unlike bakers in the past, the workers do not identify with their jobs or derive satisfaction from their tasks, precisely because the functioning

[19] The blockades I am talking about differ from the classical barricade in that they are offensive rather than defensive. The main purpose of the barricades of the 19th century was that they dispersed the state's forces so that small groups of soldiers could either be defeated with force or fraternised with and converted. But the weakness of the barricade fight, as described by writers from Blanqui to Engels, was that partisans defended particular territories (their own neighborhoods) and could not shift around as needed. See Louis-Auguste Blanqui, 'Manual for an Armed Insurrection' (marxists.org) and Engels, 'Introduction to Karl Marx's "Class Struggles in France"' (MECW 27), 517-519.

of the machines is fundamentally opaque to them. The difference between entering values into a spreadsheet and baking bread is negligible to them. Concrete labour has become fundamentally abstract, scrambling at the same time distinctions between material and immaterial, manual and mental labour:

[20] Richard Sennett, *The Corrosion of Character: The Personal Consequences of Work in the New Capitalism* (W. W. Norton & Co. 2000), 68.

> Computerized baking has profoundly changed the balletic physical activities of the shop floor. Now the bakers make no physical contact with the materials or the loaves of bread, monitoring the entire process via on-screen icons which depict, for instance, images of bread color derived from data about the temperature and baking time of the ovens; few bakers actually see the loaves of bread they make. Their working screens are organized in the familiar Windows way; in one, icons for many more different kinds of bread appear than had been prepared in the past – Russian, Italian, French loaves all possible by touching the screen. Bread had become a screen representation.
>
> As a result of working in this way, the bakers now no longer actually know how to bake bread. Automated bread is no marvel of technological perfection; the machines frequently tell the wrong story about the loaves rising within, for instance, failing to gauge accurately the strength of the rising yeast, or the actual color of the loaf. The workers can fool with the screen to correct somewhat for these defects; what they can't do is fix the machines, or more important, actually bake bread by manual control when the machines all too often go down. Program-dependent laborers, they can have no hands-on knowledge. The work is no longer legible to them, in the sense of understanding what they are doing.[20]

There is an interesting paradox here, which Sennett draws out very nicely in the following pages: the more transparent and "user-friendly" the computerised processes are, the more opaque the total process they control becomes. His conclusion should trouble any simplistic conception of the powers of visibility or the "cognitive map" as such, a problem that Jameson recognised early on, declaring "informational technology the representational solution as well as the representational problem of [the] world system's cognitive mapping".[21] The problems for Sennett's workers, as well as for our blockaders, are practical as much as they are epistemological, a matter of doing and knowing together. Unless the representations such systems provide widen our capacity to do and to make, to effect changes upon the world, they will make that world more rather than less opaque, no matter how richly descriptive they might be. And though Sennett's discussion is geared only toward the world of labour (and imbued with typical left-wing nostalgia for the *savoir-faire* and stable identities that skilled work entailed) the problems of legibility pertain as much to our blockaders as to the dockworkers at the port. To persist beyond an initial moment, struggles need to recognise themselves in the effects they create, they need to be able to map out those effects, not just by positioning themselves within the abstract and concrete space of late capital, but within a political sequence that has both past and future, that opens onto a horizon of possibilities. All of this requires knowledge but it requires knowledge that can be practiced, that can be worked out.

Our blockaders are therefore dispossessed of usable knowledge by a technical system in which they appear only as incidental actors, as points of relay and insertion which require at most a stenographic compression of their immediate environs into a few kilobytes of usable information. Bernard Stiegler, who despite an often tedious Heideggerian theoretical apparatus is one of the best contemporary theorists of technology, describes this process as "cognitive and affective proletarianization", where proletarians are dispossessed, as producers, of *savoir faire* and, as consumers, of *savoir*

[21] Fredric Jameson, *The Geopolitical Aesthetic: Cinema and Space in the World System*, (Indiana University Press, 1995), 10.

vivre. This is part of a long history of what Stiegler calls "grammatization", in which knowledge and memory is discretised into reproducible and combinatorial bodily gestures – phonemes, graphemes, keystrokes, bits – and then exteriorised through inscription in matter.[22] The digital and telecommunication technology of contemporary grammatisation is the final stage of this process, such that our memories and cognitive faculties now exist in the data cloud, as it were, part of a distributed technological prosthesis without which we are effectively incapable of orienting ourselves or functioning. In this largely persuasive account, which thankfully cuts against the optimistic readings of information technology as a progressive socialisation of "general intellect", we are dispossessed not just of the means of production but the means of thought and feeling as well.

In many ways, Stiegler shares a great deal with the rich exploration of the concepts of alienation, fetishism and reification that followed the popularisation of the early Marx in the 1960s, by Herbert Marcuse, Guy Debord and others. We might, for this reason, wonder about the latent humanism in Stiegler. Sennett, however, provides us with an important caveat against reading Stiegler in humanist terms: whereas a certain kind of classic Marxist analysis might expect his bakers to want to reappropriate the knowledge of which they had been dispossessed by the machines, few of them have any such desires. Their real lives are elsewhere, and hardly any of them expect or desire dignity and meaning from their jobs as bakers. The only person who conforms to the expected outline of the alienated worker, in Sennett's bakery, is the foreman, who worked his way up from apprentice baker to manager, and takes the wastage and loss of skill in the bakery as a personal affront, imagining that if the bakery were a cooperative the workers might take more interest in knowing how things are done. The other workers, however, treat work not as the performance of a skill but as a series of indifferent applications of an

[22] Bernard Stiegler, *For a New Critique of Political Economy*, (Polity, 2010), 40-44.

abstract capacity to labour. Baking means little more than "pushing buttons in a Windows program designed by others".[23] The work is both illegible to them, and utterly alien to their own needs, but not alien in the classic sense that they recognise it as a lost or stolen part of themselves they hope to recover through struggle. This is one of the most important consequences of the restructuring of the labour process superintended by the logistics revolution: the casualisation and irregularisation of labour, the disaggregation of the work process into increasingly illegible and geographically separate component parts, as well as the incredible powers which capital now has to defeat any struggle for better conditions, mean that it is not only impossible for most proletarians to visualise their place within this complex system but it is also impossible for them to identify with that place as a source of dignity and satisfaction, since its ultimate meaning with regard to the total system remains elusive. Most workers today cannot say, as workers of old could (and often did): *It is we who built this world! It is we to whom this world belongs!* The restructuring of the mode of production and the subordination of production to the conditions of circulation therefore forecloses the classical horizon of proletarian antagonism: seizure of the means of production for the purposes of a worker-managed society. One cannot imagine seizing that which one cannot visualise, and inside of which one's place remains uncertain.

THE RECONFIGURATION THESIS

The difficulties which Sennett's bakers (or our blockaders) encounter are not simply failures of knowledge, ones that can be solved through pedagogical intervention; as valuable as a cognitive map of these processes might be, the problems we confront in *visualising* some self-management of existing productive means originate from the *practical* difficulties — in my view, impossibilities — that such a prospect would encounter. The opacity of the

[23] Sennett, *The Corrosion of Character*, 70.

system, in this regard, emerges from its intractability, and not the other way around. In an insightful article on the logistics industry and contemporary struggle, Alberto Toscano (who has lately devoted considerable effort to critiquing theorists of communisation) faults the "space-time of much of today's anticapitalism" for its reliance on "subtraction and interruption, not attack and expansion".[24] Toscano proposes, as an alternative, an anticapitalist logistics which treats the various productive sites and infrastructures of late capitalism as "potentially reconfigurable" rather than the object of "mere negation or sabotage". No doubt, any struggle which wants to overcome capitalism will need to consider "what use can be drawn from the dead labours which crowd the earth's crust", but there is no reason to assume from the start, as Toscano does, that all existing means of production must have some use beyond capital, and that all technological innovation must have, almost categorically, a progressive dimension which is recuperable through a process of "determinate negation". As we saw above, the use-value which the logistics industry produces is a set of protocols and techniques that enable firms to seek out the lowest wages anywhere in the world, and to evade the inconvenience of class struggle when it arises. In this sense, unlike other capitalist technologies, logistics is only partly about exploiting the efficiencies of machines in order to get products to market faster and more cheaply, since the main purpose of the faster and cheaper technologies is to offset the otherwise prohibitive cost of exploiting labour forces halfway around the world. The technological ensemble which logistics superintends is therefore fundamentally different than other ensembles such as the Fordist factory; it saves on labour costs by decreasing the wage, rather than increasing the productivity of labour. To put it in Marxist terms, it is absolute surplus value masquerading as relative surplus value. The use-value of logistics, for capital, is exploitation in its rawest form, and thus it is truly doubtful that logistics might form,

[24] Alberto Toscano, 'Logistics and Opposition', *Mute* 3, no. 2 (metamute.org).

as Toscano writes, "capitalism's pharmakon, the cause for its pathologies (from the damaging hypertrophy of long-distance transport of commodities to the aimless sprawl of contemporary conurbation) as well as the potential domain of anti-capitalist solutions".

For workers to seize the commanding heights offered by logistics — to seize, in other words, the control panel of the global factory — would mean for them to manage a system that is constitutively hostile to them and their needs, to oversee a system in which extreme wage differentials are built into the very infrastructure. Without those differentials, most supply-chains would become both wasteful and unnecessary. But perhaps "repurposing" means for Toscano instead a kind of making-do with the machinery of logistics as we find it, seeing what other purposes it can be put to, rather than imagining an appropriation of its commanding heights? Any revolutionary process will make do with what it finds available as a matter of necessity, but it is precisely the "convertibility" or "reconfigurability" of these technologies that seems questionable. The fixed capital of the contemporary production regime is designed for extraction of maximum surplus value; each component part is engineered for insertion into *this* global system; therefore, the presence of communist potentials as unintended features — "affordances", as they are sometimes called — of contemporary technology needs to be argued for, not assumed as a matter of course.[25] Much of the machinery of contemporary logistics aims to streamline the circulation of *commodities* and not use-values, to produce not the things that are necessary or beneficial but those that are profitable: individually packaged boxes of cereal, for instance, whose complex insignia distinguish them from the dozens of varieties of nearly identical cereals (sold and consumed in sizes and types that reflect certain social arrangements, such as the nuclear family). How much of the vaunted flexibility of the logistics system is really the flexibility of product

[25] Marxist theories of technology often diverge along two paths, each of which can be traced to the works of Marx. The dominant view holds that capitalist technologies are fundamentally progressive, first because they reduce necessary labour time and thereby potentially free humans from the necessity of labouring, and second because industrialisation effects a fundamental 'socialisation' of production, obliterating the hierarchies that once pertained to particular crafts (e.g. e.g. Marx, *Grundrisse* [MECW 29], 90-92 [Nicolaus trans.]). In this Orthodox account, communism is latent within the socialised, cooperative arrangement of the factory, whose technical substrate increasingly enters into crisis-producing contradiction with the inefficient and unplanned nature of the capitalist marketplace. But there is also

variety, of wage differentials and trade imbalances? How much would become useless once one eliminated the commodity-form, once one eliminated the necessity of buying and selling? Furthermore, the contemporary logistics system is designed for a particular international balance of trade, with certain countries as producers and others as consumers. This is a fact fundamentally entangled with the wage imbalances mentioned earlier, which means that the inequality of the global system in part has to do with the unequal distribution of productive means and the infrastructures of circulation—the concentration of port capacity on the West Coast of the US rather than the East Coast, for instance, because of the location of manufacturing in Asia. Rebalancing the amount of goods produced locally or at a distance—if such a thing were to be a part of a break with capitalist production—would mean an entirely different arrangement of infrastructures and probably different types of infrastructure as well (smaller ships, for instance).

We might also question the reconfiguration thesis from the perspective of scale. Because of the uneven distribution of productive means and capitals—not to mention the tendency for geographical specialisation, the concentration of certain lines in certain areas (textiles in Bangladesh, for instance)—the system is not scalable in any way but up. It does not permit partitioning by continent, hemisphere, zone or nation. It must be managed as a totality or not at all. Therefore, nearly all proponents of the reconfiguration thesis assume high-volume and hyper-global distribution in their socialist or communist system, even if the usefulness of such distributions beyond production for profit remain unclear. Another problem, though, is that administration at such a scale introduces a sublime dimension to the concept of "planning"; these scales and magnitudes are radically beyond human cognitive capacities. The level of an impersonal "administration of things" and the level of a "free association of producers"

a heterodox Marxist perspective on technology, whose exemplars are writers such as Raniero Panzieri and David Noble, and whose clearest sources lie in the chapter in Capital on 'Machinery and Large-Scale Industry,' and in particular, the section on the factory. There, Marx suggests that, in the modern factory system, capital's domination of labour 'acquires a technical and palpable reality'. In the factory 'the gigantic natural forces, and the mass of social labour embodied in the system of machinery... constitutes the power of the master' (Marx, *Capital* vol.1 [MECW 35], 420-430 [Fowkes trans.]). But if machinery is a materialisation of capitalist domination—an objectification of the 'master'—then we have every reason to doubt that we can undo such domination without negating the 'technical and palpable aspect of machinery. If workers were to seize are not so much in contradiction as separated by a vast abyss. Toscano leaves such an abyss marked by an ominous appeal to Herbert Marcuse's concept of "necessary alienation" as the unfortunate but necessary concomitant of maintenance of the technical system. Other partisans of the reconfiguration thesis, when questioned about the scaling-up of the emancipatory desires and needs of proletarian antagonists to a global administration invariably deploy the literal *deus ex machina* of supercomputers. Computers and algorithms, we are told, will determine how commodities are to be distributed; computers will scale up from the demands for freedom and equality of proletarian antagonists and figure out a way to distribute work and the products of work in a manner satisfactory to all. But how an algorithmically-mediated production would work, why it would differ from production mediated by competition and the price-mechanism remains radically unclear, and certainly unmuddied by any actual argument. Would labour-time still be the determinant of access to social wealth? Would free participation (in work) and free access (in necessaries) be facilitated in such a system? If the goal is rather a simple equality of producers — equal pay for equal work — how would one deal with the imbalances of productivity, morale and initiative, which result from the maintenance of the requirement that "he who does not work does not eat"? Is this what "necessary alienation" means?

But the non-scalarity (or unidirectional scalarity) of the logistics system introduces a much more severe problem. Even if global communist administration — by supercomputer, or by ascending tiers of delegates and assemblies — were possible and desirable on the basis of the given technical system, once we consider the *historical* character of communism, things seem much more doubtful. Communism does not drop from the sky, but must emerge from a revolutionary process, and given the present all or nothing character of the production machinery and self-manage the factories, this might only amount to another mode of administering the domination sedimented inside the production machinery. The heterodox perspective is obviously in line with the conclusions of this article, but much work remains to be done in developing an adequate theory of technology. We cannot merely invert the Orthodox, progressivist account of machinery which assumes that every advance of the productive forces constitutes an enlargement of the possibilities for communism and declare, in opposition, that all technology is politically negative or inherently capitalist. Rather, we have to examine technologies from a technical perspective, from the communist prospect, and consider what affordances they really do allow, given the tragic circumstances of their birth.

international division of labour—the concentration of manufacturing in a few countries, the concentration of productive capacity for certain essential lines of capital in a handful of factories, as mentioned above—any attempt to seize the means of production would require an *immediately global* seizure. We would need a revolutionary process so quickly successful and extensive that all long-distance supply chains ran between non-capitalist producers within a matter of months, as opposed to the much more likely scenario that a break with capital will be geographically concentrated at first and need to spread from there. In most cases, therefore, maintenance of these distributed production processes and supply-chains will mean trade with capitalist partners, an enchainment to production for profit (necessary for survival, we will be told by the pragmatists) the results of which will be nothing less than disastrous, as a study of the Russian and Spanish examples will show. In both cases, the need to maintain an export economy in order to buy crucial goods on the international markets—arms in particular—meant that revolutionary cadres and militants had to use direct and indirect force in order to induce workers to meet production targets. Raising productivity and increasing productive capacity *now* became the transitional step on the way to achieving communism *then*, and in anarchist Spain, as much as Bolshevist Russia, cadres set to work mimicking the dynamic growth of capitalist accumulation through direct political mechanisms, rather than the indirect force of the wage, though in both cases economic incentive structures (piece rates, bonus pay) were eventually introduced as matter of necessity. It is hard to see how anything but a new insurrectionary process—one mitigated against by the establishment of new disciplines and repressive structures—could have restored these systems even to the labour-note based "lower phase of communism" that Marx advocates in "Critique of the Gotha Program", let alone a society based upon free access and non-compelled labour.

The traditional discussions of such matters assume that, whereas underdeveloped countries like Russia and Spain had no choice but to develop their productive capacity first, proletarians in fully industrialised countries could immediately expropriate and self-manage the means of production without any need for forced development. This might have been true in the immediate postwar period, and as late as the 1970s, but once deindustrialisation began in earnest, the chance had been officially missed – the global restructuring and redistribution of productive means leaves us in a position that is probably as bad as, if not worse than, those early 20th-century revolutions, when some large percentage of the means of production for consumer goods were ready to hand, and one could locate, in one's own region, shoe factories and textile mills and steel refineries. A brief assessment of the workplaces in one's immediate environs should convince most of us – in the US at least, and I suspect most of Europe – of the utter unworkability of the reconfiguration thesis. The service and administrative jobs which most proletarians today work are meaningless except as points of intercalation within vast planetary flows – a megaretailer, a software company, a coffee chain, an investment bank, a non-profit organisation. Most of these jobs pertain to use-values that would be rendered non-uses by revolution. To meet their own needs and the needs of others, these proletarians would have to engage in the production of food and other necessaries, the capacity for which does not exist in most countries. The idea that 15% or so of workers whose activities would still be useful would work on behalf of others – as caretakers of a communist future – is politically non-workable, even if the system could produce enough of what people need, and trade for inputs didn't produce another blockage. Add to this the fact that the development of logistics itself and the credit system alongside it, greatly multiplies the power of capital to discipline rebellious zones through withdrawal of credit (capital flight), embargo, and punitive terms of trade.

HORIZONS AND PROSPECTS

The whole is the false, in this case, not so much because it can't be adequately represented or because any attempt at such representation does violence to its internal contradictions, but because all such global representations belie the fact that the whole can never be possessed as such. The totality of the logistics system belongs to capital. It is a view from everywhere (or nowhere), a view from space, that only capital as totalising, distributed process can inhabit. Only capital can fight us in every place at once, because capital is not in any sense a force with which we contend, but the very territory on which that contention takes place. Or rather, it *is* a force, but a field force, something which suffuses rather than opposes. Unlike capital, we fight in particular locations and moments – *here, there, now, then.* To be a partisan means, by necessity, to accept the partiality of perspective and the partiality of the combat we offer.

The weak tactics of the present – the punctual riot, the blockade, the occupation of public space – are not the strategic product of an antagonist consciousness that has misrecognised its enemy, or failed to examine adequately the possibilities offered by present technologies. On the contrary, the tactics of our blockaders emerge from a consciousness that has already surveyed the possibilities on offer, and understood, if only intuitively, how the restructuring of capital has foreclosed an entire strategic repertoire. The supply chains which fasten these proletarians to the planetary factory are radical chains in the sense that they go to the root, and must be torn out from the root as well. The absence of opportunities for "reconfiguration" will mean that in their attempts to break from capitalism proletarians will need to find other ways of meeting their needs. The logistical problems they encounter will have to do with replacing that which is fundamentally unavailable except through linkage to these planetary networks and the baleful consequences they bring. In other words, the creation of communism will require a massive process of delinking from the planetary factory as a matter of survival. We will not have the opportunity to use all (or even many) of the technical means that we find, since so many of these will be effectively orphaned by a break with capitalist production. But what, then, of strategy? If theory is the horizon which opens from present conditions of struggle, strategy is something different, less a horizon than a prospect. Strategy is a particular moment when theory reopens to practice, suggesting not just a possible but a desirable course of action. If a horizon places us in front of a range of possibilities, the strategic moment comes when struggles reach a certain crest, an eminence, from which a narrower set of options opens up — a prospect. Prospects are a middle ground between where we are and the far horizon of communisation.

What are our prospects, then, based upon the recent cycle of struggles? We now know that the restructuring of the capital–labour relationship has made intervention in the sphere of circulation an obvious and in many ways effective tactic. The blockade, it seems, might assume an importance equal to the strike in the coming years, as will occupations of public space and struggles over urban and rural environments remade to become better conduits for flows of labour and capital — as recent struggles in both Turkey and Brazil have demonstrated. Our prospects are such that, instead of propagandising for forms of workplace action that are unlikely to succeed or generalise, we might better accept our new strategic horizon and work, instead, to disseminate information about how interventions in this sphere might become more effective, what their limits are, and how such limits could be overcome. We might work to disseminate the idea that the seizure of the globally-distributed factory is no longer a meaningful horizon, and we might essay to map out the new relations of production in a way that takes account of this fact. For instance, we might try to graph the flows and linkages around us in ways that comprehend their brittleness as well as the most effective ways they might be blocked as part of the conduct of particular struggles. These would be semi-local maps – maps that operate from the perspective of a certain zone or area. From this kind of knowledge, one might also develop a functional understanding of the infrastructure of capital, such that one then knew which technologies and productive means would be orphaned by a partial or total delinking from planetary flows, which ones might alternately be conserved or converted, and what the major practical and technical questions facing a revolutionary situation might look like. How to ensure that there is water and that the sewers function? How to avoid meltdown of nuclear reactors? What does local food production look like? What types of manufacture happen nearby, and what kinds of things can be done with its production machinery? This would be a process of inventory, taking stock of things we encounter in our immediate environs, that does not imagine mastery from the standpoint of the global totality, but rather a process of bricolage from the standpoint of partisan fractions who know they will have to fight from particular, embattled locations, and win their battles successively rather than all at once. None of this means setting up a blueprint for the conduct of struggles, a transitional program. Rather, it means producing the knowledge which the experience of past struggles has already demanded and which future struggles will likely find helpful.

THE LIMIT POINT OF CAPITALIST EQUALITY

Notes toward an abolitionist antiracism

Chris Chen

Without an account of the relationship between "race" and the systematic reproduction of the class relation, the question of revolution as the overcoming of entrenched social divisions can only be posed in a distorted and incomplete form. And without an understanding of the dynamics of racialisation – from capitalism's historical origins in "primitive accumulation" to the US state's restructuring in the post-World War II era – continuing struggles against evolving forms of racial rule can only be misrecognised as peripheral to an ultimately race-neutral conflict between capital and labour. Rather than waning with the decline of what is sometimes construed as a vestigial system of folk beliefs, resistance to racial subordination in the US has continued. "Race" has not withered away: rather, it has been reconfigured in the face of austerity measures and an augmented "post-racial" security state which has come into being to manage the ostensible racial threats to the nation posed by black wageless life, Latino immigrant labour, and "Islamic terrorism".

Through "race", black chattel slavery in the United States constituted "free" labour as white, and whiteness as unenslaveability and unalienable property. The formal abolition of slavery has subsequently come to define the American achievement of what Marx called "double freedom": the "freedom" of forcible separation from the means of production, and the "freedom" to sell labour-power to the collective class of owners of those means.[1] However, "race" doesn't simply complicate any periodisation of the historical origins of capitalism; it was the protagonist of a global array of national liberation, anti-apartheid, and civil rights movements in the mid-twentieth century. A planetary anti-racist offensive called into question nearly four and a half centuries of racial "common sense" and largely discredited white supremacy as explicit state policy. "Race" has been reconfigured in response to this world-historical anti-racist upsurge, and continues to exist as a body of ideas – but also as a relation of domination inside and

[1] See 'The Logic of Gender' in this issue.

outside the wage relation – reproduced through superficially non-racial institutions and policies. Two dynamics have reproduced "race" in the US since the mid-twentieth-century anti-racist movements: first, economic subordination through racialised wage differentials and superfluisation, and second, the racialising violence and global reach of the penal and national security state. Most contemporary ascriptive racialisation processes are to a great extent politically unrepresentable as "race" matters because they have been superficially coded as race-neutral – disciplinary state apparatuses, for example, defined through discourses of "national security threats", "illegal immigration", and "urban crime".

Without an understanding of the structuring force of "race" in US foreign policy and as a driver of the rise of the US carceral state in response to the end of legal segregation, one can have only a partial understanding of the institutional fusion and seemingly unlimited expansion of police and military power over the last forty years. The anti-racist critiques of recent social movements like Occupy Wall Street, and the consolidation of opposition under the banner of a politics of decolonisation, illuminate a major faultline in US political life cleaving a "politics of race" from a "politics of class". The intellectual polarisation between these two political formations has revealed the inadequacy of both Marxist approaches to class, and theories of "race" couched in an idiom of cultural difference rather than domination.

Overlapping with – yet conceptually distinct from – class, culture, caste, gender, nation, and ethnicity, "race" is not only a system of ideas but an array of ascriptive racialising procedures which structure multiple levels of social life. Despite its commitment to challenging racial ideology as the assignment of differential value to physical appearance and ancestry, much anti-racist analysis and practice continues to treat "race" as a noun, as a property or attribute of identities or groups, rather than as a set of ascriptive processes which impose fictive identities and subordinate racialised populations. To distinguish racial ascription from voluntary acts of cultural identification – and from a range of responses to racial rule from flight to armed revolt – requires a shift in focus from "race" to racism. But focusing on the phenomenon of racism tends to narrow the terrain upon which "race" is structurally enforced to personal attitudes or racial ideologies rather than institutional processes which may generate profound racial disparities without requiring individual racist beliefs or intentions.

As a result, "race" gets theorised in divergent cultural or economic terms as evidence of the need to either affirm denigrated group identities or integrate individuals more thoroughly into capitalist markets momentarily distorted by individual prejudice. On the one hand, "race" is a form of cultural stigmatisation and misrepresentation requiring personal, institutional, and/or state recognition. On the other, "race" is a system of wage differentials, wealth stratification, and occupational and spatial segregation. Whether defended or derided by critics across the political spectrum, the concept of racial or cultural identity has become a kind of proxy for discussing "race" matters in general. Conversely, dismissals of "identity politics" grounded in functionalist or epiphenomenalist accounts of "race" propose an alternative socialist and social democratic "politics of class" based upon essentially the same political logic of affirming subjects – i.e. workers – within and sometimes against capitalism. This division between economic and cultural forms of "race" naturalises racial economic inequality and transforms the problem of racial oppression and exploitation into either an epiphenomenon of class or the misrecognition of identity.[2]

Both the cultural and economic stratification theories have tended to frame racial inequality as fundamentally a problem of the unequal distribution of existing privilege,

2 See Nancy Fraser and Linda Alcoff, who stake out nuanced, though largely opposed, theoretical positions on the political possibilities and limits of 'identity politics'. As this article goes on to argue, both positions are fundamentally informed by the historical promise of a social-democratic coalitional subject, uniting labour, feminist, and anti-racist political campaigns. See Alcoff, *Visible identities: Race, Gender, and the Self* (Oxford University Press 2006); and Fraser, 'Rethinking Recognition', *New Left Review* 3 (May-June 2000).

The Limit Point of Capitalist Equality

power, and resources while continuing to posit the economy as fundamentally race-neutral or even as an engine of racial progress. A dearth of materialist analyses of the bundle of ascriptive and punitive procedures organised under the sign of "race" has meant that critics from across the political spectrum have continued to downplay the severity and extent of racial domination organised by putatively "colourblind" social institutions. Saddled with discourses of meritocratic racial uplift, "race" continues to be represented either as a cultural particularity or as a deviation from colourblind civic equality. In either case, "race" is articulated in terms of real or illusory difference from a political or cultural norm rather than as a form of structural coercion.

If "race" is thus understood in terms of difference rather than domination, then anti-racist practice will require the affirmation of stigmatised identities rather than their abolition as indices of structural subordination. Formulating an abolitionist anti-racism would require imagining the end of "race" as hierarchical assignment, rather than a denial of the political salience of cultural identities. "Race" here names a relation of subordination. The conceptual elision of the difference between racial ascription and individual and group responses to racial interpellation is endemic in much of the literature either denouncing or defending a politics of identity. From the point of view of emancipation, a social order freed from racial and gender domination would not necessarily spell the end of identity as such, but rather of ascriptive processes so deeply bound up with the historical genesis and trajectory of global capitalism that the basic categories of collective sociality would be transformed beyond recognition.[3]

A precipitous 21st century decline in the US labour share of business income, and the transition to austerity, has completely altered the terrain, the stakes, and the chances of success for not only the American labour movement but all contemporary anti-racist

[3] See 'Spontaneity, Mediation, Rupture' in this issue.

political struggles as well. The legacy of racial and gender exclusions which have structured the US labour movement has been steadily eroded at the same time that the relative size and strength of organised labour has dwindled. Because the public sector, with its robust anti-discrimination mandates, represents the last bastion of US organised labour, hostility to the US labour movement is frequently couched in racist rhetoric. As Kyriakides and Torres argue, 1960s-era visions of a Third World, non-aligned, or anti-colonial coalitional subject in the US have, in an age of declining growth, fractured into multiple "ethnically determined subjects of identity in competition not only for a shred of an ever-shrinking economic settlement but for recognition of their suffering conferred by a nation-state in which the Right won the political battle and the Left won the culture war."[4]

[4] Christopher Kyriakides and Rodolfo Torres, *Race Defaced: Paradigms of Pessimism, Politics of Possibility* (Stanford University Press 2012), 119.

[5] Barbara J. Fields, 'Whiteness, racism, and identity', *International Labor and Working Class History* 60 (Fall 2001), 48-56.

ADDENDUM: ON TERMINOLOGY

"Race" has been variously described as an illusion, a social construction, a cultural identity, a biological fiction but social fact, and an evolving complex of social meanings. Throughout this article, "race" appears in quotation marks in order to avoid attributing independent causal properties to objects defined by ascriptive processes. Simply put, "race" is the consequence and not the cause of *racial ascription* or *racialisation processes* which justify historically asymmetrical power relationships through reference to phenotypical characteristics and ancestry: "Substituted for racism, race transforms the act of a subject into an attribute of the object."[5]

I have also enclosed "race" in quotation marks in order to suggest three overlapping dimensions of the term: as an index of varieties of material inequality, as a bundle of ideologies and processes which create a racially stratified social order, and as an evolving history of *struggle against racism and racial domination* — a history which has often risked reifying "race" by revaluing imposed identities, or reifying "racelessness" by affirming liberal fictions of atomistically isolated individuality. The intertwining of racial domination with the class relation holds out the hope of systematically dismantling "race" as an indicator of unequal structural relations of power. "Race" can thus be imagined as an emancipatory category not from the point of view of its affirmation, but through its abolition.

1 A BRIEF HISTORY OF RACIAL SUBORDINATION: from *limpieza de sangre* to global superfluity

The trajectory of racial domination, from slavery to racialised surplus populations, traces a long historical arc between the colonial creation of "race" in 16th century Spanish notions of "purity of blood" (*limpieza de sangre*), and its structural reproduction under a restructured global capitalism — a history which can only be briefly sketched here. The genealogy of "race" and its precursors can be traced back to the spatial expansion of European colonialism — from the baroque racialised caste system of Spanish and Portuguese colonial administrations to the later, more Manichaean racial order produced by the British colonisation of the Americas, Africa, and Asia. The extermination, enslavement, or colonisation of racialised populations — often at the hands of a colonial class of indentured servants — consolidated "race" through the waning of European servitude and the emergence of black chattel slavery. This was the flipside of what Marxists call "proletarianisation". Marked by ongoing histories of exclusion from the wage and violent subjugation to varieties of "unfree labour", racialised populations were inserted into early capitalism in ways that continue to define contemporary surplus populations.

The cursory treatment of racial violence in the historical narration of "primitive accumulation" remains a fundamental blind spot in Marxist analyses of the relationship between "race" and capitalism. In the era of the *conquista* and in the transition to capitalism, "race" came into being through plunder, enslavement, and colonial violence. At the very same time, primitive accumulation in England produced a dispossessed and superfluous ex-peasantry, for the factory system that might absorb them had not yet been created. Many of these ex-peasants were eventually sent to the colonies, or inducted into imperial enterprises – the navy, merchant marines, etc. In the 18th and 19th centuries, more of these surplus populations were integrated into the developing capitalist economy, whether as chattel slaves or as wage labourers, according to an increasingly intricate typology of "race". Finally, after decades of compounding increases in labour productivity, capital began to expel more labour from the production process than was absorbed. That, in turn, produced yet another kind of superfluous population in the form of a disproportionately non-white industrial reserve army of labour. At the periphery of the global capitalist system, capital now renews "race" by creating vast superfluous urban populations from the close to one billion slum-dwelling and desperately impoverished descendants of the enslaved and colonised.

In the 21st century, the substantial over-representation of racialised US groups among the unemployed and underemployed – "last hired and first fired" – demonstrates the concessionary, uneven incorporation of these groups into a system of highly racialised wage differentials, occupational segregation, and precarious labour. As capital sloughs off these relative surplus populations in the core, the surplus capital produced by fewer and more intensively exploited workers in the Global North scours the globe for lower wages, and reappears as the racial threat of cheap labour from the Global South.

The Limit Point of Capitalist Equality

In the US, with the end of secure wage labour and the withdrawal of public welfare provisions, a massive "post-racial" security state has come into being to manage the supposed civilisational threats to the nation — by policing black wageless life, deporting immigrant labour, and waging an unlimited "War on Terror". The catastrophic rise of black mass incarceration, the hyper-militarisation of the southern US border, and the continuation of open-ended security operations across the Muslim world, reveal how "race" remains not only a probabilistic assignment of relative economic value but also an index of differential vulnerability to state violence.[6]

[6] See Nikhil Pal Singh, 'Racial Formation in an Age of Permanent War' in Daniel HoSang, Oneka LaBennett, and Laura Pulido, eds, *Racial Formation in the Twenty-First Century* (University of California 2012), 276-301.

2 READING WHITE SUPREMACY BACK INTO THE "BASE"

While Marx and Engels generally insisted on the need for workers to oppose racism in its more blatant 19th century manifestations, they did not attempt to articulate the relation of "race" and class at a categorical level.[7] As Derek Sayer observes, "Marx was a man of his time and place":

> Like most other Victorians, Marx thought both "race" and family natural categories (even if subject to some "historical modification"), and had little trouble in distinguishing between "civilisation" (which for him was white, western and modern) and "barbarism." His views on the beneficial results of European colonialism would embarrass many twentieth-century Marxists, notwithstanding his denunciations of the violence of its means…[8]

The theoretical relation between "race" and class has subsequently become the subject of a long debate in the varieties of academic Marxism that emerged as a "New Left" generation inspired by the struggles of the sixties entered the university. In an early and influential contribution to this conversation, Stuart Hall asserted that "race" was "the modality in which class is 'lived', the

[7] Marx's pronouncement that 'labour in the white skin can never free itself as long as labour in the black skin is branded' ([MECW 35], 305) is often quoted by his defenders, as are his denunciations of anti-Irish racism. Less often mentioned are Marx and Engels's opinions about 'lazy Mexicans' and the cause of the political immaturity of Lafargue, Marx's son-in-law, being 'the stigma of his Negro heritage' and 'Creole blood'. See Frederick Engels, 'Democratic Pan-Slavism', *Neue Rheinsiche Zeitung* 231 (MECW 8),

medium through which class relations are experienced, the form in which it is appropriated and 'fought through'."[9] Hall and other cultural theorists supplemented Marxist categories of "base" and "superstructure" with the ideas of Western Marxist figures such as Louis Althusser and Antonio Gramsci. Gramsci in particular, and his development of the concept of "hegemony"—with its room for more nuanced theories of culture, ideology, and politics—has been a central reference in academic attempts to rearticulate the relation of "race" and class. In this vein, anti-racist struggle is viewed as a contest for "democratic hegemony", which followed from the mid-twentieth century discrediting of white supremacy as explicit state policy.[10] Until recently, the Gramscian analytic of hegemony, which has informed both Marxist cultural theory and many highly influential critical accounts of "race" and slavery, has largely gone unquestioned.[11]

Recent critical writing by Frank Wilderson—part of a group of contemporary theoreticians of black politics whom Wilderson has broadly labelled "Afro-pessimist", including Saidiya Hartman, Hortense Spillers, Jared Sexton, and Joy James—sharply challenges the appropriateness of this Gramscian framework. Wilderson assesses the limits of a political economy of "race" centered on wage work, rather than on direct relations of racial violence and terror—from black chattel slavery to black mass incarceration. In contrast to a Marxist perspective that focuses on the struggle around the wage, or around the terms of exploitation, Wilderson identifies "the despotism of the unwaged relation" as the engine that drives anti-black racism.[12]

Wilderson presents a devastating critique of the relevance of a Gramscian analysis of hegemony for understanding structural anti-black violence. For Wilderson it is the focus on the wage which leads to the inability of Marxism to conceptualise gratuitous violence

362; Babacar Camara, *Marxist Theory, Black/African Specificities, and Racism* (Lexington 2008), 71-2.

[8] Derek Sayer, 'Introduction' to *Readings from Karl Marx* (Routledge 1989), ixx-xx.

[9] Stuart Hall, 'Race, Articulation, and Societies Structured in Dominance', *Black British Cultural Studies* (University of Chicago Press 1996), 55.

[10] Michael Omi and Howard Winant, *Racial Formation in the United States* (Routledge 1994).

[11] For Marxist alternatives to the Gramscian analytic of hegemony, see Bonefeld Holloway, Richard Gunn, and Kosmas Psychopedis *Open Marxism*, vols. 1-3 (Pluto 1995).

[12] Frank Wilderson III, 'Gramsci's Black Marx: Whither the Slave in Civil Society?' *Social Identities* 9 (2003), 230.

The Limit Point of Capitalist Equality

against black bodies, a "relation of terror as opposed to a relation of hegemony".[13] Wilderson is right to point out that "the privileged subject of Marxist discourse is a subaltern who is approached by variable capital — a wage."[14] This is because access to the wage was a prerequisite for both labour and later identity-based civil struggles after the end of legal segregation, throughout the 20th century. From the point of view of the classical worker's movement, racism was thus seen as an unfortunate impediment to a process of progressive integration into an expanding working class. Yet it is precisely the racialisation of the unwaged, unfree, and excluded which constitutes civil society as a space where recognition is bestowed via formal wage contracts and abstract citizenship rights for its members.[15] Thus for Wilderson "the black subject reveals Marxism's inability to think white supremacy as the base."[16]

Against a Gramscian reading of Marx, with its affirmationist focus on wage labour, value-form theorists provide an alternative framework for charting the complex interplay between direct and indirect forms of domination. If capital is first and foremost an indirect or impersonal form of domination (unlike black chattel slavery or feudalism, for example), in which production relations are not subordinated to direct social relations, there is no necessary incompatibility between this and the persistence or growth of direct, overt forms of racial and gender domination. At play here are not only unwaged, coerced or dependent forms of labour, but also, crucially, the management of those populations which have become redundant in relation to capital. Such populations are expendable but nonetheless trapped within the capital relation, because their existence is defined by a generalised commodity economy which does not recognise their capacity to labour. The management of such populations could be said to be "form-determined" by the capital relation without being subsumed by it.

[13] Ibid., 230.

[14] Ibid., 225.

[15] For a book-length critique of the fiction of 'colour-blind' and gender neutral participatory parity which governs much social contractarian thought, see Charles W. Mills, *The Racial Contract* (Cornell UP 1997); Carole Pateman, *The Sexual Contract* (Stanford UP 1988); Pateman and Mills, *Contract and Domination* (Polity 2007).

[16] Wilderson, 'Gramsci's Black Marx: Whither the Slave in Civil Society?', 225.

The "form-determination" theory of the state may also help overcome some of the limits of a Gramscian view of the state as an object over which contending social forces struggle to gain control. From the "state-derivation debate" of the 1970s there emerged an alternative view of the state as a particular manifestation of the capital relation – constituted by the separation of the indirect, impersonal relations of production from direct political power. Thus the state, with its expanded penal or carceral capacities, can impose direct relations of racial domination while for instance involving itself in the disciplinary regulation and expulsion of immigrant labour. In those relations mediated by "free" exchange, where wage labour as a commodity is traded, the state is obliged to ensure the terms of exchange and contract, while unwaged relations put one or both parties in the relation potentially outside or beyond the law. The increasingly punitive criminalisation of the purchase, sale, and transportation of illicit drugs provides perhaps one of the most infamous examples of a racialised and racialising informal economy fundamentally structured by state violence. Women's former legal status as chattel vis-à-vis marriage offers another, in which women did not traditionally have protection from their husbands within the law, but only protection from men who were not their husbands. The limited protection of this legal status as chattel was revoked in the case of black domestic labourers in order to rationalise widespread rape and sexual exploitation by white male employers.[17] In either case, the racial division of both productive and reproductive labour consistently maintains racial hierarchies within gender categories, and gender hierarchies within racial categories.[18]

The workers' movement – with its valorisation of wage-labour, work, and the worker as the subject of history – failed to grasp that wage-labour is not the only stable form of exploitation on the basis of which capitalists can profit. Capitalism has not only proven fully compatible with unfree labour – from slavery, indentured servitude, convict

[17] See Evelyn Nakano Glenn, 'From Servitude to Service Work: Historical Continuities in the Racial Division of Paid Reproductive labour', *Signs* 18: 1 (1992), 1-43.

[18] As P. Valentine has observed, 'rigorous efforts to engage with and integrate analyses of race that do not mesh seamlessly with Marxist categories' will inevitably require both rethinking some of those categories and challenging some entrenched orthodoxies of anti-racist thought.' P. Valentine, 'The Gender Distinction in Communisation Theory', *Lies* 1 (2012), 206. This article is in part an attempt to respond to this invitation.

The Limit Point of Capitalist Equality **213**

leasing, and debt peonage to gendered forms of homework and unwaged reproductive labour – *it has required the systematic racialisation of this labour through the creation of an array of effectively non-sovereign raced and gendered subjects*. These modes of exploitation are not destined to disappear with the expansion of capitalist social relations around the world – e.g. through the massive campaigns of independent states in Africa, Latin America, and Asia to subjugate local populations to projects of industrialisation. Instead they are reproduced through the creation of caste-like surplus populations, deserted by the wage but still imprisoned within capitalist markets. "Race" is not extrinsic to capitalism or simply the product of specific historical formations such as South African Apartheid or Jim Crow America. Likewise, capitalism does not simply incorporate racial domination as an incidental part of its operations, but from its origins systematically begins producing and reproducing "race" as global surplus humanity.

As Marx famously noted, the basis for "primitive accumulation", requiring the dispossession of the peasantry in England and Scotland, lay in New World plantation slavery, resource extraction, and the extermination of non-European populations on a world scale:

> The discovery of gold and silver in America, the extirpation, enslavement and entombment in mines of the aboriginal population, the beginning of the conquest and looting of the East Indies, the turning of Africa into a warren for the commercial hunting of blackskins, signalised the rosy dawn of the era of capitalist production. These idyllic proceedings are the chief moment of primitive accumulation. On their heels treads the commercial war of the European nations, with the globe for a theatre. It begins with the revolt of the Netherlands from Spain, assumes giant dimensions in England's Anti-Jacobin War, and is still going on in the opium wars against China, &c.[19]

[19] Marx, *Capital*, vol. 1 (MECW 35), 739.

While non-racially determined varieties of slave labour predated the European colonial "Age of Discovery", capitalism bears the unique distinction of forging a systematic racist doctrine from the 16th to 19th centuries – culminating in 19th century anthropological theories of scientific racism – to justify racial domination, colonial plunder, and an array of racially delineated varieties of unfree labour and unequal citizenship. The history of capitalism isn't simply the history of the proletarianisation of an independent peasantry but of the violent racial domination of populations whose valorisation as wage labour, to reverse a common formulation, has been merely historically contingent: "socially dead" African slaves, the revocable sovereignty and *terra nullius* of indigenous peoples, and the nerveless, supernumerary body of the coolie labourer.

Racial disparities have been reproduced as an inherent category of capitalism since its origins not primarily through the wage, but through its absence. The initial moment of contact between a European colonial order and an unwaged, racialised "outside" to capital has been progressively systematised within capitalism itself as a racialised global division of labour and the permanent structural oversupply of such labour, which has produced "one billion city-dwellers who inhabit postmodern slums".[20]

[20] Mike Davis, *Planet of Slums* (Verso 2006), 19.

Insofar as labour markets organise the ratio of paid to unpaid labour, "race" as a marker of economic subordination is grounded both in a permanently superfluous population and entrenched racialised wage differentials. The expulsion of living labour from the production process places a kind of semi-permeable racialising boundary bifurcating productive and unproductive populations even within older racial categories: a kind of flexible global colour line separating the formal and informal economy, and waged from wageless life. Though this wageless colour line is minimally permeable and explicit racial criteria are no longer formally sanctioned, the material reproduction of racial domination, including

The Limit Point of Capitalist Equality

the proliferation of intra-national non-white ethnic hierarchies, is grounded in intertwined processes of exclusion from the wage, the increasing criminalisation of informal economies, and elevated vulnerability to state terror.

3 RACIAL DOMINATION AFTER THE "RACIAL BREAK"

What Howard Winant and Michael Omi have called the racial "break" or "great transformation"—driven by a world-historical anti-racist upsurge of decolonisation, civil rights, and anti-apartheid social movements in the mid-twentieth century—has discredited white supremacy as explicit state policy across the globe. For Omi and Winant, racial domination has given way to the struggle over racial hegemony, and coercion has given way to consent. But fifty years after the racial "break", racial domination has also evolved. Many ostensibly "post-colonial" states have resorted to racial violence and ethnic cleansing in the name of nation-building and economic development. After the "racial break", capital and race intertwine both inside and outside the wage relation. Insofar as labour markets organise the ratio of paid to unpaid labour, "race" as a marker of economic subordination is grounded both in a permanently superfluous population and entrenched wage differentials. After the repeal of most Jim Crow laws and racialised national immigration restrictions, two anti-racist political orientations emerged. In the case of US black-freedom struggles after World War II, persistent racialised wage differentials—and racial discrimination in housing, education, and credit markets—became the target of a late civil-rights-movement politics of equitable inclusion and electoral representation. At the same time, racial exclusion from the wage, *de facto* segregation in ghettos and exposure to systemic police violence, made state institutions—like welfare, prisons, and policing—the target of a black feminist welfare-reform movement, waves of ghetto and prison riots, and a more militant politics of self-defense and self-assertion.[21]

[21] Recent studies of the history of armed self-defense in the Civil Rights Movement, for example by groups like the Deacons for Defense and Justice, have emphasised the complexity of the commitment of movement activists to Ghandian strategic nonviolence. See Akinyele Omowale Umoja, *We Will Shoot Back: Armed Resistance in the Mississippi Freedom Movement* (NYU Press 2013); Simon Wendt, *The Spirit and the Shotgun: Armed Resistance and the Struggle for Civil Rights* (University Press of Florida 2007).

Since the attacks of September 11, 2001, popular US stereotypes of the relative economic productivity of racial subgroups have justified the exposure of such groups to state surveillance, policing or incarceration – from border patrol shootings of "illegals" to black mass-incarceration. At the same time, the "post-racial" civilising mission of the US, and its prosecution of a multi-trillion dollar military campaign across the Islamic world, has been vouchsafed by a national mythology of the progressive overcoming of the legacy of slavery and legal segregation.

The changing relationship between the US state and superfluous domestic populations highlights the global, foundational role of state violence as a racialisation process. The role of the state itself as an ostensibly neutral agent of racial reform, rather than the principal agent of racial violence, provides the missing third term in theorising the relationship between race and capital. Contemporary US racial politics is fundamentally structured by the decline of US global economic hegemony and by the hyper-militarisation of a "post-racial" security state in response to three racialised "civilisational" threats: the criminal threat of black surplus populations, the demographic threat of Latino immigrant labour, and the unlimited national security threat posed by an elastically conceived Islamic terrorist menace whose adherents are subject to collective punishment, torture, and preemptive eradication. All three are directly targeted and racialised by the state's penal, citizenship-conferring, and domestic security institutions. The rise of the anti-black US carceral state from the 1970s onward exemplifies rituals of state and civilian violence which enforce the racialisation of wageless life, and the racial ascription of wagelessness. From the point of view of capital, "race" is renewed not only through persistent racialised wage differentials, or the kind of occupational segregation posited by earlier "split labour market" theories of race, but through the racialisation of unwaged surplus or superfluous populations from Khartoum to the slums of Cairo.[22]

22 To be clear, these populations are not outside but firmly within capitalism—with labour regulation enforced by an array of punitive state apparatuses—so that while the wage no longer directly mediates collective access to basic needs like food and shelter, a vast informal economy has arisen for securing the basic means of survival. In the example of the partial proletarianisation of the Chinese peasantry and the creation of a massive, 160-million-person rural migrant labour force, agricultural workers, or small peasants, have often become unwaged, self-employed informal sector workers. The historical workers' movement's dream (a dream which also sustained the US civil rights movement and an array of anti-colonial national liberation movements), of progressive incorporation into the wage, has run

4 "RACE" AND SURPLUS HUMANITY

The colonial and racial genealogy of European capitalism has been encoded directly into the economic "base" through an ongoing history of racial violence which structures both unfree and informal labour, and which binds surplus populations to capitalist markets. If superfluity, stratification, and wage differentials are deracialised and the racial content of such categories rendered contingent, then "race" can only appear as epiphenomenal, and possess a *de facto* "specificity", which severs any causal link between capitalism and racialisation. The racial typologies which emerged from and enabled the spatial expansion of European capitalism as a mode of production, have been renewed over the course of centuries by an immanent tendency within capitalism to produce surplus populations in ghettos, slums, and favelas throughout the world. After the mid-twentieth century racial "break", formal decolonisation — in places like Brazil, sub-Saharan Africa and South Asia — left in its wake developmentalist states which absorbed ideologies of industrialisation and, so also, racialised indigenous populations, ethnic groups, and stigmatised castes as peripheral to the wage relation. Such populations will never be fully integrated into capitalist accumulation processes except as bodies to be policed, warehoused, or exterminated. up against the reality of persistent structural unemployment and superfluity.

In the US, the postwar Keynesian state's grudging extension of public social provisions to non-white communities in the 1960s has now been withdrawn and largely replaced by carceral and state-mandated work regimes applied to disposable populations who inhabit the politically unrepresentable dead zones of raced, gendered, and sexualised poverty. The only alternative to low wage, precarious service work for these populations is a criminalised informal-economy abutting America's vast carceral system. The US in particular has served as a global model for a "new government of social insecurity" founded on a punitive upsurge in surveillance, policing, and incarceration in response to the disappearance of secure wage work.[23]

"Race" is thus rooted in two overlapping processes of allocation and control. Past and present racial discrimination is cumulative and distributes precarity, unemployment, and informality unevenly across the economy along "race" and gender lines. But "race" is also operationalised in various state and civilian political projects of social control which classify and coerce "deserving" and "undeserving" fractions of various racial groups while determining their fitness for citizenship. Eroding the institutional separation between policing, border securitisation, and global warfare, a massively expanded security state now sends 1 in 3 black men to prison in their lifetime, deports nearly half a million undocumented immigrants annually, has exterminated anywhere from 100,000 to over a million civilians in Iraq alone, and is now gearing up for a $46 billion dollar "border surge" which includes drone surveillance and biometric exit scanning. 21st century "race" emerges from this matrix of securitisation.

[23] Loïc Wacquant, *Punishing the Poor: The Neoliberal Government of Social Insecurity* (Duke University Press 2009). See 'A Rising Tide Lifts All Boats', in this issue, for a discussion of how such a model was developed in the case of Britain.

5 THE TROUBLE WITH "CLASS": class politics as identity politics

As a rhetoric of racial diversity has been used increasingly to conceal or even justify deepening economic inequality, recent theorists from Slavoj Žižek and Ellen Meiksins Wood to Walter Benn Michaels contend that what they call multinational or neoliberal capitalism has come to champion a "politics of race" against a "politics of class". For these critics, identity-based social movements, and liberal multiculturalism in particular, is at best indifferent and at worst hostile to what Michaels considers the more urgent problem of class inequality. Conversely, anti-racist theorists from Howard Winant to David Theo Goldberg have argued tirelessly for the irreducibility of "race" to political economy. The institutionally reinforced division between anti-racism and Marxism has a long history. It has been a commonplace of recent popular historical accounts of the political trajectory of the 1960s-era "New Left" to blame the "fragmentation" of a unitary revolutionary class subject on the emergence of various anti-racist struggles: from US ethnic nationalisms aligned with mid-twentieth century African and Asian anticolonial movements; to black feminist critiques of the centrality of white, heterosexual, middle class women's experiences in second-wave feminism; to what both liberal and conservative critics have lamented as the rise of a balkanising "identity politics".

The intellectual polarisation of theoretical traditions which address either race or class could be termed the "unhappy marriage of anti-racism and Marxism". In the latter half of the twentieth century, with the waning of Third Worldist, Maoist, Guevarist or World-Systems Marxist analyses of "race" and colonialism — and of bodies of writing aligned with and informed by mass anti-capitalist and anti-racist political movements — academic theorists have invoked Marx to reread "race" as historical contingency. "Race" typically persists in academic Marxist discourse as a social division internal to the working class and sown by economic elites in order to drive down wages, fragment worker insurgency, and create the permanent threat of a nonwhite reserve army of labour. In these accounts "race" becomes a functional or derivative component of class rule. This functionalist or "class reductionist" account of "race" has been thoroughly challenged by anti-racist scholars over the last half century, yet these challenges have customarily emphasised the irreducibility or relative autonomy of "race" as one among many equivalent though entangled systems of domination which can be simply superadded to "class". In turn, both Marxist and anti-racist theories assert, though for vastly different reasons, that there is no constitutive relation between "race" and capitalism.

Sweeping critiques of "identity politics", or of liberal multiculturalism as neoliberal mystification, conceal a deeper elision of the identitarian logic at work in a socialist and social democratic "politics of class". The classical workers' movement, with its concept of "class consciousness", was premised upon a dream that the widespread affirmation of a working-class identity could serve as the basis for workers' hegemony – within nationally constituted zones of capital accumulation – and so also for a workers' revolution. Like much contemporary anti-racist scholarship, the Marxist critique of identity politics typically *remakes capitalism as a problem of identity*, specifically of class identity, and reduces structural exploitation to distributive inequalities in wealth. Labour and identity-based struggles, assumed to be qualitatively different in such accounts, are in fact structured by the same representational logic of affirming identities within capitalism. "The 'difference' that constitutes class as an 'identity'," Ellen Meiksins Wood writes, "is, by definition, a relationship of inequality and power, in a way that sexual or cultural 'difference' need not be":

> the working class, as the direct object of the most fundamental and determinative – though certainly not the only – form of oppression, and the one class whose interests do not rest on the oppression of other classes, can create the conditions for liberating all human beings in the struggle to liberate itself.[24]

This argument from Wood highlights three interrelated problems of framing the interaction between systems of racial, gender, and economic domination which plague both Marxist critiques of "identity politics" and contemporary theories of racial difference. If for Wood race, gender and sexuality are definitionally non-economic categories of social life which index economic inequality only contingently, then it is simply a tautology that these identities are not constitutive of capitalism as such. The abolition of sexual or racial domination, here

[24] See Wood, *Democracy against Capitalism: Renewing Historical Materialism*. (Aakar Books 2007), 258; and 'Marxism Without Class Struggle?' *Socialist Register* 20 (Merlin 1983), 242.

understood primarily as vestigial forms of historical injustice, therefore would not in principle be incompatible with capitalism. Finally, the reasoning goes, the qualitative difference between class and other forms of identity rests on the fact that class identity cannot be "celebrated". And yet the argument elides a fundamental contradiction between the abolition of class inequality and an implicit agent of emancipation in the figure of the working class. While poverty may not be a form of difference which can be "celebrated", Wood nevertheless produces an implicitly affirmationist account of the working class as that social agent both responsible for and uniquely capable of ending capitalism. The question of how the affirmation of such an identity could bring about the end of class oppression, without simply reaffirming capitalism under the guise of worker self-management, is passed over in silence. Despite the attempt to criticise the logic of identity-based struggles, Wood ultimately offers what I want to call an affirmationist politics of class structurally indistinguishable from similarly affirmationist accounts of race and gender difference.

But what if we did not center anti-racist struggles on difference but on domination? To understand "race" not as a marker of difference but as a system of domination poses the question of the material abolition of "race" as an indicator of structural subordination. Both anti-racist critics of class reductionist Marxisms and Marxist critics of liberal reformist, "merely cultural" anti-racisms gloss over the strategic similarities between the increasingly desperate, defensive struggles of the US labour movement and the race and gender-based "identity politics" to which it is so consistently counterposed. As the 2011 labour struggles in Wisconsin so dramatically revealed, the US labour movement's turn toward the state and electoral politics to secure its very right to exist mirrors the extreme difficulty of securing even minimal racially redistributive programs in the aftermath of the Great Society programs of the 1960s. Which is to say that, in an era of declining membership in mass-based labour and civil rights organisations, the prospects are dim for both a "politics of race" and a "politics of class". Shifting the analytic focus from difference to domination directs our attention to the entanglement of race and superfluity, as well as the racialising impact of violence, imprisonment, and warfare. Rejecting an understanding of capitalism as an increasingly inclusive engine of racial uplift, and the state as an ultimate guarantor of civic equality, an abolitionist anti-racism would categorically reject the continuing affirmation of the fundamental respectability, productivity or patriotism of racialised groups as a way to determine their relative fitness for racial domination. Beginning from radically different histories of racialisation, abolitionist anti-racist struggles would aim to dismantle the machinery of "race" at the heart of a fantasy of formal freedom, where the "limit point of capitalist equality is laid bare as the central protagonist of racial ordering."[25]

[25] Kyriakides and Torres, *Race Defaced: Paradigms of Pessimism, Politics of Possibility*, 36.

SPONTANEITY, MEDIATION, RUPTURE

> *We do not know whether the* [contrasting] *destinies of Luxemburg ... and Lenin were to be tied to the fact that Lenin and his group armed the workers, while the Spartacists continued to view the organisation as coordination ... and the refusal to work as the only adequate workers' weapon. The essence of Leninism shifts from the relationship between spontaneity and the party to the relationship between the party and insurrection.*[1]

[1] Sergio Bologna, 'Class composition and the theory of the party at the origins of the workers' council movement' (1972).

Are present-day struggles unfolding towards revolution? We try to find our bearings, with respect to this question, in the only way we can: not only in our experience of the present, but also, by consulting the revolutionary theories of the past. However, to look to past revolutionary theories is a problematic venture: those theories emerged in response to a set of problems which arose in the course of a particular era — an era that is not our own. Indeed, the revolutionary theories of the twentieth century were developed in the course of a sequence of struggles that we call the workers' movement. Those theories do not only bear the traces of the workers' movement in general. They formed in response to the limits that movement confronted at its highest point of intensity — that is, in the era of revolutions, 1905–21.

The limits of the workers' movement had everything to do with the problem of instilling a class consciousness in a population that had been proletarianised only incompletely. Facing a large peasantry in the countryside and a motley assortment of working classes in the cities, the strategists of the workers' movement looked forward to a future moment, when full proletarianisation — attendant on a further development of the productive forces — would eradicate existing divisions among proletarians. The objective unity of the class would then find a subjective correlate. As it turned out, this dream never became a reality. The further development of the productive forces reinforced certain divisions among

Spontaneity, Mediation, Rupture

proletarians, while creating others. Meanwhile, that development eradicated the basis of workers' unity. Workers found that they were no longer the vital force of the modern era; instead, they were made over into appendages — attachments to a sprawling set of machines and infrastructures that escaped their control.[2]

Returning, however briefly, to the revolutionary high point of the last century — before the destitution of the workers' movement — may help us to understand the context in which the revolutionary theories of the past were born. On that basis, we will begin to articulate a revolutionary theory for our own times. But we should be wary in undertaking such a project today: the emergence of revolutions is, by its very nature, unpredictable; our theory must somehow incorporate this unpredictability into its very core. The revolutionaries of an earlier era mostly refused to open themselves towards the unknown — even though the revolutions they experienced never played out as they had imagined.

After all, twentieth-century revolutions turned out not to be the result of methodical projects, of slowly building up union and/or party memberships, which were expected to expand in step with the industrialisation and homogenisation of the class. Instead, the revolutionary waves of 1905–21 emerged chaotically, with self-organising struggles forming around the tactic of the *mass strike*. Neither the emergence nor the development of the mass strike was foreseen by revolutionary strategists, in spite of decades of reflection (and the historical examples of 1848 and 1871).[3]

Among the few revolutionaries who did not oppose this new form of struggle outright, Rosa Luxemburg came to identify it as the revolutionary tactic *par excellence*. Her book, *The Mass Strike*, is one of the best texts in the history of revolutionary theory. However, even Luxemburg saw the mass strike as a means of

[2] See 'A History of Separation', forthcoming in *Endnotes* 4.

[3] The mass strike of the early twentieth century had little in common with the dream of the general strike, the *grand soir*, of the late nineteenth century.

revitalising the Germany Social Democratic Party. As Dauvé points out: "if [Luxemburg] was the author of the formula, 'After August 4, 1914, social democracy is nothing but a nauseating corpse,' she proved to be quite the necrophiliac."[4]

PRELUDE: THE MASS STRIKE

The history of the mass strike is a subterranean history; it is largely unwritten. But it can be outlined as follows.[5]

In 1902, roving strikes occurred in Belgium and Sweden, as a means of pressing for universal male suffrage. The tactic then spread to the Netherlands and Russia before arriving in Italy, in 1904, as a protest against the violent repression of workers' uprisings. In Italy, workers' councils were formed for the first time. This first wave reached its high point in the enormous Russian mass strikes of 1905, which culminated in an insurrection – the first Russian Revolution – in December of that year. With the Russian example serving as the model, the mass-strike tactic circulated rapidly through European cities.

It soon appeared in Germany, the heart of Second International Marxism, where the question of the "purpose" of the mass strike – which had already been used to a variety of different ends – was first raised. For union representatives, the mass strike appeared to be an obstacle to their unions' own, plodding attempts to organise the class. A German trade-unionist declared: "To build our organisations, we need calm in the workers' movement."[6] Yet the tactic continued to spread, and its scope widened, despite the pronouncement of the Second International that it supported the mass-strike tactic only as a defensive weapon.

After the wave of 1902–07, struggles quieted down before bursting forth again in 1910–13. In the course of these two waves, union membership surged; the vote

[4] Gilles Dauvé and Denis Authier, *The Communist Left in Germany, 1918-1921* (1976), Chapter 4.

[5] See Philippe Bourrinet, 'The workers' councils in the theory of the Dutch-German communist left.'

[6] Carl Schorske, *German Social Democracy, 1905-1917* (Harvard University Press 1955), 39.

Spontaneity, Mediation, Rupture

was won in Austria and Italy, while the Scandinavian states were forced to liberalise. Anarcho-syndicalism and Left Communism appeared as distinct tendencies. The start of World War I put an end to the second strike wave, which was already beginning to peter out. But this seemingly permanent blockage turned out to be another temporary impediment. Across Europe, the number of strikes was already rising from low levels in 1915. Activity spilled outside the workplace: there were rent strikes in Clydeside and demonstrations against food prices in Berlin. In 1916, mass strikes were called in Germany, but this time in order to protest the imprisonment of Karl Liebknecht, a symbol of principled opposition to the War. By 1917, labour unrest was matched by mutinies in the army and food riots in the streets, among other actions. These actions proliferated through new forms of organisation: the shop-stewards' movements in England and Germany and the "internal commissions" in Italy.

Thus, even before the Bolshevik Revolution in October, struggle was heating up across European cities. Mass strikes in Austria and Germany were the largest ever in each country's history. People forget that World War I ended, not because of the defeat of one side, but because more and more of the countries involved in hostilities collapsed in a wave of revolutions, which surged and then receded from 1917 to 1921. We will not dwell on this final wave of struggle, except to quote the words that Friedrich Ebert, leader of the SPD, spoke to the frightened German bourgeoisie, in 1918: "We are the only ones who can maintain order"…

What can we learn from this brief history of the mass-strike tactic? Were a revolution to occur today, it would also have to emerge out of a massive intensification of spontaneous, self-organising struggles. Those struggles would have to break out and extend themselves across vast geographic spaces, in an ebb and flow that lasts for decades. It is only within such a context – that is, a context of an unfolding sequence of struggles – that revolution becomes possible, not just theoretically, but actually. It is thus also only in the course of intensifying struggles that the strategic questions of an era can be asked and answered, in a concrete way.

However, we cannot learn much more than that, from the past. The tactic of the mass strike was specific to its time, a time that witnessed: (1) an unprecedented consolidation of firms and workplaces; (2) the arrival, in new industrial towns, of recently proletarianised peasants, bringing with them certain cultures of solidarity; (3) the fight of workers to defend their control over the labour process, against mechanisation and rationalisation; and finally, (4) the fight against a persistent old regime – a fight for equality of citizenship, the right to organise, and the vote – which elites refused to grant proletarians. The horizon of struggle is very different today, yet the tools that we have for grasping the relation between struggles and revolution still bear the traces of the workers' movement.

Those tools must be re-forged. The quotation from Bologna, with which we began, touches on the key concepts of revolutionary theory, as it was understood in the course of the workers' movement: spontaneity and organisation, party and insurrection. The question that faces us is: how do we articulate the relations among this constellation of concepts today, that is, after the end of the workers' movement (which has meant also, and necessarily, the end of all the revolutionary traditions that animated the last century: Leninism and the ultra-left, social democracy and syndicalism, and so on)? We offer the following reflections on three concepts – spontaneity, mediation, rupture – as an attempt to re-fashion the tools of revolutionary theory, for our times. By taking cognisance of the gap that separates us from the past, we hope to extract from past theories something of use to us in the present.

THE COORDINATION PROBLEM

Before we discuss the key concepts of revolutionary theory, we must pause to say something about the specificity of struggle in capitalist societies. Outside of those societies, human beings are mostly organised into face-to-face communities. When they clash, they do so as communities that pre-exist those clashes. By contrast, in capitalist societies, human beings are mostly atomised. Proletarians confront one another, not as members of face-to-face communities, but rather, as strangers. This atomisation determines the character of contemporary struggles. For the basis on which proletarians struggle does not pre-exist those struggles. Instead, the foundations of struggle have to be built (out of the materials of social life) in the course of struggle itself. This feature of capitalist societies has two basic causes:

1) In the markets where they sell their labour-power, proletarians compete with one another for jobs. It is given in the nature of the exploitative relation that there are never enough jobs to go around. In this situation, some proletarians find it worthwhile to form gangs and rackets — based on gender, race, nation, creed — and to oppose other groups of workers on that basis.[7] The opposition between proletarians plays out, not only with respect to jobs and wage differentials, but also with respect to working conditions, family time, educational opportunities and so on. Intra-class competition is also reflected outside of labour markets, in ruthlessly enforced status hierarchies, on display through conspicuous consumption (flashy cars) and countless lifestyle markers (tight pants). Thus, an increasingly universal situation of labour-dependence has not led to a homogenisation of interests. On the contrary, proletarians are internally stratified. They carefully differentiate themselves from one another. Where collective interests have been cultivated by organisations, that has often re-inscribed other competitive differences in the boundaries of race, nation, gender, etc.

[7] Gangs and rackets act to ensure that some proletarians get 'good jobs' at the expense of others.

2) Labour-dependency not only issues in competition between workers, repelling them from one another. Insofar as individuals are able to secure work, the wage also frees proletarians from having to deal with one another. No longer dependent on an inheritance, wage-earners are not beholden to their parents or anyone else (except their bosses!).[8] They can escape from the countryside to the cities, from the cities to the suburbs, or from the suburbs back to the cities. As long as they find work, proletarians are free to move about as they please. They can flee the admonishing eyes of ancestral and religious authorities, as well as former friends and lovers, in order to partner with whomever they want, to pray to whatever gods, and to decorate their homes any which way. Proletarians do not have to see anyone they do not like, except at work. Thus, the community dissolves not only by force; its dissolution is also actively willed. The result is an historically unique social structure, in which people don't really have to depend on each other, directly, for much of anything. Yet, proletarians' individual autonomy is won at the expense of a collective powerlessness. When revolt ends, proletarians tend to revert to atomisation. They dissolve back into the cash nexus.

Because proletarians begin from a situation of nearly universal atomisation, they face a unique *coordination problem*. Proletarians have to find ways to band together, but in order to do so, they have to overcome the real opposition of their interests. Insofar as they have not yet overcome these barriers, they find that they are powerless in their struggle with both capital and the state. Thus, the problem proletarians face — in non-revolutionary times — is not the lack of a proper strategy (which could be divined by clever intellectuals), but rather, the presence of real power asymmetries, attendant on their atomisation. Nothing in the individual workers' arsenal can match the power of capitalists to hire and fire at will, or the proclivity of policemen to shoot, beat or jail.

[8] Not all who are labour-dependent have achieved the autonomy that comes with it. For example, proletarian women have always worked, at least for part of their lives. But for another part of their lives (especially before 1970), they were relegated to a domestic sphere, where they earned no wages of their own. Even when women did earn wages, their wages were sometimes handed over directly to their husbands. In this way, the development of the capitalist mode of production prevented women from winning the autonomy from fathers and husbands that young men were able to achieve, early on. That women, today, do earn and retain their own wages has given them an increased autonomy, even though they are still saddled with most of the domestic work.

Spontaneity, Mediation, Rupture

Workers have historically overcome their atomisation – and the power imbalances that result – in waves of coordinated, disruptive activity. But workers face a *double-bind*: they can act collectively if they trust one another, but they can trust one another – in the face of massive risks to themselves and others – only if that trust has already been realised in collective action. If revolutionary activity is exceptional, it is not because ideology divides workers, but rather because, unless revolutionary action is already taking place, it is suicidal to try to "go it alone". The ideas in our heads, no matter how revolutionary they are, mostly serve to justify – and also to help us to cope with – the suffering borne of this situation.

The seemingly indissoluble problem of struggle, of the double bind, is finally solved only by struggle itself, by the fact that struggle unfolds over time. Computationally, this solution can be described as the possible result of an iterated prisoners' dilemma.[9] Our term is spontaneity.

1 SPONTANEITY

Spontaneity is usually understood as an absence of organisation. Something spontaneous arises from a momentary impulse, as if occurring naturally. Second International Marxists believed that workers' revolt was spontaneous, in this sense: it was a natural reaction to capitalist domination, which must be given shape by the party. This notion relies on what might be called a derivative meaning of the term spontaneity. In the eighteenth century, when Kant described the transcendental unity of apperception – the fact that I am aware of myself as having my own experiences – he called this a spontaneous act.[10] Kant meant the opposite of something natural. A spontaneous act is one that is freely undertaken. In fact, the word spontaneous derives from the Latin *sponte*, meaning "of one's own accord, freely, willingly". In this sense, spontaneity is not about acting compulsively or automatically. It is a matter of acting without external

[9] See, for example, Robert Alexrod, *The Evolution of Cooperation* (Basic Books 1984).

[10] See Robert Pippin, *Hegel's Idealism* (Cambridge University Press 1989), 16–24.

constraint. We participate in capitalist social relations everyday: by going to work, by making purchases, etc. But we are free to decide not to do that, whatever the consequences may be (in fact, the consequences are sometimes severe, because our participation in capitalism is not a choice, but rather, a compulsion).[11]

Four points follow, from this re-interpretation of the term:

1) Spontaneity – precisely because it is freely willed – is inherently unpredictable. For this reason, there can be no fixed theory of struggle. There can only be a phenomenology of the experience of revolt. Of course, revolt does bear a relation to crisis, economic or otherwise, since crises make proletarians' existing ways of life untenable. But the relation between crisis and revolt is never mechanical. Revolt remains fundamentally un- or overdetermined: it never happens just when it is supposed to, and when it does happen, it often arises from the unlikeliest of corners. Discontent may simmer, but then a police murder or a rise in bread prices suddenly "triggers" revolt. However, no one knows beforehand what will be the trigger event, in any given case. This is not to say that revolt is unplanned – or that militants do not play a role in sparking revolts. In fact, militants try to spark revolt all the time. The point is that their success lies in something outside of themselves (that something reveals itself in key moments, when the human material on which militants work suddenly stops responding to their micro-management – a struggle either leaps out in an unexpected direction, or else, it wilts).[12] Who can predict when showing up at a park will lead to just another protest, and when it will explode into a civil war?

2) Spontaneity – being a break with the everyday – is also necessarily disruptive. Spontaneity appears as a set of disruptive acts: strikes, occupations, blockades, looting, rioting, self-reduction of prices and self-organisation more generally. But spontaneity is not merely a concoction of these ingredients. Spontaneity has a history, and

[11] Individuals act spontaneously, in this sense, all the time. Sometimes they have a plan and sometimes they do not. We are interested, however, not in such individual acts of freedom, but rather, in collective acts of spontaneity. That is to say, we are interested, here, only in mass activity.

[12] To point that out is not to denigrate militants: it is to remind us that while militants are an active agent in any wave of struggle, they do not hold the key to it. They solve the coordination problem much as computers solve math problems: by trying every possible solution, until one of them fits.

Spontaneity, Mediation, Rupture

in the history of spontaneity, there is a primacy of particular tactics, in two senses. (a) Tactics are what resonate, across workplaces or neighbourhoods, across countries or even continents. Someone sets themselves on fire, or some individuals occupy a public square. Spontaneously, other people start doing something similar. In the course of events, proletarians adapt a given tactic to their own experiences, but what is key is that — insofar they are adopting tactics that are taken from somewhere else — there is an interruption of the continuous flow of time. Local history becomes something that can only be articulated globally. (b) The primacy of tactics is also given in the fact that people take part in waves of disruptive activity, even while debating why they are doing so. Participants may make contradictory demands; the same tactics are used towards different ends, in different places. Meanwhile, as struggles grow in intensity and extent, participants become more bold in making demands — or in not making any at all. Barriers between people begin to break down. As the walls fall, individuals' sense of collective power increases. The risks of participation drop as more and more people participate. In its unfolding, the struggle builds its own foundations.

3) Spontaneity is not only disruptive, it is also creative. Spontaneity generates a new content of struggle, which is adequate to proletarians' everyday experiences. These experiences are always changing, along with changes in capitalist social relations (and culture more generally). That's why revolt that arises from within — spontaneously — tends to spread more widely and wildly than revolt that comes from the outside — from militants, etc. This is true, even when militants intervene on the basis of their own prior experiences of revolt (in the sixties, many militants denounced sabotage and absenteeism as "infantile" forms of struggle; in fact, they presaged a massive wave of wildcat strikes). Thus, militants place themselves in a difficult position. Militants are the human traces of past conflict, mobile across time and space.

If there are local/national histories of struggle, that is partly because militants establish continuities of experience. Strong militant formations can become agents of intensification in the present; however, in trying to apply lessons learned in the past to an ever changing present, militants run the risk of trivialising the new, in the moment of its emergence. This is a dangerous position, insofar as it remains axiomatic, for us, that we have to put our trust in the new as the only way out of capitalist social relations.

4) Spontaneous revolt involves, not only the creation of a new content of struggle, but also, necessarily, of new forms of struggle, adequate to or matching up with that content. Hegel once said, "regarding the antithesis of form and content": "it is essential to remember that the content is not formless, but that it has the form within itself, just as much as the form is something external to it".[13] That form may be incipient at first; it may exist only in potential, but it comes into its own as struggles extend and intensify. Here, too there is something creative — the emergence of a form without historical precedent. History bears witness to this fact, again and again: newly emergent struggles disdain existing forms. Instead, they generate their own forms, which are then disdained, in turn, in future waves of revolt. This feature of spontaneity, its tendency towards formal innovation, undermines any account of communisation that makes it seem as if a communising revolution would be fundamentally formless. We cannot know what forms of spontaneous organisation will play a role in — and will have to be overcome in the moment of — communisation.

Against the revolutionary theories of the past, we can say today that organisation is not external to spontaneity. On the contrary, mass revolt is always organised. To give this term a definition proper to its role in revolutionary theory, we might say that organisation is the necessary accompaniment to the coordination and extension of

[13] Hegel, *The Encyclopedia Logic* (Hackett 1991) § 133, p. 202.

spontaneous disruptive activity. But that does not mean that organisation is always formal. It can also be completely informal, and in fact, at the highest levels, it is always informal. Coordination means the spread of tactics by word of mouth, newspapers, radio, television, videos captured on cell phones, etc. (not that any particular technology is necessary: a global strike wave already spread across the British Empire in the 1930s; technologies merely afford different opportunities for struggle).

Within any revolt, debates take place around the question of organisation: "what is the best way to coordinate and extend this particular disruptive activity?" The answers to this question are always specific to the context of the revolt in question. Many individuals, whether out of ignorance or fear, ask themselves different questions: "how can we bring this disruption to an end?" "how can we wrap it up or get a win, so we can return to the familiar miseries of our everyday lives?" Overcoming ignorance and fear – coming to trust one another to act and to do so in a coordinated way, with hundreds, thousands, millions and finally billions of people – this coordination problem cannot be worked out in advance. It is only solved in and through an unfolding sequence of struggles.

2 MEDIATION

We usually come across the term mediation in its privative form, as immediacy, taken to mean, "now, at once". Again, this meaning is a derivative one. Immediacy means, first and foremost, lacking mediation. What, then, is mediation? It is the presence of an intervening term (in its early usage, the word "mediation" described the position of Jesus Christ, who intervened between God and man). To speak of the immediacy of the revolution does not mean to call for revolution "immediately", in the sense of "right now", but rather, "immediately", in the sense of "lacking an intervening term". But which term is lacking, in this case?

It should be clear that the immediacy of the revolution is not simply a matter of lacking organisation (although any revolution will be chaotic). On the contrary, disruptive activities must be highly coordinated and extensive — in a word, organised — so much so as to precipitate a desertion from the armed forces (which is the *sine qua non* of a revolutionary moment). Nor is this point clarified by saying that the revolution will take place without an intervening, or transitional period. Because in fact, there will inevitably be a transition, even if there will be no "transitional economy" or "transitional state" in the sense these terms had in the twentieth century. The communisation of social relations among seven billion people will take time. It will involve sudden surges as well as devastating setbacks, zones of freedom emerging alongside zones of unfreedom, etc. Even if communisers were to rout the counter-revolution, there would inevitably follow a period of de- and reconstruction. Relations among individuals, no longer mediated by markets and states, would have to realise themselves, in the world, as a thoroughgoing transformation of material infrastructures.[14]

For us, it is not so much the revolution as a process that should be understood with the category of "immediacy". To speak of immediacy, with respect to the revolution, is merely a shorthand for the fact that the revolution abolishes the mediations of the modern world. To speak of the immediacy of communism is thus to affirm that, unlike the revolutionaries of the past, communisers will have to take seriously the coherence of the modern world. The worker, the machine, the factory, science and technology: none of these terms appears as an unqualified good, to be opposed to capital and the state, as unqualified evils. There is no neutral ordering of this world that can be taken over by the working class and run in its interest. Thus, the revolution cannot be a matter of finding new ways to mediate relations among workers, or between human beings and nature, the state and the economy, men and women, etc.

[14] See 'Logistics, Counterlogistics and the Communist Prospect' in this issue.

Spontaneity, Mediation, Rupture

Instead, the revolution can only be a set of acts that abolish the very distinctions on which such mediations are based. Capitalism is a set of separations, or ontological cleavages – between human beings and their innermost capacities – that are subsequently mediated by value and the state. To undo these mediations is to destroy the entities that underlie them: on the one hand to reconnect everyone to their capacities, in such a way that they can never be forcibly separated, and on the other hand, to empower each singular individual to take on or divest from any particular capacity, without thereby losing access to all the others.

The actual means of reconnecting individuals to their capacities, outside the market and the state, are impossible to foresee. But that does not mean that human existence will take on an ineffable quality, a sheer flux. New mediations will inevitably be erected out of the wreckage of the old. Thus, communism will not mean the end of mediation. It will mean the end of those mediations that fix us in our social roles: gender, race, class, nation, species. Just as the end of abstract domination will not mean the end of abstraction, so too, the overcoming of these mediations will leave plenty of others intact: language, music, games, etc.

However, that is not to say these mediations won't be fundamentally transformed by the end of asocial socialisation. Take language for example, as the primordial mediation: language has been transformed by global commerce, which has led to a massive reduction in the number of languages, and to the corresponding dominance of a few: Spanish, English, Mandarin. We do not know whether the overcoming of this world will continue to maximise communication between social groupings around the world. Perhaps, instead, it will issue in a proliferation of languages. Universal comprehension may be sacrificed to make words more adequate to mutually unintelligible forms of life.

3 RUPTURE

During periods of quiescence, revolt takes place. But it remains disarticulated. The clash between classes breaks out, here and there, but then subsides. Periods of quiescence last for decades, but eventually, they come to an end. The re-emergence of class struggle announces itself in a torrent of activities. A new sequence of struggles begins. Waves of proletarian activity ebb and flow, over a period of years, as new content and new forms of struggle develop. The intensity of the fight rises, although never in a linear way, as proletarians link up, extending their disruptive activities. The articulation of those activities begins to reveal the outlines of that which is to be overcome. In this way, there is a tension towards the rupture, which throws off sparks in all directions. A rupture is, by definition, a break – a break that is qualitative in nature – but a break with or within what? Where do we locate the rupture that is synonymous with the advent of a revolutionary period?

It is all too easy to speak of spontaneous *disruption* as if it were itself a rupture, that is, with the everyday. Revolution would then be understood as an accumulation of ruptures. There is some truth in this perspective. After all, struggles never extend themselves along a linear path of rising intensity. On the contrary, the clash moves by means of discontinuities. Its dynamism gives rise to periodic shifts in the very terms of the struggle: in one moment, it may be workers versus bosses, but in the next, it becomes tenants versus landlords, youth versus the police, or a confrontation among self-organised sectors (all of these fights can occur simultaneously as well). This instability – in the very basis on which individuals are called to confront one another – is what makes it possible to call everything into question, both generally and in every specificity.

Yet these terms must be kept separate: on the one hand, spontaneous disruption, and on the other hand, the rupture, which splits open spontaneous disruption itself. The rupture forces every individual, who is engaged in struggle, to take sides: to decide whether they align themselves on the side of the communist movement – as the movement for the practical destruction of this world – or else, on the side of continuing to revolt, on the basis of what is. In that sense, the rupture is a moment of partisanship, of taking sides.[15] It is a question of joining the party and of convincing others to do the same (it is by no means a matter of leading "the people"). Just as we separate spontaneity from rupture, we must also draw a distinction between organisation, which is proper to spontaneity, and the party, which is always the party of rupture.[16]

The party cleaves its way through proletarian organisations, since it calls for the destitution of the social order (and so also, the undoing of the distinctions on which proletarian organisations are founded). The difference between organisations and the party is, therefore, the difference between, on the one hand, committees of the unemployed, neighbourhood assemblies and rank-and-file unions – which organise the disruption of capitalist social relations – and on the other hand, groups of partisans – who reconfigure networks of transportation and communication and organise the creation and free distribution of goods and services. Communist tactics destroy the very distinctions (e.g. between employed and unemployed) on which proletarian organisations are based.[17] In so doing, they initiate the unification of humanity.

And so, while revolts disrupt the old world, the rupture is its over-turning (thus, the standard term for the rupture: revolution). This overturning has both quantitative and qualitative dimensions, which distinguish it from revolt. For example, the scale of revolt is typically restricted; whereas the revolution today can only mean seven billion

[15] In *The Eighteenth Brumaire*, Marx writes of a polarisation of social forces into a 'Party of Order' and a 'Party of Anarchy'. Here, it is not a matter of pre-existing social groups, but rather, of emergent ones, finding their organisational forms in the struggle itself: the bourgeoisie and its supporters coalesce around a force that offers the best chance of restoring order, while the proletariat gathers around a force that is trying to create a situation 'which makes all turning back impossible'.

[16] The concept of the party merely registers this fact: like spontaneous revolt itself, the rupture will not proceed automatically, out of a deep or even 'final crisis' of the capital-labour relation. The proletariat will not suddenly find itself holding the levers to power, after which point it is only

people trying to find ways to reproduce themselves, in non-capitalist ways. Of these billions, even an active minority would have to number in the hundreds of millions (that is to say, if individuals are able to determine the course of events, that in itself suggests that we are still far from a revolutionary moment). The revolution will require that billions of individuals draw diverse aspects of their lives into an open struggle, which ends in those individuals calling the totality of their lives into question. The rupture calls life itself into question, but in a way that allows us to carry on living.

According to *Théorie Communiste*, the revolutionaries of an earlier era did not have a concept of rupture. They supposedly saw revolution as a matter of struggles "growing over", that is, of struggles extending themselves across society and intensifying towards a tipping point, when they would spill over into a revolution. In the course of the twentieth century, many theories of this kind were proposed (the term itself apparently comes from Trotsky, but the idea is more common among autonomists). However, those sorts of theories were not very common.[18] Most revolutionaries, including Trotsky, drew their own distinction between revolt and rupture.

So, for example, in Italy, in the course of the *bienno rosso* (1919–20), when revolution seemed like a real possibility, Amadeo Bordiga, future leader of the Italian Communist Party, announced the following:

> We would not like the working masses to get hold of the idea that all they need do to take over the factories and get rid of the capitalists is set up councils. This would indeed be a dangerous illusion. The factory will be conquered by the working class – and not only by the workforce employed in it, which would be too weak and non-communist – only after the working class as a whole has seized political power. Unless it has done so, the Royal Guards, military police,

a matter of figuring out what to do with it. Instead, the revolution will be the project of a fraction of society, i.e. the party, which solves the coordination problem in the only possible way – by abolishing class society.

[17] This is a difficult point to make rigorously. It is clear that, insofar as spontaneously self-organising struggles build their own foundations, they often connect individuals to one another in ways that belie their unity-in-separation for capital. For example, individuals may occupy a government building, even though they have no everyday connection to it. In so occupying, they may organise themselves according to a shared trait that has no meaning, for capital. The key point here is that spontaneously organising struggles disrupt the unity-in-separation of capital, but they

Spontaneity, Mediation, Rupture

241

etc. – in other words, the mechanism of force and oppression that the bourgeoisie has at its disposal, its political power apparatus – will see to it that all illusions are dispelled.[19]

In essence, Bordiga (like many communists in the twentieth century) argued as follows: by taking over the factories and demonstrating in the street, it is sometimes possible to bring society to a halt, but not to produce a rupture. The rupture will only take place when proletarians risk civil war, in an attempt to permanently transfer power to themselves. It followed that the primary task of the party was, at the critical moment, to distribute arms among the workers and to call for a transfer of power to these armed bodies. Indeed, "arming the workers" might be thought of as the key "programmatist tactic" (other such tactics included establishing political bodies of recallable delegates).[20] The link between this concept and Bologna's, quoted earlier, should be apparent.

Thus, it is clear that the revolutionaries of an earlier era did have a concept of rupture (the revolutionary was the one who, in every opening, pronounced De Sade's famous slogan: "one more effort, comrades…"). Nevertheless, it is true that, for us, such a concept is inadequate. A revolution today cannot take place by means of armed bodies taking state power – or even over-turning it, according to the anarchist conception – with the goal of setting up a society of associated workers. Even if that sort of revolution remains appealing to some, it is predicated on the will and the capacity of workers to organise around their identity as workers, instead of around other identities (i.e. nationality, religion, race, gender, etc). Workers only share a common interest to the extent that they can project a universal solution to their coordination problem ("an injury to one is an injury to all" is not universally true).

do not overcome it, in a permanent way. Thus, the tendency of distinctions of gender, race, nationality, etc., to reappear in the square occupations of 2011, that is, precisely where those distinctions were supposed to have been rendered inoperable.

18 The insurrectionists may be the true inheritors of the 'growing-over' theory of revolution. For them, the intensification of existing struggles is already the rupture. The concept of revolution is thereby abandoned as overly 'holistic' – a false universalisation in time and space. In fact, struggles universalise themselves – not by merging together, so that everyone can march behind the one true banner – but rather, by posing universal questions about the overcoming of this world. In that way, struggles themselves construct the universal, not as an abstract

Endnotes 3   **242**

Facing up to the pressures of competitive labour markets, workers did construct their common interest, in the course of the twentieth century, by building workers' organisations, which were linked together through the workers' movement. That movement forged – from among a multitude of specific workers' experiences – an actually general interest. But the actuality of this general interest was predicated on two things. First, it was predicated on winning real gains, both within capitalist societies and against an old regime, which sought to exclude workers from the polity. Second, it was predicated on a lived experience of many proletarians: they identified with their work, as the defining trait of who they were (and they imagined that, with the extension of the factory system to the entire world, this identity would become a common human condition). Workers felt that they shared a common destiny as the vital force of modern society, which was growing all the time.

All that is now in the past. A massive accumulation of capital has made the productive process ever more efficient, rendering workers ever more superfluous to it. Under these conditions, capitalist economies have grown slowly, due to chronic overproduction; at the same time, most workers find it hard to win any real gains, in a context of high levels of unemployment. Moreover, this superfluity of workers has found its correlate in a changed experience of work itself. Insofar as they are employed, most proletarians do not identify with their work as the defining trait of who they are. Either they are peripheral to a more or less automated production process – and thus, cannot see themselves as the vital force of modern society – or else they are excluded from production altogether, and toil away in dead-end service sector jobs. This is not to say that there aren't still proletarians who dream of doing similar jobs in a better world, where they could organise their work democratically. It is just that this minority can no longer claim to represent the future of the class as a whole – especially

object of an idealised revolution, but as the concrete object of an actual revolution.

19 Amadeo Bordiga, 'Seize Power or Seize the Factory?' (1920).

20 Certain communists have taken a different tack. They take it as their primary task to identify and infiltrate what they perceive to be the 'key' economic sector(s), the part that represents the whole. Militants within that sector will supposedly be able, at the right moment, to intervene decisively, to produce the revolution, or else to prevent the betrayal of the revolution (which was supposed to come from elsewhere). See, for example, Monsieur Dupont's *Nihilist Communism*, on the question of the 'essential proletariat' (Ardent Press 2002). These are false solutions to real problems, but again, for that reason, they will find their actual solutions in time.

Spontaneity, Mediation, Rupture

when so many proletarians are un- or underemployed, or else are lost in the informal sector, where seventy percent of workers are self-employed, because they cannot find jobs.

As a result of these transformations, the revolutionary horizon of struggle is itself transformed. It must be something other than what it was. We can neither remain who we are, nor take over things as they are. That is all the more true, insofar as the apparatuses of modern society (factories, networks of roads and airports, etc.) — which proletarians helped to build — have turned out not to presage a new world of human freedom. On the contrary, those apparatuses are destroying the very conditions of human life on earth. It is difficult to say, therefore, what would constitute a communising tactic, replacing the programmatist tactic par excellence, namely the "arming of the workers" or "generalising the armed struggle". We know what those tactics will have to do: they will have to destroy private property and the state, abolish the distinction between the domestic sphere and the economy, etc. But that tells us nothing about the tactics themselves. Which will be the ones that break through?

In the end, communising tactics will turn out to be whichever tactics finally destroy the link between finding work and surviving. They will reconnect human beings and their capacities, in such a way as to make it impossible to sever that connection ever again. In the course of struggle, a process may unfold, somewhere in the world, which seems to go all the way, to bring an end, once and for all, to capitalist social relations. Just as today, proletarians adopt and adapt whatever tactics resonate with them, so too, some proletarians will adopt these communising tactics. However, these tactics will not extend the struggle. On the contrary, they will split that struggle open, turning it back against itself.

If there are such breakthroughs, anywhere in the world, it is possible to imagine that, as a feature of partisanship, communist parties will form (or will align themselves with the new tactics). They may not call themselves parties, and they may not refer to their tactics as communising tactics. Nevertheless, there will be a separation out of those who, within struggle, advocate and apply revolutionary tactics, whatever they may be. There is no need to decide in advance what the party will look like, what should be its form of organisation, if it should be formalised at all, or whether it is just an orientation shared among many individuals. Communism is not an idea or a slogan. It is the real movement of history, the movement which — in the rupture — gropes its way out of history.

CONCLUSIONS

The concept of communisation marks out an orientation: an orientation towards the conditions of possibility of communism. The concept enjoins us to focus on the present, to discover the new world through the critique of everything that presently exists. What would have to be overturned or undone, in order for communism to become a real force in the world? There is both a deductive and inductive way of approaching this question: (1) what is capitalism, and therefore, what would a communist movement have to abolish, in order for capitalism to no longer exist? (2) What, in the struggles and experiences of proletarians, points towards or poses the question of communism? In fact, our answers to this first question are shaped by our answers to the second. Proletarians are always fighting capital in new and unexpected ways, forcing us to ask, again, "What is capital, such that people are trying to destroy it, like that?" The theory of communisation sets itself up, in relation to these questions, as a set of propositions, regarding the minimal conditions of abolishing capitalism. These propositions can be enumerated, briefly, as follows:

(1) The unfolding crises of capitalism cause proletarian struggles both to proliferate and to transform in character. (2) These struggles tend to generalise across society, without it becoming possible to unify concurrent struggles under a single banner. (3) In order for fundamentally fragmented struggles to pass over into a revolution, communising measures will have to be taken, as the only possible way of carrying those struggles forward. (4) It will thus become necessary to abolish class divisions — as well as the state, distinctions of gender and race, etc.— in the very process of revolution (and as the revolution). Finally, (5) a revolution will therefore establish, not a transitional economy or state, but rather, a world of individuals, defined in their singularity, who relate to one another in a multitude of ways. This last point will hold true, even if those individuals inherit a brutal world, ravaged by war and climate catastrophe — and not a paradise of automated factories and easy living.

We must recognise that this set of propositions is rather weak: a starting point rather than a conclusion. It should also go without saying: these propositions tell us nothing about whether a communist revolution will actually happen. Having gone through a conceptual topology of revolutionary strategy, the question remains: does any of this affect what we do? Do these reflections have any strategic consequences?

Today, those who are interested in revolutionary theory find themselves caught between the terms of a false choice: activism or *attentisme*. It seems that we can only act without thinking critically, or think critically without acting. Revolutionary theory has as one of its tasks to dissolve this performative contradiction. How is it possible to act while understanding the limits of that action? In every struggle, there is a tension towards unity, which is given in the drive to coordinate disruptive activity, as the only hope of achieving anything at all. But, in the absence of a workers' movement — which was able to subsume difference into a fundamental sameness – this tension towards unity is frustrated. There is no way to solve the coordination problem on the basis of what we are. To be a partisan of the rupture is to recognise that there is no collective worker – no revolutionary subject – which is somehow hidden but already present in every struggle.

On the contrary, the intensification of struggles reveals, not a pre-existing unity, but rather, a conflictual proliferation of difference. This difference is not only suffered; it is often willed by participants in struggle. Under these conditions, the weak unities of this or that anti-government front – which are imposed on so many differences – merely offer yet another confirmation that, within struggle, we remain disunited. In that sense, we might even say that, today, all struggles lead away from revolution – except that it is only through activation, intensification, and failed attempts at generalisation that unification may one day become possible, in and through a revolutionary rupture with struggle itself.

This observation raises a paradox. There is nothing for us to do but support the extension and intensification of struggles. Like everyone else engaged in struggle, we may seek to introduce a new content into our struggles. We may try out new tactics and forms of organisation (or else, we might adopt tactics and forms of organisation from elsewhere, when they occur in a way that resonates with us). We may put forward what we believe to be the watchwords of the moment. In any case, we understand that the limits of our own power are the limits of everyone else's participation: the extent of their coordination, the degree of their mutual trust, and the intensity of their disruption.

But we also recognise that, as we participate in struggles – as we organise ourselves – we are pushed towards or fixed into identities from which we are fundamentally alienated. Either we can no longer affirm those identities, or else do not want to, or else we recognise that they are sectional and for that reason impossible to adopt among the broad mass of humanity. Struggles pit us against one another—but often not for reasons that we experience as absolutely necessary. On the contrary, sometimes, we come to see our differences as inessential—the result of a fractious differentiation of status or identity, within capitalism.

In facing these limits of struggle, we are completely powerless to overcome them. The trouble for activists is that an awareness of limits appears as loss and defeat. Their solution is to desperately force a resolution. We recognise, by contrast, that the fight will not be won directly, by leaping over the limits. Instead, we will have to come up against those limits, again and again, until they can be formalised. The impossibility of solving the coordination problem—while remaining what we are, in this society—must be theorised within struggle, as a practical problem. Proletarians must come to see that capital is not merely an external enemy. Alongside the state, it is our only mode of coordination. We relate to one another though capital; it is our unity-in-separation. Only on the basis of such a consciousness—not of class, but of capital—will revolution become possible, as the overturning of this society.

In the meantime, what we seek is not premature answers or forced resolutions, but rather a therapy against despair: it is only in wrestling with the limit that proletarians will formalise the question, to which revolution is the answer. As it stands, ours is thus a meagre offering, based more on speculative argument than hard evidence. Except among a tiny minority of participants, a concept of communisation (or a concept bearing its essential characteristics) has not yet arisen within struggles. We are still speaking of a new cycle of struggle in the worn-out language of the old. We can refine that language as best we can, but we have to recognise that it is nearly, if not completely exhausted.